MASTER MARINER

MASTER MARINER

A life under way

CAPTAIN
PHILIP RENTELL

SEAFARER BOOKS

© Philip Rentell 2009

Published in the UK by Seafarer Books Ltd
102 Redwald Road • Rendlesham • Suffolk IP12 2TE

www.seafarerbooks.com

ISBN 978-1-906266-13-4 paperback

Design and typesetting:
Louis Mackay / www.louismackaydesign.co.uk

Editing: Hugh Brazier

Text set digitally in Proforma

Printed in Finland by WS Bookwell

Contents

Foreword
by Sir Robin Knox-Johnston

There are far too few books written about the merchant navy by its officers and men. To most people ashore the merchant navy is something that is there, but seldom seen except in ports, and forgotten once the vessel has disappeared over the horizon. Most seamen look upon their life as being normal, and therefore unexceptional, so not worth writing about. And yet the seaman's life, away from home for months and facing nature in the raw, is far from ordinary, and the all too few books that describe life at sea are the more valuable as a result, as they show a snapshot of the extraordinary life led by seamen.

The merchant navy was a great career. Challenging, exciting, often too exciting, boring at times, and yet there was always change. Different ports in different oceans and incidents in the daily lives of a crew always provided interest.

Although Philip Rentell went to sea as I was leaving after a happy thirteen years, his account of his life as a cadet and watch-keeping officer mirrors my own experiences, even if we were in different companies. Shipping companies in the merchant navy can be compared to regiments in the army: each had its own history, traditions and uniforms. Up until the British merchant navy began its disastrous decline in the 1970s, most officers spent their entire career with a single company. The highly professional officer corps of the merchant navy was, as Richard Woodman has so clearly put it, fatally dispersed across the oceans of the world and only came together for the dreaded Board of Trade examinations for second mate's, mate's and master's certificates.

It could never be organised as a single group, and as the ships disappeared more and more highly trained officers left the sea. Philip Rentell stayed on, and his account shows those of us who did leave the sort of life we might have led had we remained at sea. I read this book with huge enjoyment – and just a little bit of envy.

Foreword
by Captain N C H (Jimmy) James, RN

It is reckoned that some ninety per cent of Britain's trade is carried over the sea into and out of our islands. In addition, in these days of increasing discomfort and problems facing those who choose air travel, travel by sea, especially for a cruise holiday, has become more and more attractive to more and more people.

These facts re-emphasise the importance of the tradition that Britain is, as she has always been, a maritime nation. To satisfy the demands of the merchant navy, men and women of a very high calibre are required to fill the many appointments available at sea. Lessons must be learned as to how their tasks are to be best performed. One way to learn those lessons is to read of the experience of people who carry out the tasks now and who have the expertise and competence to teach trainees to perform well, and to lead and command ships' companies.

It is also true that because of the traditional enthusiasm for maritime affairs in Britain, people want to read of the exploits of our mariners and of the way they cope with the continuing dangers and complications of life at sea. Passengers are always inquisitive, and want to know what their captain does and how he controls his ship and staff.

This book is perfect for both purposes. It is written by a man who has vast experience of life at sea. From being a young cadet in cargo vessels, through being a watchkeeper and navigator of the most famous cruise ship of our time – the *QE2* – to being the master of a wide variety of passenger ships, and now the captain of a very traditional cruise ship, the *Saga Ruby* – Philip Rentell has it all.

I had the privilege of working with Philip at sea in the *QE2* at the time of the Falklands War, and now have had the additional privilege of watching him perform every facet of his duties in his present appointment. He is one of the most competent and far-thinking people in his profession, and this book explains why he is so respected and admired. I can assure any reader that they will learn from this book – and enjoy themselves as they are being educated.

Preface

Here lie some of the anecdotes and salty tales that make up forty years of earning one's crust from driving vehicles that float. The answer to many a question may be found within – 'What made you go to sea?' 'What does your wife feel about you working on passenger ships?' 'Have you ever had any dangerous moments?' 'If you're down here talking to us, who's up there driving the ship?'

Ten years ago I compiled a little book of 'ruminations from a passenger-ship captain'. I called it *Not Yet*, to express the hope that I would spend at least a few more years at sea – and *Master Mariner* brings my professional life right up to date, with my current employment on the magnificent classical cruise ships of Saga, the *Saga Rose* and *Saga Ruby*.

I was urged to write a book by the many passengers with whom I have shared tales at my dining table on board. There are two other reasons why I felt compelled to commit words to paper. The first is because I knew so little of my father's life and his ancestors, and I believe it is important that I should record something for the sake of my son and any children that he may have. The second is because I would like to encourage the young men and women who come to sea today to stick to their chosen profession. Life at sea is often far from easy, but those who persevere will have their own tales to tell when they eventually retire. They should then feel a fine sense of achievement, having worked in an environment that can be merciless, and proud that they have been in a profession that still deserves the greatest of respect.

Master Mariner is not meant to be a diary or an autobiography. Neither would I like to think that this was the sum total of my professional life to date – and of course there are some tales which I cannot tell! The book records just a few memorable moments from a busy career. It takes the reader from my early days of being wet behind the ears to almost twenty years in command. So far I have kept the water from getting into my boots, as well as my ships. Long may it continue, and to those many colleagues I have met upon the way may I wish that 'You always have at least six inches of water under your keel.'

Writing the first half of the book has involved some dredging of the memory, but since my first command in 1990 I have tended to record the stories shortly after the event, usually in sufficient time before they became just a hazy blur. Everything recounted here is true – though I have changed one or two of the names.

'Driving the new hotel, 1987' was originally published in the magazine *Cruise Digest*, and '*Cunard Princess*: a week down Mexico Way' appeared in *Ships Monthly*. 'Ruminations from a master' was first published in the Nautical Institute magazine *Seaways*, as were the two final chapters, describing cruises to Antarctica and Greenland – and these are in fact edited versions of two extracts from the 'Master's blog' that is published on the Saga website. Also included are two papers that I wrote for Nautical Institute command seminars in 1995 and 2000. I am grateful to have been able to reproduce all of these. I also wish to thank Express Newspapers for allowing me to reproduce an extract from the *Scottish Daily Express*, and the publishers of the other brief newspaper reports included.

There are many people I should like to thank for their assistance, including of course the two distinguished mariners who have so kindly contributed forewords – Sir Robin Knox-Johnston and Captain 'Jimmy' James, whom I was very pleased to have on the bridge many times during a recent cruise around Africa. Joan Crosley and Richard Woodman, in correcting the text, both kindly saved me from including a number of errors (but any that survive are mine and not theirs). Bob Curtis let me use his photos of Brixham pilot boats and Tony Davis supplied his photograph of *Cunard Princess*. Patricia Eve and her team at Seafarer Books have given me much encouragement and have produced what I hope will be received as a fine book. I am grateful to the many colleagues and friends I have made over the years, too many to mention of course, but who have all been important members of the team. Finally, I thank my wife Helen, and our son Richard Trevelyan, both of whom have been the linchpin in my life and the reason I always call our home the port I love the most – and the one to which I always want to return.

———

Sea life, I am happy to say, continues to be challenging, interesting – and still the vocation I always wanted it to be. As the last few words of this book are hitting the keyboard I am taking the *Saga Ruby* around Africa. It has been a fascinating experience, calling at places I haven't seen since the mid seventies and even, on the east coast, ports I have only visited on my first trip to sea as a cadet back in 1970. We have had to divert because of a cyclone, cancel a port in Madagascar because the Foreign and Commonwealth Office have said the country is too dangerous for UK nationals. Preparations have had to be made to avoid the modern-day pirates off the coast of Somalia, and all that without even mentioning the hectic day-to-day schedule of a modern cruise-ship captain.

From Greenland and Spitsbergen all the way down to the Antarctic, and around the world from east to west and west to east, calling at hundreds of ports, many for the first time, the last few years with Saga have been as rewarding as I could have hoped. Saga has been a great family for the crew and officers, as well as for the many passengers who keep returning. As I approach what I expect to be the final years of my vocation, I am certain that there is nothing else I would rather be doing.

Saga Ruby, Mombasa, February 2009

Cadet

Worcester

'**S**o why did you go to sea?'– not quite the most asked question, but nearly.

My father was a newsagent/tobacconist in Birmingham, as were his father and grandfather before him. I was brought up in the heart of England and only ever saw the sea when I visited my mother's parents in Cornwall. In fact the only possible connection I might have had with the sea was my maternal grandfather's job during the late 1920s, when he worked as a rivet catcher in the Falmouth ship repair yard.

I went to a very progressive comprehensive school in the mid 1960s. Apart from the Duke of Edinburgh award scheme and various other outdoor pursuits, there was a chance to go cruising along with children from different parts of the country, usually around Easter time. I was fortunate enough, when I was just thirteen, to spend ten days on the British India ship *Dunera*.

After a voyage from Southampton to Vigo, Lisbon and Cadiz, I probably needed little further convincing that this was going to be my career. Somehow I could not face following my father into the family business. As a child, I hardly saw him, because he left home so early and returned so late – and I probably saw more of him when I was 'detailed to help' in the shop at weekends and during the school holidays.

My first aspiration was to become a radio officer. Eventually, after three more cruises over the next few years, I settled down to finding out exactly what qualifications I needed to become a deck officer, and how my education had to continue once I'd left school. The local careers office knew nothing, and even the man from the Shipping Federation tried to put me off.

———

In September 1969, aged nearly eighteen, I was one of just under a hundred new cadets to join the training ship *Worcester*, moored in the Thames off Greenhithe in Kent. We were to be the last full intake for the old ship, which had been built as a training ship in the early 1900s, used as a submarine depot ship at Scapa Flow during the Second World War, and was now owned by the Inner London Education Authority. Along with an old abbey and a swimming pool ashore, the establishment was officially named the Merchant Navy College.

I had been for an interview over a year before, but because of my lack of a maths O-level it had been decided I should remain at school to improve my qualifications. That initial introduction had been an eye-opener, and my mother was not convinced that I would be suited to the obvious boarding-school regimentation of this floating institution. I can assume, however, that then, like now, when I got something into my head it became a challenge – and, to this day, failure or withdrawal is not something that I easily accept.

More than anything, the *Worcester* was character-building. I was placed in a small group of young men who were to study for their Ordinary National Diploma, while the remainder were taking their Ordinary National Certificate. From the beginning I found the academic side difficult, and it was quite obvious to me that I would be thrown out after one term. The physics and electronics was another language, as I had struggled at school to get a general science O-level even at the second attempt. Naturally maths was just as frustrating, but some of the more practical subjects – such as general ship knowledge, navigation, seamanship – were more to my liking. I quickly learned to drive boats and enjoyed the outdoor activities on the river, even though they were completely new to me. (I found out many years later that my mother had not encouraged me to join the Scouts because

Philip Russell Collection

Worcester

she thought all the scout leaders were homosexuals.)

By the end of the first term the last of the old boys left. They had completed their time and were finally joining whichever shipping company would take them. Even if they had only reached the minimum standard, they had had a good grounding in seamanship and all would make good officers eventually.

Along with the rest of my small class, I was made a cadet captain. I was placed in charge of Mizzen Division, and the responsibility, such as it was, took time to sink in. The confidence to give orders came quickly, but it was not always easy.

I struggled on with my lessons, was not thrown out, and survived the year. Academically I was not brilliant, and eventually I was transferred to the ONC course for the remainder of my three-year cadetship. In fact it made little difference, for an OND or an ONC was only useful if you left the sea altogether. The real goal for us was a second mate's certificate, the final examination that would allow the cadet to go to sea as a junior officer and take a watch on the bridge.

In the meantime, life on the *Worcester* continued, and it was an experience not easily forgotten. The good times probably did not outweigh the bad, but at the end you knew you had been through the mill, to a proper training ship and not some mamby-pamby polytechnic.

The ship had been built out of iron and steel to resemble a larger version of Nelson's *Victory* and, needless to say, was slightly lacking in modern-day comforts. When the winter came the chill easterly wind rushed down the Thames across Long Reach, and would come racing through every hole in the ship's side, penetrating the accommodation deck and blowing straight through anything in its way – including us. The orlop deck was one through space where the deck boards had been rounded by continual polishing, with the bunks separated by steel lockers into groups of five or six. Towards the stern was a billiard table wedged up in an attempt to make it horizontal, but it was still affected by the passing river traffic, which at times gave the ship a gentle roll.

The cadet captains had a private little recreation room to which we could retire away from the other lads, and that was next to the hospital – where the capable but not so attractive matron ruled the roost. There were many stories invented about her sexual exploits with previous cadets, but of course there was never a cadet that could give me first-hand details of his experiences!

Among the strange characters we had as lecturers was a certain Mr Fuller, apparently known as 'Fruity Fuller' to the older boys. Within a few weeks of our arrival he took us to the swimming pool situated in the college grounds ashore in order to demonstrate the function of the inflatable life raft. The raft was already floating in the pool, and after changing he told us to take off our trunks, jump into the water, swim out to the raft and climb in.

We were all very 'green', and although we thought this a little strange we complied with his request. Once inside the raft, the flaps were closed and he, also naked, proceeded to explain that because of the enclosed environment, the raft would soon heat up and thus the cold wet bodies without clothes would soon get over any degree of hypothermia we might have suffered by being in the ocean and remaining in wet clothes.

It was at this moment that another class of senior boys unexpectedly came into the pool area, saw what was happening, and started blowing wolf whistles. Looking back, it was really very funny, but at the time I think we were just embarrassed at what fools we must have seemed to have been duped like that. Fuller did attempt to assist one of the cadets, who by this time had left the raft and, because he could not swim, was shuffling along the wall bar. Needless to say, with so many of us around, nothing untoward happened, but it was my first insight into what could be considered an 'alternative' society.

Our time off was limited to a few hours in the evenings, when many of the boys who had a few bob went into the village to the nearest pub. Every other weekend was free after Saturday morning divisions, and so for the first few months I took the opportunity of visiting a young lady in Rochester whom I had met the previous summer. That relationship tailed off and, after a dance we had organised, I started heading the other way to visit another lady in Northfleet. Regrettably she had other plans and went off to be a Bunny Girl in the London's Playboy Club – a pity really, because her father was an interesting man, the skipper of the last open-wheelhouse London river tug.

We really didn't have much time for protracted affairs. Apart from the studies, which didn't get any easier as the months progressed, we were obviously also expected to do all sorts of nautical things. I was in the rowing team for my division, and we had to train by rowing large whalers, which were very heavy. There was a race called the 'Houlders Oars', which had formerly seen the *Worcester* cadets pitted against another nautical institution,

HMS *Conway*, but they had no team to offer so it was competed for in-house. Our division put up a good effort, but we were placed second.

Undeterred, several of us volunteered to row in a charity race from Gravesend to Southend Pier and back, a distance of twenty-five miles. These whalers had fifteen-foot ash oars, so the work was back-breaking and blister-forming. We made the pier by early afternoon, had a short break and struggled back. It was probably one of the most physically demanding things I have ever had to do – and I have never felt the urge to repeat the exercise!

As in all boarding schools, there were always one or two of the boys that were brighter, clumsier, less liked, etc, than others. I was fairly fortunate, for apart from being a bit dimmer than the others in my class I was never actively disliked – I don't believe! The chief cadet captain, however, was a bit of a prat. He took his role very seriously and eventually became ostracised by the others, to such a degree that all sorts of tricks were played against him.

A few of the boys ganged together and started filling in all sorts of coupons in newspapers – and very soon some strange articles of women's underwear, along with catalogues, job applications and free samples of this and that, started landing on board, much to the amusement of all. Eventually the captain called us all to a meeting and insisted that this tomfoolery had to stop, otherwise there would be serious trouble.

One early morning we actually carried the cadet captain, in his bunk, down the companionway to the deck below, which was just above the level of the river. His bunk was placed next to the old submarine access door, which was then opened to allow the full force of an easterly gale to blow right over him. He had been asleep until that time and, needless to say, there was much laughter all round when he woke.

In general, life on board the *Worcester* was relatively routine and, apart from a few odd bods, all the boys left after one year as young men and went on to a variety of companies. I was fortunate in that I was accepted by British and Commonwealth, a company which had well over eighty ships at that time, including five large passenger liners on the South African route. I left the college in July 1970 and joined the cargo ship *Clan Malcolm* on 28 August – the first of a great many vessels I would have the pleasure (sometimes the dubious pleasure) to work aboard.

First tripper

The *Clan Malcolm* was the first of a number of vessels I would join as cadet, or 'gadget' as we were unceremoniously referred to by the other officers. My father took the day off on 28 August 1970 and drove me to join the ship, which was berthed in Hull docks. I'm sure he must have had a lump in his throat as he left me there on board, about to start a way of life that was as remote to him as it was to me.

The ship had just returned from a foreign voyage and was starting a 'coastal' period. It would call at a number of UK ports, first to unload the cargo brought back from West Africa and then to load a new cargo of manufactured goods bound for Kenya

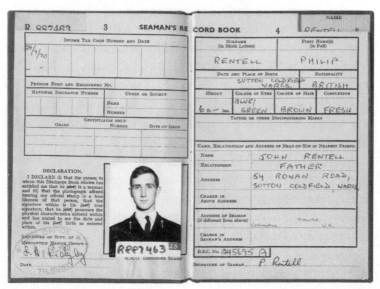

and Tanzania. There was another brand new cadet, a 'Jock', and we were to share the same cabin with yet another chap from Plymouth. Three young lads at the start of an adventure in life, but all very different in their attitudes, and in their ability to come to terms with what would turn out to be almost nine months together in a new life at sea.

The next day Jock and I, having been told by the mate to familiarise ourselves with the ship, were standing at number one hatch on the forecastle watching the busy scene of a working port. The sound of sirens could be heard, and eventually we saw a couple of fire engines tearing round the other side of the water. We casually remarked that there must be a ship on fire somewhere – but they rapidly got closer, and very soon pulled up alongside our ship. We were so green that we had been oblivious to the fact that the dockers had reported that number four hatch, loaded with fishmeal from Walvis Bay, was smoking quite nicely the deeper they got into it. Apparently that cargo was prone to spontaneous combustion, and the temperature had reached a point where extensive precautions were necessary in order to quell the flames that could erupt at any time.

Work continued, and after some time the ship was made ready for sea, not to foreign and romantic parts, but to continue round the UK coast. We were bound for Birkenhead, with a passage first round the north of Scotland and through the Pentland Firth. When we arrived it was realised that the ship would be alongside in Hull for at least three weeks, so the mate decided to send us off for a spot of leave, most likely to get us out of his hair rather than for our personal benefit.

It was some weeks later when my father put me on the train at Birmingham's New Street station, I can remember quite distinctly his advice about not 'going with strange women' – though I really didn't know what he meant, as any advice about 'ladies of the night' up to that point in time had been nil.

There was a wonderful confusion, or so it seemed, about the loading of a general cargo ship. Tween decks, lower hold, deep

Clan Malcolm

tanks, and eventually above deck, were all stowed in meticulous fashion, and where any gaps lay between crates, packages, sacks, drums, etc, the carpenter was busy 'tomming up' with bulks of timber, referred to as dunnage, to prevent collapse in heavy seas. The rounded hull and framed bulkheads necessitated platforms and bulkheads to be constructed, mainly with an endless supply of six-inch nails, to ensure no part of the cargo could touch the steel, which would sweat as we reached the tropics.

The cadets were used as labourers to assist wherever necessary, learning the trade from as close to the bottom of the skill ladder as you would ever want to be. Hard work, and every day we seemed to be learning or doing something new until eventually it was time to sail and leave the UK a long way behind us. We knew not for how long. One trip to East Africa and back should take about four months, but if we did a 'double-header', back up to the Mediterranean to discharge and load again, who knew how long it would be before we returned to home shores?

South

After a week or more we arrived at Las Palmas for bunkers, a six- to eight-hour stop to fill up with cheaper fuel oil, which would take us all the way to our first discharge port, Mombasa. A voyage that would take four weeks and see us rounding the Cape of Good Hope, skirting the South African coast, up past Portuguese Mozambique, Tanzania and eventually Kenya. After an afternoon sailing, the ship developed a technical problem in the engine room and had to come limping back into the Las

Palmas anchorage with 'not under command signals' flying, to lie for a few days in sheltered waters while parts were delivered and repairs effected.

Long days at sea eventually drift into each other. The ship starts to gradually cook as we approach the tropics, the sun burns down and, with no air conditioning, various constructions are rudely assembled to gather some of the precious ship-generated breeze into sweltering cabins. Dirty clothes and sweaty socks have to be quickly dealt with to ensure the unpleasant odours don't become a cause to gag as we return to our three-berth 'box'.

We ate to appease a huge appetite, and our crew from Pakistan produced good wholesome food, including typical dishes from their own country. I was a faddy child apparently, but any sign of that had long since gone, and I ate everything that was put in front of me. We were always hungry. Plates of toast and jam would come out for 'smoko', just a few hours after breakfast. Ten minutes before lunch, a quick wash-up, into decent uniform and ready to attack the starter, main course, curry, pudding, and anything else on offer, before being turned back out on deck, changed ready for work. Dinner was at six and we were hungry again by eight.

We could have a beer in the evening but we were limited as to how many we could have in a week, and our salary of around £8.50 a month did not lead to expensive tastes or over-indulgence. The one thing I do remember with some unpleasantness was the tea. Fresh milk did not last long after our departure, so condensed milk or 'cony-ony' was used, quite disgusting when I look back.

Although much of our time was spent on deck, soogying, chipping, painting and greasing, we also had to spend some time on the bridge, watchkeeping. Here the officer of the watch would attempt to make us proficient in taking compass errors and sun sights, in radar position fixing and chart work, plus maintaining a conscientious lookout, perhaps one of the most boring but vitally important aspects of the deck officer's work.

Landfall

Eventually excitement grew as we approached our destination, but the port was congested and the master was told to anchor. We lay there for three weeks, sweating at our work. The mate ensured we were never at a loss for something to do – and helping the carpenter secure spar ceiling in the forward deep tank comes to my mind as one of the most exhausting tasks. Great lengths of timber were bolted to the side of the tank to ensure subsequent bagged cargo would not touch the steel, get wet and go rotten. The temperature inside the airless tank was well over a hundred degrees and I must have lost weight with the amount of sweat I produced. In this tropical climate revolting salt tablets had to be taken with our meals to ensure our continual wellbeing, but they just made me feel sick.

Eventually our turn to berth came around. We heaved anchor late one very sunny morning, approached the entrance and took our harbour pilot aboard. I guess our time as colonial rulers had come and gone, but there were still some indications that these far-flung outposts of a forgotten empire were home to many expatriates, as the pilot was as British as the rest of the officers on board. He guided us professionally through the narrow entrance, between the shoals of coral and sand, taking us to the inside anchorage where we were to partly discharge our cargo. I remember the old harbour tugs, still painted brilliant white in an effort to reflect the heat, and the dhows and barges which seemed to be on endless business being taken out to unload ships in the inner anchorage then back alongside the shallower berths, where the bigger ships were too deep in their draught to dock.

Ashore

My recollections are of sweating and coping with the heat while on cargo work duties, attempting to find the sultry shade at every possible opportunity, then looking forward with great anticipation to going ashore in the evening to the 'Mish'. This was the Mission to Seafarers, the Christian club that welcomes sailors of all nationalities to a place where they can relax and have some time ashore in safe and pleasant surroundings. The Mission in Mombasa was particularly pleasant, with swimming pool, snooker table, table tennis and a small bar where a local beer could be bought at a reasonable price. Over thirty years later my wife Helen and I would travel to Peru on a sponsorship challenge to raise over £5000 for the same organisation.

But sailors' tales are made up of more than a lazy few hours at the Mish. We had the odd evening 'up the road', the Kilindini Road as it happened. This was the main street running into the centre of the city and passing under two impressive crossed tusks which I presume had been erected in colonial times to represent the great elephants that inhabit the interior. I was told we had to go to a few bars, a sort of pub-crawl really, to places that sailors often frequent for pleasures not necessarily entirely of the alcoholic kind.

After a beer in one or two, we ended up in the Sunshine Bar, a place of great reputation up and down the east coast of Africa, and I was to learn just how green I was. The place was black inside, and as our eyes adjusted to the darkness we realised that the only lighting came from a few scattered ultraviolet neon tubes. Their light turned our T-shirts white while the remainder of our clothes and everything else in the bar remained black. We grabbed the only free table, or so it seemed, though there were handbags on the chairs. We placed the bags on the table, sat down, ordered a round and waited for the drinks while being deafened by some contemporary local music bellowing out from huge speakers. Then my embarrassment started, when a number of local ladies came to retrieve their bags and seats. But they didn't seem to mind our presence; they just gathered around and quickly started becoming quite familiar. So familiar, in fact, that I found one sitting on my lap, one arm draped around my shoulder while the other hand was rubbing its way up and down my trouser leg.

Of course, they were friendly because their particular trade warranted not just social intercourse. I was inexperienced in this sort of blatant foreplay to financial transactions for pleasures of a more intimate nature. A few of the other guys just lapped it up, and I guess we all had a good laugh, mainly induced by the varying quantities of alcohol we had taken in the last few hours. I was grateful my embarrassment was hidden by the darkness, and fortunately a number of us fairly soon decided enough was enough and it was time to make a dignified retreat. We headed back to the ship and safety – but not without a couple of the lads deciding that the pleasures of the flesh were necessary to ensure that their 'trip up the road' was a complete success.

I would imagine our exploits then were no different to what the younger folks get up to these days – it just so happened that we had this period of our adolescence in vessels far away from home. But I feel sorry for the younger seafarers of today. In those days it was not uncommon for sailors to pick up a sexual problem, but it was one for which there was a ready cure, and by the time you returned to 'Blighty' things had usually returned to normal.

Naturally, as time goes by, you don't always remember the grind of the daily work and the hot nights where even one sheet was too much to allow sleep to come for more than a few precious hours. But I do remember a safari trip. As we were a training ship with twelve cadets on board, it was decided that we should be given an opportunity to see the interior. Consequently we embarked in a couple of minivans that were to transport us off to the Amboseli Game Park for a couple of nights. After what seemed an interminable time bouncing over not the best of roads we arrived the first evening to be given small chalets, two or three beds in each. They were very Spartan, with a mosquito net over each bed, so we dumped our gear and a couple of us went off to explore. Before long we were halted by the bellowing of a ranger not far behind us. Our first mistake had been not to check out the safety procedures, and we were told in no uncertain terms that wandering around where elephants are prone to trek is a good way of becoming rather dead. After supper we retreated to our chalets, only to find that all the flying insects of the night had taken up residence and were covering the mosquito nets. They had been attracted to the single lamp, powered by the camp generator, which we had unwisely left on. It was a strange sensation carefully pulling the net to one side, sliding onto the bed and attempting to secure the opening with all this wildlife creeping around just inches from your face. Sleep does not come easily when you think your going to be bitten to the bone during the dark hours. Of course it eventually did, and we awoke early the next morning as the sun rose – with not an insect in the room.

We had a great time, saw all sorts of wildlife, met the people of the Maasai tribe, lived in the bush, and just gained more experience of life outside our home country – what a privilege.

We must have been alongside almost three weeks, but eventually it was time to leave. We were not going that far, just down to Dar es Salaam in Tanzania. Even there we had to anchor for a few days before going alongside to discharge. We were in the tiny port of Mtwara for New Years Eve, then in Lourenço Marques, and finally down to what was then considered civilisation, Durban.

South Africa in those days was very much apartheid, and it came as something of a shock. Some of the people we spoke to considered it was the only way their country would survive, as they had heard of the other African countries slowly falling into corruption and disrepair because of the inability of local governments to sustain any sort of continued growth. Maybe over the years their view has changed, but one thing I was made aware of was that the Blacks did not have compulsory education, whereas the Whites did. Without educating their people no country will prosper.

But South Africa was great for the sailor, with bustling streets, plenty to do and, so it seemed, plenty of young ladies who were happy to meet us. We arranged a few parties on board, inviting nurses down from the local hospital – great fun had by all. Life is cruel, however, as we had no sooner met someone we liked than again we would have to sail. East London, Port Elizabeth, Cape Town were all ports we called in to load cargo, and the cargo was bound for Mediterranean ports. We were on a double-header!

Northbound

We headed off into the deep Cape rollers, with the ship secured down against the massive swell coming up from the Antarctic Ocean. All cargo had been secured both below and above deck, not a thing moved despite the inclinometer's great deviations. The trade winds pushed us north, and eventually the seas became calm enough for one to walk about without constantly grasping for the handrail. Our first discharge port in the Mediterranean was to be Gibraltar, where we had just a little cargo but where, more importantly, we would replenish our fuel bunkers.

But we first had to make a call at the islands of St Helena and Ascension, those British outposts in the South Atlantic. There is no berth to take a ship of any size in St Helena, so vessels anchored and cargo was unloaded using ships' derricks onto small barges that were then towed ashore. The rate of discharge depended entirely on the swell conditions, and it could become a protracted operation. For us it was a couple of days, and that gave the cadets time to explore the island. Our training officer managed to arrange for an open truck to be fitted out with seats, and all twelve of us took a boat ashore and clambered into the back, not forgetting a case of beer to ensure liquid replenishment during the expedition. (A case of beer was a compulsory addition in those days to any venture ashore longer than a few hours.)

It was a great day, as St Helena is such an unusual place. It is noted, of course, for being the last home of Napoleon, and indeed we visited where he was kept prisoner, as well as the grave in which he was originally buried. The house was a small museum, with some interesting artefacts inside. We visited Government House, where we did not meet the governor but did meet a huge tortoise in the garden that had apparently been alive during the time of Napoleon's internment. It is a mountainous island, and so we had a very scenic drive which returned us to an incredible set of nine hundred steps, Jacob's Ladder, which led down into Jamestown, the only town of any significance, nestled in the valley below. To go down was hard enough; to come up must have required incredible stamina.

I think my strongest memory, though, comes from the evening ashore we had in the community hall. It was Saints Day and a band was playing music to suit all tastes; they were the Syncopated Saints, and they were equipped with electric guitars capable of making a very loud noise. The locals danced the night away, dragging us up onto the floor in a way I was not to repeat until Peru some thirty-two years later. Great fun, only curtailed by the call of our boat beckoning us back to the ship.

We carried fifty or so locals on the two-day passage up to Ascension and, in line with the normal custom, these folks slept on the open boat deck either side of the engine-room skylights. Apparently many of the men went away to work on Ascension, mainly at the American airbase at Wideawake, which became famous as the busiest helicopter base in the world for a few weeks during the Falklands crisis in 1982.

Gibraltar was almost like going home. These were days when the British Navy were still using the rock as a base, the shops had a sort of English feel to them, and of course the policemen were dressed the same as at home. We were not there for long but we managed to try a local pub and buy a few bits and pieces we had been missing for four months – Cadbury's chocolate, for example.

The Mediterranean was pretty cold, as it was winter. We had cargo for Barcelona, Livorno and Genoa, and in all these places there was time to do some sightseeing – the Leaning Tower of Pisa, a few miles outside Livorno, a day's skiing in the Italian Alps and a run ashore up the Ramblas in Barcelona – and that was another education. During the day the Ramblas is a beautiful tree-lined avenue running between wonderful old buildings, but at night in the early 1970s it seemed to be lined with bars, all bustling until well into the early hours.

One of my cabin mates homed in again on the female pleasures, and there seemed to be plenty of opportunity, stunning young ladies in every bar and on every corner – but then of course after a few beers they all looked great. Yet when we returned to Barcelona a few weeks later to load cargo, the American Sixth Fleet was in town. The ladies had gone, the MPs had replaced them on every corner and in every bar – and even so their sailors seemed to be far worse for alcoholic wear than we ever managed to be. We reckoned it was because the US Navy had a dry ship policy: when the boys eventually got ashore they couldn't handle more than just a few beers. Our nautical training included the social necessity of being able to hold one's liquor!

South again

The next few months shot by. The charming city of Cadiz was our last port in Europe before going south. We were only going as far as Lourenço Marques this time, but we called at the South African ports both on the way and on our eventual homeward voyage. By this time the five of us who had joined in Hull were the senior cadets, and another six had come aboard in the Med to replace those who were going back home and to college. Naturally we felt quite superior: we had crossed the line, we had stories to tell of adventures in Africa. Leave the party arranging to us: we know the contacts, the girls, the bars. Nonsense of course, but it impressed one or two of them. The others were not so gullible as to take our ramblings for anything but one-trip cadet bravado.

And so, after a few more months, I completed my first voyage at sea, a great learning experience in more ways than one, exciting on occasion, but also at times tedious, boring and even lonely. I think most of us have done a lot of soul searching at that age – Is this really the career for me? Will I end up like the senior officers? Do they actually like what they do for a living?

The only thing I was sure about was that I should finish what I had started. Getting to the end of the first road involved more sea time and a great deal of study before I might end up with a second mate's ticket, the first certificate which allows young cadets to become young officers and be responsible to the master for keeping a safe navigational watch for eight hours a day. It was still a long way off, and I wasn't sure I was academically bright enough, but if it was going to take a kind of stubborn staying power, I knew I had it.

The *Clan Malcolm* returned to Avonmouth on 4 June 1971, and I was to take four weeks' leave before my next appointment, so my father picked me up from the ship and drove the couple of hours back up the M5 to Birmingham. We had been together down that same road three years before in order to take my sight test at the Mercantile Marine Office in Bristol, the dreaded lantern test that reveals whether you can distinguish the coloured lights of ships at night. As I look back over almost four decades at sea I often ask myself the question, what would I have done if I had failed that sight test? At the time I had been so nervous it had been very touch and go. What if?

Bowater's

When I travelled up to Scotland to join my next vessel I was not to realise that by the time I returned home after another seven months I would have served on three ships, all belonging to the same subsidiary of British and Commonwealth Shipping, the Bowater Paper Company. As the name implies, the ships were all involved in the paper trade, carrying in the main either newsprint in great rolls or paper pulp in compressed bundles of about a cubic metre.

Bowater's had originally run their own ships, and although relatively small they were lovely vessels, almost yacht-like, with accommodation for a few passengers and an 'owner's suite'.

Nicolas Bowater

Times were changing, though, and as their fleet started to age and contract I presume it was not felt practical to operate a shipping company within a paper company – so the management of the remaining ships was handed over to B&C. The two main trading patterns were from the Baltic running cargoes down to the paper mills on the River Thames, and with products from the paper mills of Newfoundland to the eastern seaboard of Canada and the USA.

The *Nicolas Bowater* had been refitting in a Glasgow dry dock. I arrived on board on 2 July 1971 in the knowledge that the ship was expected to sail the following day for the USA, my first trip across the Atlantic. In a ridiculous way I felt almost like Christopher Columbus on his voyage of discovery: for the first time I was going to see at first hand this land of opportunity we had all heard about since our early school days. Other chaps who had sailed on the ships before had talked of good times ashore, and I was really looking forward to experiencing them. Our first destination was to be Charleston, South Carolina, for a cargo of paper pulp.

The crossing must have been fairly routine, and when we reached the US coast the ship anchored in the Cooper River for a day or so. I was posted on bridge anchor watch, on my own. I must have impressed the chief mate with my abilities, or perhaps he was a lazy so-and-so and didn't want to get up at four o'clock in the morning. Anyway, even though I felt almost petrified in case anything should happen when the ship was theoretically under my sole responsibility for the first time, I did the watches. Much to my absolute relief, the ship did not sink, drift away, catch fire or run aground.

Paper pulp is loaded very efficiently using what are referred to as chain slings, lifting up about eight or ten of these cubic-metre blocks at a time. Inside the ship they were dropped unceremoniously into the hold, quickly released from the chains and rolled into position so that you eventually end up with a solid mass of white pulp filling every possible space like bricks in a wall. Of course, paper in this form can absorb a great deal of water, so it was imperative that when loading the hold was complete, the hatch covers were securely closed and completely watertight so that any rough seas that the ship might meet on its next voyage should not be able to seep down into the hold. If the pulp became wet it would swell to such a degree that hatch lids could be forced off, structural damage to the ship might occur and of course the cargo would become useless.

My time ashore to experience America was very short, as this type of cargo could be loaded very quickly and within three days the ship was full to her marks. But one night we did manage to go to a local club, a disco the like of which I had never seen before, as the floor was illuminated by coloured stripes all flashing in time with the music. I wasn't over-impressed when I went to get a beer, however. I was refused on the grounds that I was under twenty-one, the age limit at which young Americans became eligible to buy a drink in a public bar. Even in the UK I had never been questioned before, and I had been going into pubs since I was about sixteen years old.

We sailed, not to enjoy the pleasures of the North American coast but to Durban in South Africa. I was a little disappointed. I'd 'done' South Africa, I wanted to get to see other places – and besides, Durban was a heck of a long way. In fact it would take twenty-eight days of steady steaming to get there, a whole month at sea. Could I stand the routine and the boredom?

Of course I had to, there was no choice. On arriving in Durban we went straight alongside to discharge and to be told that we were loading a full cargo of Rayon pulp, which looked almost identical to the paper and was stowed in just the same manner. After ten days and a few evenings ashore we set off, bound for the USA again, another twenty-eight days at sea. In fact we repeated the whole round trip twice, finally ending up in Mobile, Alabama, some time in late November. Five months had gone by, somehow without us really noticing it, as the officers were a good relaxed crowd who were easy to get on with.

North America

On arrival in Mobile the company-appointed local agent told us we were lucky to get in, as the dockers were going on strike and the port would be closed. Unlucky for the poor ship owner perhaps, but not for us guys, who seemed to have seen far too much water in the past five months. The chief mate, an Australian who smoked like a chimney, decided we should have a party and duly contacted the agent to organise same. The women were staff and friends from the agent's office and it was decided Friday lunchtime would be most suitable, with the weekend coming up and no sign of any serious cargo work being done in the near future.

The ladies had been told it was to be a traditional British fish-and-chip lunch, in newspaper, so I think that might have encouraged a few who may have had second thoughts about going on board a cargo ship full of sailors who hadn't seen much of the opposite sex for some considerable time. But the agent was advised of a serious proviso when inviting the ladies: there had to be one whose task would be to socialise with the captain, George Trowsdale.

At the appointed hour a convoy of large American cars drove into the dock and parked alongside the ship, and about a dozen ladies, plus the agent, proceeded to make their way up the gangway. Of course they were received warmly, and for the first hour or so good manners simply oozed out of the officers. Drinks were served in the cosy lounge normally reserved for the few passengers the ship might take from time to time, the fish and chips arrived and were devoured with great relish, with these Southern ladies all commenting on 'how cute it was'.

Then we noticed George sloping off with a slightly more mature lady, who had obviously been instructed in her duty as she had been in deep conversation with the 'old man' for some time. They went down to her car, extricated a suitcase and made their way back on board. As they passed the lounge on the way up to his cabin we pretended not to notice, but there were big grins on all our faces. George had 'scored' – no wonder they called him 'Trousers Trowsdale'.

In fact we never saw the captain until Monday. I guess he must have had a very tiring weekend. We made friends with the ladies and were invited back to a number of parties in the few weeks we stayed in port. I had a very close friend who drove me around and showed me the area in her big open-top American cruiser. One party sticks in my mind, and that was when we were all invited to the home of the captain's lady friend, only to be met at the door by her husband. Nothing was said, he and his wife were perfect hosts, and we only found out a few days later that, because the husband could apparently no longer 'perform', his wife had threatened divorce, which he could not face. I'd like to believe it was because he loved her so much he couldn't bear to live without her, but maybe it was because of the settlement he would have to make if they did separate. Anyway, he was prepared to accept her 'playing away' provided she stayed with him – an amicable arrangement, I suppose.

We eventually sailed after discharging our cargo. A sad goodbye, but we were all looking forward to our next port. We had been told the runs to Durban were finally over and we should proceed to Corner Brook in Newfoundland, where a cargo of newsprint would be waiting. At long last, I was to visit the port all the Bowater boys talked about, and Christmas was coming up.

Corner Brook

We arrived on a crystal-clear cold day in this beautiful place set at the mouth of the Bay of Islands. The city is twenty-five miles inland from the open waters of the Gulf of St Lawrence, the landscape of the region is rugged and the scenery spectacular, with mountains filling the horizon in all directions. The surrounding coastline holds magnificent fjords, jagged headlands, thickly forested areas and many offshore islands. We were to go alongside a wooden jetty right next to a large paper mill that was very atmospheric – tall chimneys belching out steam from the plant inside, the noise of working machinery. The smell of the lumber being processed was so rich and sweet it felt as though it could be cut with a knife.

Trees were brought down from the forest and the mill dealt with the entire process of converting them to pulp or, as in the case of our cargo, newsprint. Great rolls about four feet high and two feet in diameter were brought to the quayside by specially adapted forklift trucks that had a set of jaws to clamp each roll. The ship's derricks were rigged in what is termed a union purchase arrangement to lift the rolls into the hold, but great care was needed by the stevedores to transfer, lower and position the rolls, ensuring they suffered no damage. Damaged rolls would be rejected if they could not fit the machines of the newspaper printing press.

The small town and the surrounding hills were covered in snow and, although the day we arrived was clear, there was plenty of snow to fall during our stay. It was very cold at night, and everything appeared to be frozen, even some of the ballast tanks that I had to sound every day to ensure there was no ingress of water. There might have been, but my sounding rod always came up dry, and because of the temperature it was even difficult to remove the brass plug in the deck at the top of the sounding pipe.

After a day's work we always tried to have a nap before going ashore, as it seems did the young local folks, as the only disco didn't open its doors until ten o'clock at night. Making friends was very easy, as the girls were always keen to meet the few sailors that came into town, and we stayed until closing time at two in the morning. I met a lovely girl, a young primary-school teacher, and several times I was invited back to her parents' house. We would take the short journey in her car, sliding around on the icy roads before creeping in to the lounge downstairs to sit by the boiler and drink coffee. The relationship was all very proper, and despite any other intentions I might have had, she would always ensure I was on my way back to the ship by four. I can still clearly remember struggling the mile or so through the snow, dressed in just about every bit of clothing I had to keep out the cold, through the mill and back on board. After less than a couple of hours' sleep I had to be back on my feet to sound those damn tanks. Tired but happy, as I recall.

So we had Christmas Day there, and it was, as might be expected, a somewhat alcoholic celebration. One tinged with some sadness, however, as I had had my marching orders. I was due to go back to college to take my next study course in January, but the ship was to remain on the eastern seaboard. The company therefore planned to transfer me to the 3,917 gross ton *Gladys Bowater*, one of the smaller paper carriers that had come across the Atlantic and was expected to return to the UK. The ship, unfortunately, had been through some very rough weather and was now sitting in the dry dock in Halifax, Nova Scotia. Amongst

Gladys Bowater

other steelwork repairs, it had to have several hundred rivets in the forepart of the hull replaced.

Late in the afternoon of 27 December I picked up the regular taxi service that ran to the tiny airport at Deer Lake. I think the driver realised I was tight for time, because he careered off down the road at a great rate of knots, hardly taking his foot off the accelerator until we came to a sudden halt at the airport some hour and a half later. For most of the journey there had been no sign of the road in the headlights, just a long ribbon of packed grey ice stretching endlessly into the distance, with the ever-present forest hugging our intended path. That was some drive: he knew what he was doing, but it was better than many a fair-ground ride I've been on since. The plane was waiting, the props were turning, I just made it, much to the mirth of the stewardess at the door, who I suppose had seen this sort of situation many times before.

By the time I reached the ship it was late. The taxi driver didn't know where it was and we seemed to drive around half the city of Halifax before he returned to the dry dock. There it was, so small you could just see the masts and the funnel poking up over the top of the dock walls. In the officers' bar there were still a couple of guys and I managed to scrounge a beer before I found a cabin, unpacked and finally got my head down.

I was to be there only until 6 January. The ship was late coming out of the dry dock and the owners decided to change its itinerary for one that would keep her on the Canadian coast. We did actually sail, but only round to Liverpool, Nova Scotia, another tiny port where paper was processed and loaded. In the meantime, however, the New Year festivities were coming up and a party was organised for New Year's Eve. The ladies came from the local Young Women's Church Association – whether they were determined to offer some degree of Christian charity to us poor sailors stuck on a vessel in dry dock many miles from home, or just wanted to party, I never really found out. We all had a very good time, but not long after midnight there were just a few of us stalwarts left standing, I managed to chat to a very pleasant lady who had come out to Canada from Wales. We got on famously – so much so that she was able to see at first hand how small the bunks are in a cadet's cabin, so she took me back to see her spacious apartment. They say there's a warm welcome in the Welsh hillsides, and I'm pleased to report that this indeed is correct even in the expatriate of the species. As a result of our party, the socialising was reciprocated and our new-found friends extended hospitalities.

Yet again I felt I was making up for too many lonely months at sea, but then I was given a flight ticket back to Newfoundland. Upon arriving at Liverpool I hopped in a cab, was driven back to Halifax airport and flew to Stephenville, another small airport not so far away from Corner Brook. Here I joined *Constance Bowater*, a sister ship to the *Gladys*. She had almost finished loading and was shortly to leave for the UK.

North Atlantic

There was no time to see my recent acquaintance as we headed out for one of the worst-weather trips I have had to experience. The North Atlantic is rarely anyone's friend in the middle of winter, and the next twelve days were going to be no exception. The ship was tiny compared to any average container ship you see these days, and we seemed to be stuck in one huge low-pressure system. All the way across, she rolled, pitched, bounced and even dived continuously. There was almost as much water coming over the deck as you might expect on a submarine. One minute we would be on the crest of a huge swell, able to view several miles into the deep grey distance, with only the white spume blowing off the peaks of the mountainous waves to give any colour to the leaden sky. Then the ship dived or fell into the trough, and solid walls of water came up on either side like massive hills suddenly erupting to block the view.

On board, sleep was snatched for minutes at a time. The only way to stay in your bunk was to wedge the mattress up with lifejackets on the outboard side, while you lay in the valley between the mattress and the bulkhead with your insides heaving with the violent movement. When you closed your eyes your body felt as though it was being thrown through space by the forces of some external gravity. When the bow came crashing down after a particularly large head swell your whole body seemed to come to a sudden stop, but it felt as though your insides wanted to continue their vertical or transverse journey.

Down below in the engine room the engineers were struggling with the overspeed governor on the main engine, as at times the propeller almost came out of the water, the load came off and the engine tried to accelerate beyond the designed specification. Because the governor could not keep up, an engineer had to be down regulating the speed on the throttle sticks. On the bridge conditions were foul. During the day it was just not very pleasant looking out of the windows, and at night you couldn't see where the next great wave was coming from. Inside the ship anything that could not be tied down had long ago found the lowest part of the cabin or lay smashed on the deck. There was no point in trying to tidy up even if you were physically able to hold on long enough to do so.

After forever, or so it seemed, the old man took her up through the Minches, that wonderful stretch of relatively calm water which protects part of the west coast of Scotland from the Atlantic swells. Bliss. We could sit, eat, stand, lie down and even go to the heads in comfort. But it wasn't to last, for the ship went through the Pentland Firth straight into the teeth of an easterly gale, and we ended up making less than 7 knots – and at one stage, because of the strong tide, it was actually recorded that we were going backwards over the ground. Two more long cold days we struggled against wind and tide – but eventually of course it all came to an end and we pulled into Grangemouth on the morning of 20 January 1972.

The voyage had taken almost twice as long as it should have, but on the train south it somehow just seemed like a bad dream. Within a few days I was off to London and the School of Navigation at Tower Hill. Our digs were at the King Edward VII Hall on the Commercial Road down in the East End, better known as the 'Stack of Bricks'. I guess I've known better places, but the guys I was with were all around the same age so we had some fun, studied fairly hard and all eventually returned to our ships to finish the sea time we required before we could sit our first ticket. I even managed to learn a little Cockney – but then I had a good teacher, who used to pick me up in her Triumph Herald for evenings out at some not too distant pub.

Final sea time

To complete the sea time I was to do another two relatively short voyages down to South Africa, first on the refrigerated cargo vessel *Rothesay Castle*, which I joined in Hamburg in late April 1972, and then on another 'reefer', the 10,538 gross registered ton *Southampton Castle*. I have always felt that British and Commonwealth Shipping gave cadets a good all-round training because they had such a variety of ships, and these two were to broaden my knowledge and experience further.

The *Rothesay* was built to take either general or refrigerated cargo. We carried the former southbound and the latter northbound, as it was the citrus season in the Cape and we loaded mainly oranges in Cape Town. Fruit has to be carried very

Southampton Castle

carefully to ensure that it does not ripen before arrival at the discharge port, so it is chilled to stop the process or slow it right down. This means the refrigerated holds have to be monitored very carefully by the refrigeration engineer, who adjusts the machinery to change the temperature just a degree or so, finally bringing it up just prior to arrival so that by the time the fruit reaches the customer it is ripe and ready for eating.

On 5 August I signed off in Drammen, Norway, and flew to Germany to join the *Southampton Castle* in Hamburg, where she was alongside loading. An unusual event, as the vessel was on the Mail contract from the UK to the Cape and it was only as a result of a dockers' strike in Southampton that she had been sent to the Continent. With the ship fully laden we sailed for the English Channel and Dover, where we were to pick up the few passengers.

This ship was one of a pair of the fastest reefers afloat. They were able to reach a service speed of close to 24 knots, enabling them to fit in with the other five larger passenger cargo vessels which in those days maintained a weekly service from Southampton.

Accommodation on board for a maximum of twelve passengers was an afterthought from the original builder's plan, but it was added at a later date when it was decided the ships would also make calls at Ascension Island and St Helena on the way north and south. On this voyage we were to carry the young wife of the newly installed doctor at Jamestown. She was very pleasant and allowed me to become perhaps a little too familiar; it came to nothing, of course, and I felt rather foolish after she departed. The weeks passed by, we discharged and loaded, then on the way north from Cape Town our help was summoned to look for a light aircraft that had come down somewhere of the coast of South West Africa. In the early hours a light was spotted in the area of its last known position, and we sailed over to find a life raft with both pilots safe inside. They were taken on board, fed and watered, and remained with us until St Helena.

Apparently they were on some kind of fishery research flight and both engines of their Beechcraft packed up when they changed over fuel tanks. How and when they returned home from the island I never found out, as there certainly were not that many calls by ships and, as today, there was no airfield.

I disembarked in Southampton in the middle of September, and within a few days was back at the School of Navigation to finish my studies and take my second mate's ticket. I had sailed for the last time as a cadet. After another six months at college I would board my next vessel as a watchkeeping officer.

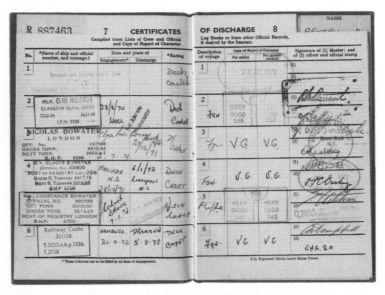

Second mate

Watchkeeper: *Clan Ranald* and *Kinnaird Castle*

My discharge book indicates that I returned to sea after my college course on 27 March 1973. I joined the refrigerated cargo ship *Clan Ranald* in Southampton for a voyage to South Africa as un-certificated third mate. Although I had passed the oral section of my second mate's 'ticket' I would have to make a second attempt at the maths paper (yet again my Achilles heel), but a pass in orals was enough in those days to guarantee a place as a junior watchkeeping bridge officer, thus gaining valuable experience at a comparatively young age. I was just 21.

The one thing that stands out in my memory of this voyage is the apparent total unconcern of the master regarding my ability to navigate the ship single-handed. We left Southampton Water and sailed down the Solent, passing through the Needles Channel with the Isle of Wight on our port side and heading southwest towards Ushant and the Bay of Biscay. It was dusk and the captain, once the pilot had disembarked, hung around for the shortest of time, handing the 'con' of the ship to me and just telling me to give him a call should I be concerned about anything.

I presumed he had other more important business to attend to, but in retrospect I expect he was pretty tired after a long day and was looking forward to sitting down in his comfortable chair with a large whisky or gin in his hand.

Within an hour it was dark, very dark, and also very clear,

which is not always such a good thing. Lights from other vessels can be seen for great distances, so great in fact that the radar may not be able to pick up and show the targets. In those days radars were relatively simple, with no automatic radar plotting aids, no satellite position input and often not even an automatic speed input. Bearings were taken with an electronic bearing line or manual cursor, distances with a variable distance marker, and these were either plotted onto a separate chart or a chinagraph pencil was used to mark them onto a special plotting screen which could be attached above the cathode ray tube of the radar. This screen was illuminated from underneath, and could be switched on and off at will.

Needless to say, if there were more than just a few targets the plotter became very busy with the thick pencil marks, and in spite of all the instruction and practice we had had as students in plotting ships and attempting to find their point of nearest approach it often became a rather useless confusion of smudged lines, which made accuracy somewhat hit and miss.

As we continued our journey towards the west and areas of increased traffic, I was aware of lights just about everywhere. I could see ships at a distance much further than the range on which the radar was set, some bright and clear, others a mere glimmer. The bright ones are not always the closest, as they can be small fishing boats far away with powerful lights hanging over the side to encourage the fish to their nets. And a not so bright one might of course be a small yacht at a close distance. Vigilance was required.

Fair enough I suppose, but then as we approached Portland I detected many echoes on the radar screen, but without any apparent lights visible from the bridge. Looking at the chart, I could see our vessel was in the area where high naval activity might be expected. The naval base at Portland was close by, and I guessed the boys were on exercise. My rudimentary tracking showed some vessels making high speed and in some form of convoy. As they approached and passed us, just a faint glimmer from their navigation lights could be seen. And then a small radar target, travelling quite slowly, turned out to be a submarine. One minute it was there, the next it must have submerged, the light had gone, as had the radar echo. All rather unnerving to a very junior first-trip mate.

The warships started to send up flare signals, and then were talking to each other in Morse by use of the Aldis light. Then I could see one of them was trying to attract my attention by flashing the letter U at me, the International Code letter for 'You are standing into danger!'

I could see nothing that might indicate a problem, neither on the radar nor on the chart. The water was certainly deep enough, and my position fixes indicated we were on track. The light flashed again. That was enough – I called the captain.

He came fairly nonchalantly to the bridge, had a cursory look around, noticed that most of the warships had now passed our beam and were clearing astern. The phantom light flasher had disappeared and the radar was showing just a few targets way ahead in the distance. Not much for him to do but go back down again. He made little comment then or the next day, and I presume he had observed many inexperienced mates on his ship before and was happy for them to learn their own lessons without wanting to give them some protracted lecture about calling him needlessly just because their nerves were getting a little frayed.

The voyage to the Cape was fairly routine, a quick run down to the South Atlantic, full load of chilled deciduous fruit and back up to Southampton to unload – and where I was to pay off on 15 May. I joined the *Kinnaird Castle* in Tilbury later the same day. The company knew I needed to go back up to the Shipping Office on a certain day to re-sit my paper, so another trip south was not on the cards.

The *Kinnaird* was an older cargo vessel 'coasting' around the UK, and I was on board for about six weeks until paying off in Glasgow on 27 June. A coastal voyage in many ways was a good way to learn the more practical aspects of cargo stowage and handling, plus getting to understand the many frustrating practices that some of the militant unionised stevedores turned to in order to earn an extra shilling or have a more 'relaxed' physical day.

In the early 1970s strikes were often called for what were considered by us to be the most pitiful of excuses. For example, a docker might have been sent ashore for stealing from the cargo, so the rest would stop work until he was reinstated, even if he was on a different gang and on a different ship. I heard that extra 'embarrassment' money had to be paid if, for example, a quantity of urinals had to be loaded. Breakfast breaks lasting up to an hour were taken just 45 minutes after work commenced. If a cargo to be loaded consisted of alcohol, then there was always a problem of one sort or another. A sling containing several cases of whisky would be dropped sufficiently fast by the crane operator to ensure a case would land hard on the deck of the hold and bottles would break, an open invitation for the remaining bottles to disappear.

After leaving the ship I took the maths paper again, and passed.

Reina del Mar

I remember phoning up the office after receiving my results, and they asked me what sort of vessel I would like to work on next. At that time the Union Castle Line, a part of the British and Commonwealth group, had six major passenger ships, and I stated that I felt I had had enough of cargo ships for a while, so could I go on one of the passenger vessels? I was straight away offered the *Windsor Castle*, which was one of the regular mail vessels running to South Africa and due to leave in a few days' time. That was a little too soon, I said, was there anything else? When they suggested the *Reina*, as she was affectionately known, I just about fainted. This ship was a cruising vessel, and everyone's idea of a dream to work on board. They said I should work for a few weeks as fourth officer, second on a watch, and thus 'learn the ropes', then I would go up to third officer, in charge of a watch.

To get such a ship was lucky at the best of times, but to do so just after obtaining my licence was amazing. I was still twenty-one years old and would have the responsibility of keeping a safe navigational watch on a ship with probably over 1,400 people on board. Even now, I am still surprised at my luck, but it was a great thrill and a terrific experience for a young man.

The cruising calendar

Reina del Mar had been built in 1956 for the Pacific Steam Navigation Company (PSNC) to operate a liner service from the UK to South America. The advent of the jet aeroplane had sealed the fate of that run and, after a few attempts at breaking into the cruise market, Union Castle Line finally chartered her. The calendar was basically made up of two-week cruises out of Southampton to the Atlantic Isles, Spain, Portugal, North Africa and the Mediterranean during the spring, summer and early autumn. In the winter the ship would leave the UK for South Africa and then operate cruises to South America from Cape Town.

The ship had a reputation for being particularly friendly, and there were many passengers who would come back and cruise time after time, including such notable names as the comedian Harry Worth and Jean Alexander, the actress who played Hilda Ogden in the TV soap *Coronation Street*. The ship had an atmosphere that resulted in a following, and many of the crew had been with the ship for a long time – and those that left often came back to visit. It was a very happy ship to work on, and consequently there was never a problem finding new staff or reliefs. My own relief was another young officer who had gone on to do a nautical science degree and was more than willing to work during his university vacation time.

Social events

There was a great deal of socialising on board, along with a considerable amount of drinking, which rarely got out of hand, and we all seemed to adapt to working with copious quantities of alcohol in our bodies. The biggest problem was sleep, or the lack of it. I started on the 4–8 watch with the senior second officer as my 'boss', I had a tiny cabin just behind the bridge, originally designed no doubt for use as a pilot's cabin on those rare occasions when a pilot would 'stay over'. It was behind a heavy steel door which, when opened, just about filled the whole space. After the evening watch it was customary to quickly change, have a few drinks in the Coral Lounge, which was reputed to have the longest bar afloat, then go down to dinner.

Dinner in the tourist-class restaurant was always an event, with the wine flowing and much telling of stories and rude jokes. The British stewards were usually OK but I remember a surly grey-haired chap who had obviously been around a long time and was not over-impressed with us young 'upstarts'. After dinner the group invariably drifted on to have 'stickies' in another bar and then to watch whatever entertainment was organised for the passengers. In contrast to my later experience on Cunard Line ships, the entertainment was rather homespun. There was the small band of Ronnie Carroll and his singer wife Celia Nicholls (who, I remember, had a very large bust), and another chap who played the accordion, but in the main the purser's staff put on the entertainment. A cruise director, Robbie Rutt, had a dedicated few staff who would could perform and other officers supplemented these when there was a need for a larger chorus or a bigger show. 'Singing Waiters', 'The Can-Can', 'Morris Dancing' etc were all performed, along with other favourites one might expect from the music hall. By the time our officers went up on the makeshift stage they had consumed vast quantities of booze, to give them confidence, so the mistakes were often far more entertaining than the original show.

After a few weeks on board I moved up to the 8–12 watch,

and a bigger cabin on the deck below the bridge, which became my home for the rest of my stay. There were no toilets or showers in the cabins, so it was a short hike down the corridor, but no-one minded as we were all great friends – most of the time. The cabins were quite small with a single bunk, a sink and a porthole looking forward onto the games deck.

I probably fell in love many times on that ship, but the first was with a girl called Sarah who came on board to operate the disco equipment. She was very outspoken and a real character, but I think a little too much so, and consequently she only stayed for about six weeks before being fired. By that time, however, our relationship had started and she would come down to Southampton every time we returned from a cruise, staying the night in my cabin, where I had managed to get another mattress to make a larger bed on the deck. When we sailed for South Africa in November she stood on the quay as we departed. All very emotional.

Incidents
During one morning watch, we had left the Strait of Gibraltar and were heading west prior to turning towards the north for Lisbon. There had been many other ships, but by 1130 hours there was just one relatively close, about half a mile on the starboard bow going the same way. I was writing up the deck logbook on the folding table at the bridge front when I looked up and immediately became aware that this vessel was now at right angles to our track and much closer than before. The ship was making a tight turn to port, crossing our bow and then appearing to continue back in towards our port side. I altered course to starboard, but the other vessel kept closing. The master, Captain Reggie Kelso, was on inspection, so I sounded a short ring on the alarm bells, his signal to come to the bridge straight away, and rang the engine room telegraph. The other ship had cleared our bow by the time the captain came racing up the port bridge wing steps. But I could see that unless I went hard to port the

Reina del Mar in Valetta

ship would hit us somewhere behind the wheelhouse. Captain Kelso was unable to speak because he was out of breath, but he could see me having the quartermaster turn the wheel towards the other ship. Very quickly our stern skidded out of harms way, at about the same time as the other ship went full astern. She cleared us by forty or fifty feet, much to my relief, and Captain Kelso, after I had explained the sequence of events, praised me for making the right decision. Some fifteen minutes later, when I had retreated to the deck bar for a gin, the doctor came up and asked what had happened. He had been looking out of the hospital porthole at the time, and all he could see was a cargo ship apparently coming straight towards him.

Three other events occurred within about six weeks that made me feel that I might be jinxed. The first was when we were undocking in some North African port. The starboard anchor had been used when the vessel docked, and I was in charge of the forward mooring deck party. We let go the ropes and started to bring the anchor home, and as it cleared the water I gave the signal to the carpenter on the windlass to slow down the capstan, and then turned to advise the bridge on my radio that the anchor was clear of the water. They did not at first hear so I had to repeat myself, and as I did so the anchor came up into the hawse pipe at great speed and with a tremendous thump. The carpenter had not slowed down the capstan. I feared the worst, and gave instruction for the anchor to be walked out – but it would not move.

The next day we tried all sorts of ways to free the jammed stock of the anchor, but it was firmly wedged into the hawse pipe. We had no joy, and in fact several days later a welder had to come on board and burn a large hole into the hawse pipe where we believed the anchor stock to be wedged. The anchor was freed, then the hole was welded back up again – but I felt a fool for letting it happen in the first place.

The second incident was when we left Guadeloupe in the Caribbean. A rope had been passed out to a mooring buoy in the stream, and it was the intention when we left the berth to heave on the rope to pull the stern clear of the dock. Again I was on stations, but this time down aft. We heaved on the rope and the stern came away nicely, but when the captain instructed for the rope to be let go and retrieved from the buoy things did not go according to plan. We slacked off the rope to allow a native craft to come alongside the buoy, and though it was getting dark we could see one man jump onto the buoy. But he was having problems letting the rope go. The ship started moving ahead so we slacked more rope, and I explained the situation to the captain, this time Alistair Sillars, over the radio. Still no joy, and the ship was still moving ahead. The bosun's mate had put a turn around the windlass ready to bring the rope back on board, but as fast as he slacked off the ship's forward momentum kept putting strain on, and the man on the buoy eventually jumped back into his boat.

We had paid out a great deal of rope, but the captain still had not slowed down. The rope was beginning to jump dangerously and I shouted for the men to get out of the way before it parted. Captain Sillars gave instruction to just let the rope go over the side, but it was too late as one of the sailors had already made fast another rope to the tail. I watched with surprise as one man came up with his knife and tried to cut the rope – I had visions of the rope parting and the whiplash taking the man over the side. Fortunately another sailor brought an axe, and one blow caused the bar-tight rope to part, disappearing over the side. We had lost over one and a half lengths of good mooring line, probably worth well over a thousand pounds even then.

The third event was the most expensive. We were docking in Venice and I was aft. A local tug had come in and taken our towing spring on the port side to assist the ship as we berthed. We were close to being in the position required when secure and I was supervising a spring and sternline on the starboard side. The captain called on the radio to see if the port side was clear so that he could go astern on the port engine. I automatically said yes, as I knew I had no lines in the water on that side. However, unknown to me, the tug had slipped our wire, and as the port engine went astern it pulled in the wire, which wrapped itself around the port propeller. Too late I realised what had happened as I saw the floating rope tail being drawn into the ship's side, and I barely had time to tell the bridge to stop the engine before, with a big bang, the wire snapped at deck level.

Fortunately the ship was to be alongside in Venice for two days, as it took all night for the wire to be burned free from its position around the propeller. Yet again I felt an absolute fool – but it is these events which, in the end, make you a better officer and an experienced future captain.

Heading south

The run down to Cape Town was via Madeira, that lovely Portuguese island in the Atlantic. The ship was to take bunkers and leave some mail, and after we arrived alongside I sat down with the senior second officer, George Paxton, for a beer before lunch. A problem developed, and the double-bottom tank used for holding the fuel was ruptured. At first we were aware only that there would be a delay in sailing, so we decided to continue drinking, and only much later did we find out that the oil spill in the engine room had resulted in the sealing of the forward machinery space and the shutting down of pumps. This in turn resulted in a sewage back-up into the lowest passenger cabins, where 'grey water' was coming out of sinks and showers and flooding the carpets.

All the purser's staff were turned to, helping to move belongings and trying to clean the place up. We took a walk down to have a look and quickly made an about turn. We had probably drunk far more than we should have, and it wasn't until the ship was just about ready to leave that George remembered about the mail. The next fifteen minutes saw us literally throwing the bags over the boat-deck rail onto the dock forty feet below. It was a right shambles, and I'm sure there must have been at least a few broken Christmas presents.

South American cruising
We made three cruises out of Cape Town with South African and Rhodesian passengers. The average age was probably no more than thirty-five to forty so they were a young and attractive crowd – and it was fun!

Each cruise was thirty days' duration, ten days across the South Atlantic, ten days on the coast and ten days back to Cape Town. On each voyage we called first at Rio de Janeiro, staying four days, then a day at Santos, three days in Buenos Aires and two days in Montevideo, Uruguay. It was beautiful relaxed cruising and many friends were made with the passengers who were on board for the month. Needless to say there were also many romances. In fact it was almost impossible for any of the bachelors, and sometimes the married officers, not to end up between the sheets with one girl or another.

On the second voyage I spied a very attractive lady on the first night, who, it turned out, was four years older than me, divorced, and very willing to have a partner for the duration. We spent much of the first ten days together, but by the time we reached Brazil I had become bored with her company, which was typical of my somewhat silly attitude in those early years. I tried to let her down gently but she was very upset. In the end, after about five days, the boys took pity on her and pushed her into my cabin when I was having an afternoon nap. My physical inclination overcame my mental one, and that was the end of our separation. I seem to remember that by the time we had returned to South Africa I was physically exhausted.

All the ports were very interesting, particularly Rio and BA, and in both places I managed to do a little exploring. On our second cruise it was carnival time in Rio. The atmosphere was electric, and it was incredibly noisy most of the time as our ship was docked on the tourist wharf right at the bottom of the main street, the Rio Branco. Taped samba music played constantly, and it felt as if we were being drugged by the incessant beat. Passengers and crew had a wonderful time ashore, but somehow I found it all a little overwhelming. I did go ashore one evening with friends when the parades were going past, but the streets were so crowded that it seemed you could just get swallowed up in the mass of sweating humanity. I did not at all feel comfortable. Another evening we took a bus ride to the beach area, careering around corners at breakneck speed. It is no wonder they have a saying in Rio – 'There are only two types of pedestrian in this town, the quick and the dead!'

The atmosphere in all the ports was very Mediterranean. Santos was dirty and a typical sailors' town of squalid bars and poverty; BA had an air of bustling business and Latin efficiency; Montevideo was notable for its incredibly aged buses and cars, many over fifty years old. They were all so totally different to the African ports I had visited before.

We made friends with a group of South African air force pilots who came on one of the cruises, and after they disembarked they made a fly-past of the ship when we left Cape Town. We usually had only one day to re-supply the ship before leaving on the next voyage, but I remember that Alistair Sillars managed to convince the company we needed an extra day alongside after the second South American trip – to give us all a rest, I think the excuse was!

Eventually we left for the last time and returned to the England for the spring and a three-week cruise to the Caribbean.

Second season

After we returned to our Mediterranean schedule I was promoted to junior second officer and given the 12–4 watch. This was a real killer, because I was young and didn't want to miss any of the entertainment. I socialised even more and rarely went to bed before the night watch. I can vividly remember staying in the disco to the last possible moment and giving myself just two minutes to race back to my cabin, change and get onto the bridge for midnight. I always felt great at that time, but of course by one in the morning the combined effects of too much booze and the darkened bridge made me feel very sleepy. It was often a real struggle to keep my eyes open, a struggle I did not always win.

One particular night I came to the bridge and sat down (fatal) between the radars on a sloped plotting table. We always considered that if we dozed off sitting on this table we would fall off the back of it and therefore wake up, albeit with a headache. However, I looked at my watch at one, thinking the time was really dragging, and then looked at it again and it was two o'clock. I must have been asleep. I was stunned into awareness, never thinking this would happen, but it had – and that day I vowed I would never again go onto the bridge having had too much to drink. What had concerned me most was that we were actually only five hours away from the busy Strait of Gibraltar. Another lesson in the learning curve of life, luckily won without mishap.

We went to the West Indies on one voyage, my first time and a total delight. One day an old lady passenger died and, as we had no morgue, she was sewn up in canvas that was weighted at one end. It was traditional for the bosun's mate, or whoever did the job, to receive a bottle of whisky – and it was also traditional for the last stitch to go through the nose.

Although it had been anticipated that we would bury the lady at sea that night, we received a message telling us to land her in

Antigua, our next port of call. The corpse duly went ashore, but just an hour before we were due to sail the next day she came back – in a coffin. That night arrangements were again made to pass the lady over the stern. The ship was slowed and turned to alleviate some of the wind blowing across the deck.

I came on the bridge at midnight and was shortly afterwards told by the mate to resume the course and speed. I turned the ship back towards the moonlight, but when the chief officer arrived on the bridge he remarked that there had been an unusual event. The coffin, upon hitting the water, had broken apart and no one was sure that the lady was still weighted down in the canvas. We were now heading back towards the spot, and I spent the next ten minutes scanning the waves to see if I could see the corpse floating in the moonlight.

———

My time on board was accumulating, and I realised that soon I would have to go back for my first mate's examination. Looking back, I believe that I had become physically tired of being on board the *Reina*. I had experienced many things, drunk far too much and somehow become a different person, one that I didn't really like. The ship had been good for me in many ways, but I knew it was time to leave.

Elbe Ore

When I eventually left the *Reina* I was very much wiser in many ways, not all of them to do with the art of navigation or seamanship. I had a relatively short amount of sea time to complete before I could go up to college and study for my chief mate's licence, and I knew there would be another oral exam. I anticipated that the examiner, realising that I had spent my intervening time on a cruise ship, was likely to hammer me with questions about cargo vessels or tankers. I asked the company to place me on a different kind of vessel. They did, and what a culture shock it turned out to be.

The *Elbe Ore* was an eleven-hatch bulk carrier that could carry up to 84,000 tonnes of cargo. It seemed absolutely huge when I joined as second mate in Rotterdam on 28 November 1974. Everything seemed massive. The bridge, engines and accommodation were at the stern, so the bow was almost 800 feet ahead of the wheelhouse. The eleven hatches disappeared into the distance and the windlass machinery on the bow seemed to be an insignificant lump of metal when in fact each link of the anchor chain was over a meter long.

My cabin was like a stateroom, the bridge was big and the bridge wings were even bigger, while the engine room was of cathedral-like proportions. A grand affair perhaps, but the trade was not, for the ship was on long-term charter to the German company Krupps and was in the business of bringing large quantities of iron ore to Europoort at the seaward end of the Maas River, from where it was transhipped to feed the iron and steel manufacturing plants in the Ruhr valley. When I arrived the ship was being discharged by several large cranes with grabs that could pick up twenty-five tonnes at a time, and the deck was covered with the dirty grey ore which had spilt from the grabs as they continued their seemingly never-ending task. I was to find that the ore dust not only blew everywhere outside, but even got carried into the accommodation no matter how much we tried to clean off our boots and overalls before entering. Even my large but spartan cabin with its lino floor had a fine dusting of the gritty substance.

Within two days the full cargo could be discharged and the ship was on its way again to pick up the next cargo, and there seemed to be plenty of inhospitable ports around the world where it was available. This was no passenger-ship excursion to sunny climes and sandy beaches. My first destination was to be Narvik in northern Norway, way north of the Arctic Circle, and in December.

Grey North Sea weather was followed by the long haul up the Norwegian coast before eventually sailing into Vestfjord, leaving the spectacular Lofoten islands to port and finally entering Ofotfjord with Narvik near its head. The almost continual darkness of winter must be disturbing to many and is surely one of the reasons why the region is losing its youth to Oslo and the more hospitable south.

Once docked, and with the formalities completed, the loading was quick to start. The first pour of ore from the huge elevated conveyor belts fell up to fifty metres into the empty hold below, making the most resounding crash. Everyone on board knew that loading had started, as tonnes of ore hitting steel reverberated through the ship like a minor earthquake.

The chief officer, a rather dour chap with whom I was to have a few problems later in the voyage, had worked out a loading and de-ballasting plan which necessitated thousands of tonnes of ballast water being gradually pumped or gravitated out of the ship as the cargo was loaded. The ballast was in the ship to ensure the vessel's stability on the voyage north; it was kept in wing tanks on either side of each cargo hold and also in two of the holds. The smaller one contained 11,000 tonnes, the larger 14,000 tonnes, and on opening the hatch it was like staring down into a very large black swimming pool. The hold ballast pumping system required the manual opening of large valves operated by a spoked metal wheel situated on the deck. Because of the weight of the water and the extension of the valve spindle it could take up to ten back-breaking minutes using a special wheel key to open a valve fully. The smaller wing tanks were above the water line and, by opening a smaller valve, the contents of each tank could be dumped or gravitated over the ship's side.

Throughout loading or unloading, the ship's horizontal trim would vary depending on how quickly and into which hold the ore was poured. To avoid undue stress developing within the hull of the ship the de-ballasting plan had to be followed conscientiously. Cargo watch was therefore quite a busy time, running

Elbe Ore

the length of the deck, and then down into the pump room (a six-storey space containing pumps and their controls) or into the engine room to check the valves situated in the bilge tunnel.

The bilge tunnel ran the length of the bottom of the ship from engine room to fore-peak tank, and contained all the pipework connecting bilge, ballast and fuel tanks. The space was only about five feet high, with the pipes led along the bottom plates, so going from one end to the other could take twenty minutes with much banging of head on various bits of ship which protruded into the space from tank or frame. The space was dimly lit, damp and rusty; it was not for the faint-hearted or those suffering from any degree of claustrophobia as it could be up to forty-five feet below the surface of the sea outside.

On one occasion, during ballasting, the cadet had reported to me that the forward wing tank was showing a sounding that would indicate it was full when it should not have been because of a cracked seam in its upper section. The only way to prove the point was to investigate, so I led him down through the engine room and into the tunnel. The first part was about a foot deep in water as a result of the ship being trimmed by the stern, and after ten minutes or so we could hear what sounded like a minor waterfall echoing down the tunnel. I continued for some way until I could just make out in the dark distance the dim light reflecting from water pouring out from near the top of the wing tank. I needed no further convincing. If we had continued to ballast, the water would have filled the tunnel and then made its way to flood the engine room. We retreated, but even so by the time we had returned to the entrance our boiler suits were soaking wet and our energy almost depleted. The Indian pump-man looked at us with some incredulity, but was hastily sent to work to ensure the ballasting of the tanks was both stopped and then reversed.

Time ashore was very rare on this ship. Cargo watches were twelve hours in every twenty-four and port stays were usually no more than two days. Huge mechanical loaders on the quayside could pour up to 10,000 tonnes of ore per hour into the ship's holds, and often it was difficult to take the ballast out quick enough to keep pace. All eleven holds were not loaded because iron ore is a heavy bulk cargo (as opposed to grain, for example), and there was always plenty of space left in each hold when loading was completed. Like all ships we were only allowed to load to our 'marks', the line on the ship's side introduced by Samuel Plimsoll in the nineteenth century to prevent greedy ship owners from overloading their ships in order to maximise profit, but which in turn resulted in ships having an increased chance of becoming a sinking coffin in the event of bad weather.

The normal routine was to load seven alternate holds, the remainder being kept empty. The stability of the ship during and after loading was carefully worked out using a mechanical instrument called a 'lodicator'. The chief officer in his calculations not only had to control the fore and aft trim of the ship, but also had to take account of the sheering stresses at the bulkheads between a hold containing 14,000 tonnes of cargo and an adjacent hold that remained empty. In simple terms, the empty hold had a force of buoyancy acting upwards while the loaded hold had the vertical force of the ore acting down. If every hold had been half-filled, then the overall centre of gravity would have been low, which in turn would have made the ship very 'stiff', or prone to a relatively quick rolling motion in bad weather. Heavy rolling is not only uncomfortable for the crew but can result in stress that is beyond the designed limit for the steel structure. The resulting damage could be catastrophic, with the ship even breaking up and sinking. By loading alternate holds, the centre of gravity of the cargo is raised because each pile of cargo is higher within the hatch.

Over the next few months we were to return to Rotterdam many times, but the cargo was always loaded in a different port. After Narvik we proceeded to the coast of West Africa, where we berthed in a place known as Nouadhibou in Mauritania. We were there over New Year, having spent Christmas at sea, but there was little to see except the loading jetty with a desolate landscape behind, and certainly nothing to go ashore for even if we had had the chance.

An Atlantic crossing in January can be uncomfortable at the best of times, but we were sent off to Canada for one cargo. Port Cartier and Seven Islands are two ports in the Gulf of St Lawrence, not so far apart about 250 miles on the seaward side of Quebec. We were to take a part cargo in both, I presume because of draught restrictions and the availability of the ore.

After the wind and rain of the Atlantic we rounded the southwest corner of Newfoundland and the temperature dropped rapidly. Sea ice was forecast, and as we proceeded through the murk of the winter day we started to pick out the smaller ice floating on the surface. In the calm conditions the sea took on an oily appearance as it started to freeze, until eventually as we passed into the gulf itself the sea had large patches of ice with less and less water visible between them.

Speed was later reduced to around 10 knots and, as we passed the island of Anticosti to starboard, the night was dark and crystal clear, the sea was completely frozen over and a coating of snow made the surface appear like a white desert illuminated by the light of the full moon. As I looked behind, the ship had left a perfectly straight wake of dark broken ice and water disappearing into the distance many miles astern. That sight will remain in my memory forever.

An early-morning arrival off Port Cartier required us to anchor the ship in the bay opposite the loading berth. We anchored in clear water, but the next ship ran her bow into the ice until all way was taken off the vessel. They dropped the anchor, which landed on the ice and went no further. For a while it was left sitting there surrounded by its chain, an amusing sight. With the large tugs available, berthing some hours later was not a problem. We took a part cargo and proceeded the few miles down the coast to Seven Islands in order to complete the loading. Here the ore loaders were very high, which meant we could discharge all our ballast before going alongside. The distance between the loader and the hatch coaming is known as the air draught, and this must be at least a good six feet to prevent the loader coming into contact with the ship and causing serious damage.

The pilot, however, had great difficulty in getting the ship alongside the dock. The ice near the dock was very thick, and it rose and fell twelve feet or more with the tide, but as the ship was pushed by the tugs towards the berth, the ice became crushed and built up between ship and quay. He was eventually satisfied with the ship lying somewhere between six and ten feet off, and our heavy steel wires on tension winches held the ship in place. The loaders reached out over the ship and could be adjusted fore and aft to go to different hatches, but also across the ship in order to place the ore in the hatch over one side or the other. To ensure the vessel remained upright there were two lights the loader operator could see, one on either side of the accommodation block. If the ship listed one way the light on that side would come on and he would adjust the pour to the other side of the hold.

In Seven Islands the loaders were rated at around 25,000 tonnes per hour each, an incredible rate. Fortunately for us the intense cold had for the time being put one out of action and the other was working at less than fifty per cent. Even so we were on our way within thirty-six hours. Again we transited the ice field, and this time the captain, 'Corky' Bennet, was very cautious as he had a large ship with a draught of around forty-six feet under his command, and with the momentum this weight of ship contained, heavy ice could cause serious damage to the bow if we hit it too fast. Corky was an unusual character. I had met him on a trip when I was a cadet. He was the only man I'd met who wore a monocle and turned up the waxed ends of his moustache.

The clear skies had given way to low grey clouds mixed in with a murky visibility, not a real problem regarding position fixing and avoiding other traffic, as our radars were fine, but they could not see where the ice started or finished. The best way of proceeding through intermittent sea ice is to slow right down as you approach and increase speed gradually once surrounded. Corky took a while to leave the watchkeepers to their own devices on the bridge, but eventually relaxed sufficiently to spend most of the time in his cabin. We became rather accustomed to all this ice and it became routine, but once I failed to slow down sufficiently, and as we hit the next ice raft we could feel the jolt throughout the ship. With the bow so far away and quite high it was impossible to see what was on the water right in front for up to quarter of a mile, I guess I had not kept a really vigilant watch with the binoculars or just thought it didn't seem so bad. Corky phoned the bridge and suggested I should be a little more careful with the speed.

By the time we approached Newfoundland and had cleared the ice area, we all felt as though we had come back from some great Arctic expedition.

The return Atlantic crossing was through some very rough seas and fierce winds, and even though the ship was loaded to maintain the highest acceptable centre of gravity, she rolled and heaved in a most uncomfortable way. We seemed to be held in the vice of a huge depression that crossed with us across the ocean. The view from the wheelhouse windows was at times disturbing as the front end of the ship could be seen to bend and twist as we rode over swells which at times must have been at least sixty feet or more between peak and trough. Bulk carriers are built with their strength longitudinally for this very reason and, much like a ruler, they can quite safely bend to a slight extent to compensate the sea swell passing around and under the hull. Even so, it was on my mind as to how much the ship could bend before the inevitable happened; bulk carriers have a notorious record of being lost at sea, usually in heavy weather.

In the end the voyage was completed safely, although I remember one of the lifeboats and the ship-to-shore gangway were damaged by a particularly large wave that tried to climb up the side of the ship one night. In addition, when we arrived in Rotterdam we found that most of the 'booby hatches', those entries into each hold whereby personnel could climb down a ladder for inspection purposes, were cracked at the corners. The ship had twisted or 'racked' so much during the voyage that these areas of relative weakness had fractured.

During my time on board I was to make good friends with most of the other guys, but I always had a problem with the chief officer. He had a big problem getting up to the bridge at four in the morning – in fact I don't think he managed it once, and sometimes it was up to thirty minutes before he arrived. I was permanently on the 12–4 watch whilst at sea, which meant I never got a full night's sleep, and continually doing extra time during the hours of darkness started to wear me down. He was always reeking of alcohol, so I believe that was his problem, and any reference I made to time keeping got a surly if not downright rude response. The master was no help, and in the end I wrote to the company and asked to be relieved. After one more voyage, this time up to Kirkenes, a Norwegian port not so far from Murmansk on the Barents Sea, I finally left. It was 3 March 1975 when I departed from the ship in Rotterdam, and for the first time I didn't look back as the taxi to the airport left the dock.

I was hauled into the London offices of the company and rebuked for not following proper channels and informing the master of my letter, then told it takes two to cause a problem so I was in part to blame for this personality clash. I was not impressed. They posted me to the coastwise *Clan Macintyre* a week or so later. I joined in Avonmouth and left in Liverpool after two weeks, having gained enough sea time in my discharge book to take my next ticket, and in sufficient time to go to the Brunel Technical College in Bristol, where I would study from April to December of 1975.

That period was one I found frustrating in different ways. The girl I had intended to live with during my study time had, during our time apart, decided a Greek food and beverage manager was more to her liking, and the work at college proved to be very tough. In their wisdom the Department of Transport had recently decided that the mate's ticket should include not only electricity as a core subject, but also electronics. It might as well have been Egyptian as far as I was concerned; it was certainly not a language I had either studied before or understood.

When it came to the exam, covering six subjects over three days, I passed the electricity but failed the electronics. I took it again a month later, passed the electronics but failed the electricity, and also failed the stability paper – which was unforgivable, really, even though the subject of stability is not particularly easy and has some very confusing formulas to learn and apply. There was nothing for it but to go back to sea for a trip, earn some money and return refreshed – perhaps!

Clan Macnab

I joined the *Clan Macnab* in Birkenhead on 21 December. She was a general cargo vessel of some 9,168 gross tons about to complete loading a mixed cargo of machine parts, household goods and various other sundries, including a few heavy lift items of sixty tonnes or more which were stowed on deck.

We sailed on Christmas Eve and consequently spent a fairly

subdued Christmas off the Western Approaches making our way down to the Bay of Biscay and the Mediterranean bound for the Suez Canal, Jordan, India and Sri Lanka. The weather became gradually warmer. The Med is not as hot as some people think, but the seas were kind to us and by the time we reached Port Said at the entrance to the canal the early-morning temperature was a very pleasant 70 degrees plus. The canal transit was straight-forward and interesting, as it hadn't been so long since it had reopened after the second Arab–Israeli war. Signs of destruction could easily be seen, with a few burned-out military vehicles still lying on the raised banks, and as we passed through Suez, bombed-out buildings were evident.

The Suez Canal is not as glamorous as some would wish to think, although if you are a watcher of people then observing the day-to-day routines of the local folk can be interesting. Wealth is not in any way evident among those who make a living on or beside this particular stretch of water. There was a pilot change towards the centre of the canal at Ismailia when the chap who joined in Port Said left us. We then passed through the Great Bitter Lake, where one ship trapped by the war still lay at anchor awaiting its eventual fate. The second pilot finally disembarked at Suez, the city that marks the southern end of the canal. The transit had lasted about ten hours.

During the next night we passed down the Gulf of Suez, with its oilrigs evident by flames reaching for the dark sky from their tall gantries. Before daylight the waters of the Straits of Gubal passed under our hull as we turned north again and into the Gulf of Aqaba. After anchoring off the rather shabby Jordanian port of Aqaba all romantic thoughts generated by Peter O'Toole and Lawrence of Arabia disappeared and we were left to our own devices, staring rather enviously through the binoculars at the lights of the thriving Israeli city of Eilat, just across the water. After a few days it was our turn to berth at the congested wharf and discharge a relatively small amount of cargo, including some heavy lifts from the deck. These included a large steel boiler-like

Clan Macnab

construction that must have been almost thirty feet long. With
our own derricks it was carefully landed onto two flatbed trailers and then pulled along the wharf – until the local stevedores
realised that it could not get around any corners or through the
main gate. The following morning we noticed it had been unceremoniously rolled off the trailers and dumped against a crum-
bling block wall.

Our stay was a short one, and soon we were steaming back
down the Gulf with the Sinai Peninsula on our starboard side
until we entered the Red Sea for a steamy two-day passage down
to Jeddah. There we expected to take bunker fuel, but when we
arrived the anchorage was extremely crowded with ships of all
types, most waiting for a berth to unload their cargoes. It was
period of great affluence for Saudi Arabia, and many goods and
commodities of all types were ordered and brought in ships.
However, the ports were neither large enough nor modern
enough to unload their cargoes quickly and ensure minimum
delays for the ship owner, a problem I was to see again a few
years later in West Africa. In Jeddah there must have been well
over a hundred large ships anchored between the reefs, and for
one period they resorted to unloading certain cargoes by helicopter – which must have increased the final cost of the cargo
many times over.

We approached slowly, and after several calls on the VHF
radio to 'Jeddah pilot station' a small scruffy motorboat came

slowly chugging towards us. The pilot ladder was hung over the side and a gentleman in an off-white kaftan climbed aboard. The captain greeted him with cautionary surprise and said he was expecting a pilot. The gentleman said he was the pilot and that we could proceed to the inner anchorage. When pressed as to whether there was a berth available for us to take fuel the pilot prevaricated and said that after anchoring we would find out. Time is money in our business and the captain was not prepared to hang around for an unknown number of days just to take fuel when he knew we could get it down the coast in Aden. He sent the pilot off the bridge and the last we saw of him was his little boat chugging back in the direction from which it had come.

We turned our bows back to sea and continued our journey southwards towards the southern end of the Red Sea. We passed through the strait of Bab-el-Mandeb and continued towards Aden. At that time this Yemeni port was basically run by the Soviets, and there were no problems or delays when our Russian pilot boarded. Within an hour we had turned, docked and were taking fuel.

Throughout the voyage so far there had been some memories that kept coming back, sometimes when I was alone on the bridge at night as the moonlight gave a surreal and calming effect to the vastness of the open sea. I had had a good friend on the *Reina del Mar*, a junior electrical officer who had left for promotion and joined this very vessel less than six months ago. During a stopover in Aden he had been on duty while the vessel was bunkering, probably at the same berth we were in this day. Apparently there had been a hairline crack in a fuel-line sight glass. As the fuel was being pumped aboard the crack allowed a fine mist of fuel to escape. A vapour cloud is believed to have ignited over the hot exhausts of a generator, causing a small explosion just as my friend opened the door to the machinery spaces. The fireball first consumed the oxygen in the engine room and then headed through the open door, setting him on fire as it passed. It is believed that, in his pain, he ran up to the forecastle and then back until he was rescued and taken up to the captain's cabin, where the master's wife managed to get him in a bath filled with cold water.

He was later taken ashore to the well-equipped Soviet hospital. The company arranged for an aircraft to be flown down from the UK to pick him up and, against the wishes of the Russian doctor, he was taken to the airport on a stretcher. His heart stopped on the way out to the plane, the doctor tried everything he knew to keep him alive, but there was no recovery. A young man, with all his life before him, who died in a foreign land – and my sadness at the news of his death came back to me then. It was as though his spirit and I were to be together once again at the place of his death, and from that day I don't believe I had any doubts or worries about being on the same ship again. I still remember his beaming smile, the attraction he had for the ladies, and the occasions I had to cover for him when he had more than one of them on the go at the same time!

Leaving Aden, our track took us just north of the impressive but desolate-looking island of Socotra, reaching 1,503 meters out of the sea. As we steamed deeper into the Indian Ocean the northeast monsoon picked up and gave the ship a gentle relaxing motion, as well as a welcome breeze that came through the bridge doors and into the wheelhouse. Bombay was our next port and after making our arrival the master was told to anchor in the dangerous goods anchorage.

We had a deck cargo consisting of drums containing a compound which was to be mixed in small quantities with petrol before its sale to the customer. This stuff was highly poisonous, and we had been given special instructions and equipment in case of a spillage on deck. The drums were discharged with our own derricks two at a time into an old wooden dhow that was brought alongside. As the night wore on I noticed the boat was taking water so I stopped the discharge and told him to move off and back to the shore. The skipper had been trying to get sawdust down and into the leaking seam, an obviously tried and trusted method that didn't seem to be having much success this time.

The boat cast off, but a few hours later we heard a message over the harbour radio warning of a fire and sinking in the bay. Apparently our friends had been rather nosy, and in their efforts to check what was in some other boxes they had taken from us, they found a white powder. I assume they realised that it could be no use to them, so they threw it back into the boat. Unfortunately it must have landed into the flooded part of the cargo space and the white powder, which was a compound that caught fire when mixed with water, ignited. The drums went to the bottom of the harbour and, because of the poisonous nature of their contents, had to be recovered. A manufacturer's representative was flown out to supervise the salvage, which, I learnt later, took six months.

Colombo in Sri Lanka followed, and then up to Madras on India's east coast to complete our cargo discharge. I can remember long ten-hour shifts on cargo watch at night, hot, tiring and tedious. One morning, however, I made a point of visiting the town. My intention was to just walk, but as I left the dock gate a chap with a rickshaw-type pedal bike pestered me. I gave in, hopped on the back, and we were soon on our way. By seven in the morning the streets of Madras were coming alive, the choking fumes of cars and bikes mixed with the pungent smells of cooking food and the odour of open sewers. It appeared that the whole spectrum of human life could be seen by the side of the main road, with shanty housing disgorging poor people as they prepared themselves for another squalid day.

From some I received only a quick casual glance as my guide pedalled past, no acknowledgement or even an awareness that we were there, just feet away. But others could see there might be a chance and shouted for money, holding out their hands, palms upwards. Little scruffy children wearing only rags followed the bike for a short distance until giving up their quest, plump naked babies were held in the arms of thin brown mothers, or with more rotund grandmothers, their long grey hair tied back in a bun. Washing water in stained metal jugs was sent cascading into the gutters to mix with rice and other food waste.

My chap pedalled around the streets for almost two hours, stopping here and there so that I could take a few photos, mainly of the Hindu temples, which were very colourful and yet rather shabby. The temperature was already well over seventy degrees when we started, and by the time we returned to the ship it was very hot indeed. I felt exhausted, and grateful that I had taken the ride. I think I only gave him the equivalent of a couple of pounds, but it was twice what he asked for so I left him a happy man.

The ship continued up the coast to the state of Andhra Pradesh and the town of Kakinada to load tobacco, a full cargo that was going to take several weeks. We anchored outside the tiny port, which was too small to take us alongside. The stevedores came out in a series of wooden sailing boats, and our deck was to be their home until loading had been completed. They built a small wooden hut overhanging the stern rail – the thunder box, a simple solution to an everyday problem, and no running water required!

The holds had been cleaned during the sea passage, and the carpenter had made wooden platforms above the bilges, as the tobacco was packed into wooden boxes about four foot long by two foot square. Sailing dhows towed out from the shore were secured alongside, often two or three deep, and then the stevedores would swarm down to their designated positions and commence the transhipment. Their work was a joy to see, heavy manual work but organised and efficient, a typical example of many hands making light work. Labour was cheap in this part of the world, and the possibility of mechanising the process had not even been considered. Each box was carefully stowed into the hold so that only the bare minimum of unused space could be seen, even around the pillars supporting the decks and at the turn of the frames. As each dhow became empty it was taken out of the line and went on its way, with its huge sails filling to the trade wind.

The stevedores stopped only when all the dhows that been brought out that day were gone. They had their own cook, and a fire was made up on a clear part of the deck in order to prepare their food, which of course seemed to consist of rice with a few scraps of meat or fish. They slept in any space they could find with just a coarse blanket and I never saw a change of clothing – not that they wore much anyway.

When the loading was complete the holds looked like they were full of building bricks cemented together in a perfect fashion. The full cargo was bound for Avonmouth, Liverpool and Belfast, but I remember the stevedore foreman could not pronounce these places; it came out as 'Avonmouse, Liverfool and Belpast'.

The voyage home was uneventful, and by the end of April 1976 we were heading up the Bristol Channel and into the lock at Avonmouth, where I was relieved fairly promptly in order for me to go and resit my mate's exams. Before I left the ship I saw with horror how the British dockers took out this almost perfect stowage. They sent a wire from the dockside crane down into the hold, took it around each box of tobacco in turn and simply heaved until it was dragged out of its stowage. The amount of damage done to the cargo was unbelievable, with boxes split apart as wires tightened or crushed as they were caught between pillars and hatch coamings. With a little extra thought and care the cargo could have been brought out intact. I felt there was perhaps an animosity on the part of the dockers because the care taken in loading would have caused them to take longer to complete their allocated task if it was done properly.

I tried to take my exams without spending any revision time at college. It didn't work, so I opted to go back to college, living the life of the hermit with an old lady who did bed and breakfast for students. After a month I tried again and at last I passed, so I started to look for a new employer. I felt I needed a change, and British and Commonwealth was fast being run down.

Gallic Minch

I looked around for a company where I thought I might be promoted to first mate. In the mid-seventies there were still a good number of jobs on offer for British officers. Denholm Maclay were advertising for mates on mini-bulkers, cargo ships of less than 1,600 tonnes designed to carry cargo in bulk. The contract time was for ten-week trips, and that appealed, so I made enquiries and was invited for an interview in Glasgow.

Denholm Maclay was an offshoot of the Denholm Group, a large shipowner and management company. I was offered a mate's job straightaway, but felt I could better serve if I were to complete a few weeks as second mate, thus familiarising myself with the trade.

They appointed me to a twin-hatch bulk carrier, the *Gallic Minch*. The intention was that I should complete ten days or so, take a short break, then return to another vessel as mate. The ship was owned by Gallic Shipping, a small independent ship-owner in London who had Denholm Maclay manage the vessel, which in turn was on long-term charter to Jebsens of Norway.

The ship, because of her small size and shallow draught, could go into many ports larger vessels could not enter. I was to join in Gunness, a village on the River Trent, some considerable distance from the Humber and Hull, which the ship would have had to pass to reach its destination. I joined the ship at a small wharf after a tedious journey by rail. The second mate was eager to leave, but he introduced me to his new wife – the previous voyages having been their honeymoon. When I saw the size of the cabin I was surprised that they had managed to live in such cramped conditions, and amazed that they were still speaking to each other.

The voyages were too numerous to mention, save to say that it was normal to have two or three discharging ports a week and that we operated from the northern point of Norway down to Poland, Germany, Holland, Belgium, England and northern France. The cargoes were bulk commodities of varying types, coal, iron and other metallic ores, and a white powder, the name of which I forget, which was used in the manufacture of glass.

My initial enthusiasm soon evaporated when we got to sea, for being a small ship she was very much affected by the sea conditions – as was my stomach. Watchkeeping was basically five hours on the bridge followed by five hours off, a very tiring routine, as the longest sleep I could hope to get was not more than four and half hours, and then I still had to eat. The food was at best mediocre, but usually quite poor. The master, a fairly young chief officer who had come out of Ben Line, had to fire the first cook. His replacement was 'helped' aboard in Rouen; he stayed for about six weeks, during which time I don't think he was ever sober. He had a habit of putting far too much salt into the food during cooking, until eventually the captain told him to leave the salt out altogether. He complied, but substituted vinegar

Gallic Minch

instead. The food was ghastly, and not exactly what you needed on a rough day.

Ten days came and went without any indication of a relief or promotion, and when the captain finally asked what was happening the company told him just to keep me on board for the full ten weeks. I was not impressed.

Collision

The runs through the fjords of Norway were interesting, and it was customary to take a local pilot for the duration of our stay in the inside waters. On one voyage, I distinctly remember, we had unloaded our cargo at some remote wharf at the end of yet another fjord, and sailed light ship to pass mainly within the sheltered waters to another loading berth some six or eight hours away. There had been little need to ballast down after discharge because of the short run, and consequently the ship was very 'light', with the bulbous bow well out of the water and trimmed down by the stern. The aged Norwegian pilot was on the bridge as we approached a small town at the junction of two fjords. We had to turn to starboard to enter a narrow buoyed channel, which led under a modern road bridge connecting the town with the land on the opposite side.

The pilot had brought the speed down to about 7 knots, and we made a steady course into the channel. Beyond the bridge lay a small port, and coming away from one of the jetties we noticed a red-hulled cargo ship, even smaller than our own. The ship appeared to be making for the channel to which we were now committed, so our pilot, believing we could clear the way for her entrance, increased speed to full ahead. Our speed must have increased to at least 10 knots through the narrow confines of the buoyed channel, but it soon became apparent that we would not clear before the other ship arrived – nor did it look as though she was slowing down. Her bridge looked deserted, but sailors could be seen battening down the hatchboards.

We could neither slow down nor alter course to avoid the

impending collision. To turn would have swung our vessel into the pier of the bridge, to slow down would have just delayed the inevitable. The rapidly unfolding situation was met mainly by a feeling of disbelief, as the crew of the other ship realised, too late, what was about to happen. The point of impact was going to be where they were working. They scattered in every direction as our pilot advised at the last minute to go hard to starboard and full astern on the engine. The stern had just cleared the last buoy on the port quarter, but our actions made little difference. The bulbous bow rammed into the starboard side of the other ship with a sickening crunch.

Our momentum appeared checked, but there was just a moment between that first impact and the continued forward movement of our vessel. The bulb had penetrated the steel shell and then continued for another six to ten feet until we were finally stopped by the main body of our forecastle. The engine, still turning astern, then started to pull us backwards out of the hole we had created, and as our ship gathered sternway the bow swung to starboard, the forces acting on the propeller creating a turning moment.

For a few short moments we stood, as though riveted to the spot.

The other vessel took a distinct list to port and the oval hole, which must have been at least eight feet by four, came out of the water. I can only presume that the cargo on board had shifted, thus preventing the vessel from sinking rapidly where she lay. In fact she continued to move slowly forward and made for a small jetty on the opposite side of the fjord. The pilot turned to the master and indicated that as the ship appeared to be OK we might as well proceed on our way! Needless to say that took us completely by surprise, and I can remember saying, 'But that's hit and run, isn't it?'

We put a boat down, and the mate went over to the other vessel which, by that time, had been secured alongside. Details were exchanged, and a truck loaded with steel plate and welding gear could be seen coming across the bridge. After a few hours at anchor, and no doubt some awkward phone calls by the master to the company, we continued on our way. Damage to our ship was negligible, as the reinforced bulbous bow had taken the full impact.

Strange as it may seem I can remember very little in the way of official enquiry. Soon after the incident I had written down the events in a bridge notebook, and that was taken as evidence. There was a brief interview some two or three weeks later, and that was the last I ever heard concerning the incident.

Grounding

Life continued much as before, with one port following another, the weather sometimes good, sometimes not so good. A few days in Gdansk, a depressing port in Poland, come to mind, but only because it was a public holiday, the skies and the scenery were grey, cargo work was slow and most of the locals I saw seemed to be drunk on cheap vodka.

We had another run up the River Trent with a full cargo. The pilot had advised us to wait for the next tide but the captain insisted we proceed. Unfortunately there was not enough water as the tide receded and we grounded halfway up towards Gunness. Much use was made of the engine operating astern and ahead, but to no avail. We were there for the night, and at low water we settled onto the mud with about a five-degree starboard list and down by the head, a most unusual situation for a ship and very noticeable when lying in your bunk.

The next day the ship came off the mud in her own time and we continued up towards the wharf. As we approached, the intention of the pilot was to drop the starboard anchor and use it to swing the ship through 180 degrees and then dredge the anchor down to the berth, not an uncommon manoeuvre with little ships in constricted waters. Unfortunately he miscalculated and let the anchor go when the ship was still running at about 4 knots, the ship started to swing but the chain ran out with great momentum with sparks, rust and dried mud flying in every direction. Somewhere near the fourth joining shackle the cable parted, the chain continued over the gypsy and disappeared to the muddy waters below. The ship, by this time swinging across the river with the engine going full astern, ran gently onto the bank, the pilot being fairly resigned and informing the captain that it was the only option left if we were to swing the ship around and dock against the tide onto the wharf, which is what eventually occurred. There was no damage to the bow this time either.

———

By the time I had completed ten weeks on board the *Gallic Minch* I was quite determined that the coastal life was not the one for me. I had come from an established deep-sea company looking for quick promotion, and instead I received my first introduction to the more industrial and unsympathetic side of our business, where time is money, and personal feelings and company loyalty don't mean a damn. The people on the ship were just there to fill up the numbers, and provided you had some sort of licence you had the job for as long as you could stand it. I handed in my notice when they asked me to go back to another ship after only two weeks. The office were most surprised, particularly when I also refused promotion to mate. A few days later I was on the books of Palm Line.

Palm Line

After being bounced around on the North Sea I decided I wanted short voyages, but with sun. I was interviewed and accepted by Booker Line, the Liverpool company that ran to the Caribbean, but they wanted me to join a vessel on charter and the trip would have been three months. At the time I was in the process of buying my first home, and needed to be back in the UK to complete, so after being in Liverpool one day I found myself in London the next, where I was interviewed by Palm Line and offered a job as second officer on board their ship *Ikeja Palm*. Palm Line, a traditional company running mainly general cargo ships down to West Africa, was an offshoot of the industrial giant Unilever. I was about to be introduced to the joys of the West African trade – yet another eye-opener!

Ikeja Palm

Even before I reached my first ship things were interesting. I had to join the *Ikeja Palm* on 15 December 1976 in Antwerp. I reached Heathrow early on a rather foggy morning to find things pretty chaotic, and I settled down for what was probably going to be a long day. I wasn't wrong. The British Airways flight was cancelled because of fog on the other side of the channel. After several hours my flight was called to the information desk and informed we were all being placed on a Romanian Air Services flight. Interesting, I thought, no other carrier was heading that way because of the weather. The ageing One-Eleven took off OK and the stewardess came around with the in-flight meal, which consisted of a small bar of bitter dark chocolate and a cup of water served from a wine bottle. After about half an hour the pilot came over the public address and, in heavily accented English, advised us that there was fog at Antwerp and we would be landing at Amsterdam Schipol. Well, not much of a surprise there, I thought, the other carriers were obviously not flying there for the same reason.

I have to give it to the guy: either he was very good or he was just running out of fuel, because I looked out of the window all the way down and never saw the tarmac till we hit it, literally. It must have been the hardest landing I have experienced, including any of my own. The plane touched down while seemingly still at a forty-five degree angle to the ground before continuing at great speed with the engines screaming on reverse thrust along the runway. Everything was shaking so much that anything loose was bouncing around, lockers fell open and the oxygen mask above dropped a few inches from my nose. Maybe all perfectly normal for the Romanians, but the rest of the passengers and I all breathed a long sigh of relief as the plane eventually came to a halt.

It was late, dark and a long way from where I wanted to be. A bus was laid on, and five or six hours later we rolled into Antwerp. The dock system here is vast, and any agent detailed for my collection had long since gone home. I found a taxi and after many stops and enquiries we eventually found the ship. I heaved my gear up the gangway around one-thirty in the morning. A couple of guys were still in the officers' bar and welcomed me with 'We wondered where you were, want a beer?'

The *Ikeja Palm* was a comfortable and traditional cargo ship of 5,816 gross tons, five hatches, normal derricks, or sticks as we used to call them, and a good crowd of guys who had been in the company for a while. I was to do two runs on this ship and, although the ports were pretty bad in the main, the atmosphere on board was always great, fun chaps who could find a joke in even the most uncomfortable of situations.

We sailed from Antwerp with a full cargo of general goods bound for Lagos in Nigeria. As second mate I was not the lowest-ranking officer and was therefore quickly accepted as one of the lads. My time with British and Commonwealth was a huge benefit when it came to understanding how this company worked, and my recent move was considered perfectly understandable.

After ten days or so we approached Lagos and, even though we were on what was known as a liner trade, where we should have expected to berth on arrival, we were instructed to anchor. Shades of Jeddah came to mind, as there were anchored ships all over the place. Over the past year or so I had heard stories of hundreds of ships being at anchor off Lagos, some for more than a year. Most of them were fully loaded with cement, destined for the rapidly growing construction industry that had resulted from Nigeria's huge oil revenues of recent years. In fact we

Ikeja Palm

were pretty sure there was a big scam going on, for if a ship had a full cargo and was delayed because the port had insufficient capacity or infrastructure to discharge the ship, the shipowner would receive demurrage, or financial remuneration, to offset the losses incurred as a result of the ship being effectively taken out of normal revenue-earning service. Many unscrupulous shipowners bought very old ships destined for the scrap yard, obtained a one-off cargo of cement bound for Lagos, knowing the ship would earn demurrage for effectively doing nothing. Apparently the hold life of a cargo of cement can be measured in weeks rather than years, which of course meant that when the cargo was eventually unloaded it was good for nothing.

We fell into the routine of being at anchor, with watches being maintained on the bridge and down below as normal. In fact we were perhaps a little more vigilant than normal, as this was a period when pirates were often reported in the area. These people were not of course the swashbuckling heroes of the eighteenth century, but modern-day rogues who were apparently armed with weapons left over from the war in Biafra. They had been known to board unsuspecting ships at anchor and rob the crew at gunpoint. Murders had even been reported.

And so it was one night, around about one o'clock, that I heard a distress message coming over the VHF emergency frequency, also commonly referred to as Channel 16. A captain on a small ship anchored almost fifteen miles off the coast was saying he needed help for his chief engineer, who had been shot. There was no response from any shore station, perhaps because the local port radio was not manned at night, or more likely because the guy on duty was asleep. I went on the radio and relayed the message in the hope that, because we were so much closer to the land, a mobile station might pick me up. I was lucky, and soon a British voice came back. He was a cargo superintendent who had a portable VHF and was on his way back home after what had been, no doubt, a long day at the docks.

Between the two of us we arranged for a work boat to be manned and sent out, but the Danish captain of the coaster was told that he needed to bring his ship much closer to the port as the boat could really not go much further than the outer breakwaters. In due course the ship approached and the engineer was landed. When things had settled down I talked to the captain again and asked what had happened. He told me, in his lilting Danish English, that the chief had joined just ten days ago, but it transpired the man had a drink problem. The captain had stopped him getting any more beer or spirits, but the chief was turning violent. It came to a head that night when, as the captain stated, 'He came down from the bridge to my cabin with the shotgun, but I was too quick for him and shot him with my pistol!' The captain then had to go down to the engine room, start the main engine himself, and rush back up to the bridge and carefully navigate the ship towards the harbour entrance.

Quite a turn of events, I thought, and if this is what long anchorages did for you I really wasn't interested. To my knowledge we had no guns on board our ship and probably just as well. I was later informed that the chief engineer survived the gunshot wound.

A day or so later we went into the inner anchorage for a night, tantalisingly close to the bright lights of (what appeared to be) civilisation. The following morning, having been at anchor for over ten days, we went alongside the wharf in Apapa. The bustling grimy city of Lagos lay across the water some half a mile away. I couldn't quite understand why, after we had started to open the hatches, a great rush of stevedoring humanity came surging down the quay towards us. The explanation was that we were carrying almost 4,000 tons of beer on pallets and the word had spread. Over the next few days we found that more and more cases of beer were getting damaged, and the smell in the holds was becoming very pungent in the tropical heat – and it wasn't just alcohol. The dockers were not very pleasant at the best of times and after consuming copious quantities of pilfered booze they were just horrible. They were aggressive and lazy, sleeping and peeing in dark corners, and it was not very pleasant to have to go into the hatch and check the unloading. During one night I went down and found a large bag full of beers stashed up between the steel deck beams. I confiscated it and went up on deck and threw it into the river, much to the surprise and anger of the dockers nearby, who insisted it was Nigerian beer and I had no right to take it. Apparently it is quite normal when taking cargoes of this nature to West Africa for shippers to allow a forty per cent loss through pilferage.

Lagos and its surroundings had been connected by a new elevated highway, built with tons of cement above what only could be described as a shanty town of mud huts covered by corrugated iron. What corruption there must have been; the money would have been far better spent rehousing the extremely poor people and constructing decent roads at ground level. Traffic was chaotic and, to alleviate some of the problems, restrictions were in place. If your car had an even number at the end of its registration then you could only drive on even days within the city area, and vice-versa for odd days.

Watching local TV and hearing various stories, I came to believe that Nigeria had been rushed into the modern era as a result of its oil wealth, but all that was coming to a close as revenues were affected by the oil price reductions, and corruption had hastened the process of boom turning to bust. I was pleased to leave after a week or so alongside, and from what I hear things are no picnic there now, over thirty years later.

On my second voyage on the *Ikeja Palm* we were sent on a totally different itinerary, down first to Freetown in Sierra Leone, where we picked up about a dozen 'Kru Boys'. These men were to assist our British sailors when the derricks had to be rigged and worked together for the loading and stowage of logs and packaged timber.

Leaving Freetown, we proceeded further into the Gulf of Guinea, first to Abidjan on the Ivory Coast, then Takoradi and Tema in Ghana (which had originally been the Gold Coast). Lome in Togo followed, then Cotonou in Benin, Douala in Cameroon, and finally we reached as far down as the port city of Matadi in Zaire, which is approximately one hundred miles up the Congo River and just south of the Equator.

The Kru Boys were of great assistance, and our 'white' crew took their presence as almost being an excuse for working the minimum amount of time possible. The 'Boys' lived in a mast house on deck that had been kitted out with bunks, and worked a good twelve hours plus a day. There was much preparation needed to prepare the lifting cables, blocks and hooks prior to the heavy-lifting derricks being ready for use, and when moving around the deck you had to make sure not to trip over wires running to winches, or heel blocks set at head height just above what had previously been an access way.

As I look back, these ports tend to merge into one great experience. Abidjan was French-speaking, which made it seem quite sophisticated. Takoradi and Tema still had that ex-colonial British feel about them, but we had a very busy schedule of discharge that gave us little time off. Another problem was the third mate, who knocked himself out during a friendly soccer match between ships. He had been put off work for a few days and the chief officer and I were splitting the working day between us.

The moment we finished discharge in Tema the captain sailed.

It was late in the evening, and by the time my duty supervising the letting-go of ropes on the forecastle (known as stations) was over, it was time to take the 12–4 bridge watch. I was peeved that the old man didn't even consider doing the first hour for me. I managed to keep awake, but only caught a short kip after my watch, as we were arriving in Lome at daybreak and again I had to go forward. We had berthed by eight o'clock and were taking a quick breakfast prior to starting cargo, when we found out that the dockers did not work on a Sunday in this port.

No further excuse was needed. Breakfast went on to having a quick beer before an intended lie-down. However, this developed into a long session of reminiscences told by these experienced West Coast men, very funny stories that had us in fits of laughter. Then arrived a second mate and a purser from another Palm Line ship who were being put up at a beach hotel along the coast. Apparently their captain had left quicker than expected when cargo had finished as he intended to catch the start of the next working day in Cotonou, sixty miles up the coast. I presume he thought that the guys, who were legitimately taking shore leave, could soon catch up in a taxi. Unfortunately, because of a territorial dispute, Togo and Benin had a policy of not allowing anyone to cross the border. The two officers had been stuck for ten days.

By early afternoon everyone had probably had too much to drink, but we were invited by these two chaps to come back to their hotel. We did, and proceeded to continue our story telling at the very pleasant beach bar, having been told that the company would be picking up the tab. I made the stupid mistake of diving into the pool at the shallow end, and as soon as I had done it I knew something was wrong. I thought I'd broken my nose, but in fact I had split my forehead open. When I surfaced there were gasps of horror from the other guys – it did look quite impressive, apparently. They fixed me up with a couple of sticking plasters when it should have been stitches, and the alcohol dulled the pain, but I was lucky I didn't lose consciousness. Common sense took over, and we all beat a hasty retreat to the ship.

After the discharge of general cargo was complete the ship started to load local produce. Before loading cocoa in sacks the holds had to be scrupulously cleaned, and I remember that the local inspectors made us clean ours twice. The cocoa was loaded using rope slings from a barge that was brought alongside. I decided during one long hot and boring nighttime cargo watch to scramble down the rope ladder and inspect the barge. I turned my bright torch into the void space at the stern and to my consternation I could see a coppery reflection from below. It shimmered, and I realised that I was looking at cockroaches, the big ones we called Bombay canaries. They literally covered every square inch of deck space – so, as far as I was concerned, all our own efforts at cleanliness were rather pointless.

Another cargo of pulses for one hatch were brought up a makeshift gangway, one bag at a time over the shoulders of the stevedores. At the hatch coaming another chap slit each bag, and the contents were poured into the lower hold to become a bulk cargo, not a particularly quick operation. The top six feet of the hold were filled with bagged cargo, layered in the shape of a bowl over the bulk in order to prevent the cargo from shifting in heavy seas.

The high point of the voyage was the passage up the Congo River. It took most of the day to get up to Matadi, and even though the river was quite wide in places, the current was strong. The river pilots were very good, placing the ship accurately to avoid problems with turbulence and bank effect, which can cause even the most powerful of ships to go aground. We loaded heavy logs with our derricks, quite an operation, requiring a certain skill and experience on the part of the winch men at either end of the hatch. They would have to drive four winches to coordinate the lifting, transfer and lowering of logs thirty or forty tons in weight.

The river was quite wide near the city where it flowed sluggishly towards the sea, bringing down with it from up country all sorts of vegetation and the odd dead animal. The tropical sunsets were magnificent, looking across the river towards the distant hills, but the smells from the city were not so pleasant.

Before too long we were making our way northwest to Freetown to disembark the Kru Boys – and then back home. My discharge book records that I paid off in Glasgow on 21 June 1977. It was a day I remember well. Our sailors were off like a shot as soon as we berthed, but the officers had to wait for their coastal reliefs. The deck equipment in the meantime had been set up for discharging the logs from the lower hold. Then the stevedore foreman came into the mess and said there was a change of plan and the packaged timber from the tweendecks would come out first, so could we move the heavy-lift derrick (referred to as the 'jumbo stick'), as it was right over the hatch? This had to be carefully done to avoid the multi-sheave block and hook being stuck in the air with insufficient weight on the hook to get it down again.

I went on deck to find one of the dockers heaving up the hook. I ducked around a heel block to tell him to stop, but didn't duck sufficiently and gave myself a good crack on the head. That removed any sense of humour I might have had, and perhaps I was a little brusque in my request for him to desist. In return I was given a handsome tirade of Glaswegian vocabulary. Needless to say I backed off before the language was reinforced by something more physical. In the end all was well, the cargo was started and I caught the train down to Birmingham. After a long spell of leave I joined, for the one and only time in my career, a tanker.

Matadi Palm

In fact the *Matadi Palm* was not a regular oil tanker, but had been designed specifically for the carriage of vegetable oils on the trade between West Africa and Europe. I joined in Rotterdam on 5 September 1977 after the ship had completed a discharge of cargo. The chief officer was supervising the loading of refined vegetable oil to take back down to Nigeria. I began to understand the trade when I realised we were basically picking up the raw product in one place, taking it to Europe, where it was refined, and taking the refined product back to the place where it had originated.

Even so, the cargo was always split up into parcels that had to be loaded separately and kept in individual tanks, thus creating quite a work-up for the mate to ensure each grade was not contaminated with another of a different quality. Loading was fairly simple: hoses from the shore were not connected to the cargo manifolds but were laid across the deck with the end dropped into the manhole hatch. Fortunately the pressure was never very high, otherwise the hose would have snaked all over the place. A nice simple clean cargo that made very little mess, and consequently the decks were clean and well painted, a far cry from the *Elbe Ore* and her filthy foredeck covered in iron ore.

I was to make a couple of voyages on this fairly new ship. It was pleasant enough, but there was no great challenge with the cargo work and we were only in port for a relatively short time, with very little chance to go ashore. In West Africa we usually picked up palm oil, a creamy brown liquid extracted from a certain type of palm tree and used as a basic ingredient in many types of vegetable oil. One problem was that we had to maintain the cargo at a particular temperature, or it would solidify. The tanks had steam coils inside to ensure the temperature of the cargo, and I was told an unusual story when I joined. When the ship had been built a design error had allowed the steam to be introduced into the coils from the top. Naturally, as the steam went further down the coils it started to cool, so much so that before it reached the bottom of the tank it was already too cool to keep the cargo heated and liquid. The first cargo the ship carried ended up as a solid mass below halfway and of course could not be pumped out: it had to be dug out by men with shovels. A strange mistake to happen, considering the ship was not the first tanker the company had had in service.

When the cargo was discharged there was always a residue inside the tank, these residues could be fairly considerable, depending on the type of oil. It was therefore necessary for some of the men to go down into the tank and, using squeegees, push the residue towards the strum box and the tank suction. This was known as puddling, and I was told good money could be earned by volunteering to be one of the puddling gang. In fact, a rota had always to be drawn up by the mate as volunteers inevitably exceeded the number required.

When puddling the hot oils more money was earned, something like ten pence per ton of tank quantity split between however many men went down there, but it was hot, tiring work and it could take an hour or so a tank. Refined vegetable oils were less viscous and did not need to be heated so the figure was around seven pence per ton. The crew were in every tank, as was the mate, so they could take home several hundred pounds a trip. The other officers made a little less, but it was very welcome to go home with a tax-free 'wedge' in your pocket.

The one cargo no-one wanted to puddle was fish oil. Occasionally the ship took a small quantity, maybe six hundred tons or so, loaded from a fish factory ship. On my last voyage we stopped off in Tenerife on the way north and went alongside a factory ship for about twelve hours. The fish oil was extracted from the fish brought to the factory ship from trawlers in huge fishing fleets. They spent months at the fishing grounds, controversially catching anything and everything that came into their nets. The fish were sorted, gutted, packed and frozen by the factory ship, and anything that could not be used for any other purpose was converted to oil. Because the whole process was carried out at sea in all weathers, these big ships were far from looking pristine. Rust was everywhere, and the smell was almost overwhelming.

Upon arrival at Rotterdam it was normal for the crew going on leave to discharge the cargo and puddle the tanks. The fish oil left a greasy yellow stain that soaked into your skin along with an odour that took days to disappear. Catching the short flight back to the UK was something of an embarrassment because we could see fellow passengers turning their noses up when they came to sit nearby. The one benefit from carrying fish oil was of course financial, as we earned fifteen pence per ton for puddling duties.

I signed off in January 1978, vowing not to return to tankers if I could help it, but not knowing at the time that this ship would be the last cargo ship of any kind on which I would serve as a watchkeeping officer. The following month I went down to Ramsgate and joined Hoverlloyd for an extended season as relief navigator.

Hoverlloyd

One of the most interesting jobs I have had was as a second officer for Hoverlloyd, a company operating large SRN4 hovercraft between Ramsgate in Kent and Calais, France. I had first seen one of these ungainly looking machines in 1969 when I was still on my pre-sea training. I was interested even then because of their unusual characteristics, not really a ship, but neither a plane.

By 1977 I had a first mate's certificate and was working for Palm Line, running between the UK and the Continent to West Africa– interesting ships but hardly romantic destinations. Hoverlloyd advertised in the late autumn for seasonal navigators for the busy periods in the coming year. On 15 November, my twenty-sixth birthday, I drove down to the International Hoverport for my interview. The day was very windy and the hovercraft service had been cancelled, a good thing perhaps, as it had been the intention of the company to take me over on a familiarisation trip. Knowing what I do now, I would almost certainly have been as sick as a dog, and that would have been the end of the whole business.

Captain Roger Syms was my 'interrogator', and I was his first victim. We started off very well, and I even suggested some of the questions he should ask. By 1130 we had had a chat, walked around one of the craft on the pad, had another chat and then retreated to the bar. My birthday was of course used as an excuse, and I met a few of the other flight crew, finally leaving around 1430 having been offered the job. I was elated, knowing it was going to be an interesting time ahead with a good crowd.

Initial training and techniques

In February I went back to do my initial training, which was to last approximately a month. The navigator's position in the control cabin was behind the captain and flight engineer. Two basic radars were all that was used, chartwork being neither necessary nor possible with speeds of over 60 knots and considerable vibration. A designated track across the Goodwin Sands and the Channel was maintained where possible by parallel indexing technique, using the navigational buoys to keep a horizontal minimum distance of one mile between opposing tracks. With closing speeds of 120 knots plus, the hovercraft on opposing tracks had to ensure this distance was not reduced. Because of the speed and the amount of traffic, it was normal practice to use the six-mile range of the radar, not the normal twelve miles, since with that coverage it was just about impossible to track the increased number of targets.

I had only one crossing with another navigator, then I was on my own. The navigation was not particularly difficult, but the collision avoidance was a different matter. The captain had no radar, nor would he have time to use one, and he relied totally on the information being fed to him from behind. The company standing rule was not to pass closer than one mile ahead or half a mile astern of a crossing vessel, which caused problems in thick weather when ships tended to follow one another up the Channel about a mile apart. In reality we would aim for a ship then at the last moment sideslip under her stern.

A certain amount of skill had to be developed to get this technique to work well, as a hovercraft when turned would continue on its previous course for quite a distance. God only knows what

SRN4 hovercraft at Ramsgate

the other ships thought if they were tracking us on their radar or listening to the growing roar of four Rolls Royce turbines coming at them through the murk!

Information was passed back and forth in the control cabin via radio, as the noise caused by the four great propellers was deafening. We wore headphones with boom mikes, and it was important to give the captain just enough information for him to picture the general situation, without flooding him with useless paraphernalia.

Early crossings

Some of my initial crossings in February and March were close to the limits of wind and wave height – force seven and eight feet – and in fact by the time we arrived in the middle of the Channel they could be considerably over. The craft were most uncomfortable in bad weather, and sometimes it was necessary to strap into the specially designed seats. Needless to say, the contents of my stomach were shifted in a vertical direction on more than one occasion. The first time, I remember, was during an early-morning flight when I felt the 'overwhelming desire' after about thirty minutes. Even though I tried to fight it, I succumbed, but only for a minute, and a bag was always kept handy for such purposes. In these poor weather conditions it was imperative to resume conning as soon as possible. By the time we arrived in Calais

– late, of course – I had regained my composure and felt relatively normal. I climbed the ladder to the car deck and walked into one of the passenger compartments, clutching my little bag. The worse-for-wear passengers had all left, no doubt vowing never to return, and the six stewardesses were all recovering with the aid of a brandy (this was eight o'clock in the morning). I made my entrance, held up my bag and asked if anyone would care for Cornflakes. Most of the girls feigned disgust and revulsion but the head girl rushed over, took the bag and said, 'Oh! You poor thing, would you like a drink?'

During that first month I worked with many of the captains, enjoying their differing experiences and attitudes, enjoying the work, fine-tuning my own abilities and getting a great deal of satisfaction from the responsibility. The final test before qualifying was a return crossing while navigating from behind closed curtains. Going out on 19 March was fine, and the return went well until we were within about six miles of Ramsgate, when I picked up many targets outside the harbour, some crossing our track. The captain could of course see all the yachts quite easily, as it was a fine day with a clear blue sky, but I had to weave my way through them using the radar to advise him, at one stage having to slow down and stop. The ground controller at the hoverport, who could see us in the distance, called up to ask if we had a problem. I eventually navigated the craft through to clear water and made the base. The captain said I might be a little less than refined, but at least I was safe!

The season
Three of us who trained up at that time were passed for working on the craft, and our abilities were put to the test over the busy Easter period, after which we were given a month off as our services were not required until the summer schedule started in earnest towards the end of May. By then another ten navigators had passed through the training system, and three or four more had failed, I presume because they couldn't mentally adjust to

the different style of radar operation and the need to cope with many targets at high speed.

For a three-month period during the summer the flight crews were designated teams, and I was fortunate to have Dennis Ford as my captain. We all worked well together and I only regret never continuing our friendship or even exchanging Christmas cards. Our average week would consist of three days when three return crossings were made and two days of two crossings. On a three-crossing day the Civil Aviation Authority ruled that we must have a break of two hours after two trips had been completed, so those days were quite long, but the two-trip days were finished in under five hours.

I used to get quite a kick out of walking across the apron to the craft, climbing up to the control cabin and making ready for sea. Over in Calais the craft would only be on the ground for twenty minutes, forty cars off, forty on and up to two hundred and forty passengers off and on, plus we would take fuel. The crew consisted of three on the flight deck, six stewards and six car-deck men, whose responsibility it was to lash and unlash the vehicles.

Among of the more unusual problems we encountered were the bait diggers who went about their business on the mud in Pegwell Bay, the stretch of coast just to the south of Ramsgate where the hoverport was situated. At low tide there was a mile or so of beach to cover before reaching open water. The local fishermen would dig anywhere to obtain fresh bait, even within ten feet of the concrete apron. In misty weather they could not be seen until the last moment and quite often continued happily digging with hovercraft roaring past only yards away, feigning complete indifference. There was a well-found rumour that one was actually knocked over face down into the mud as a craft turned off the pad and sideslipped onto its departure course. Although no doubt rather upset, the gentleman in question survived unscathed.

On occasion, to obtain our duty-free allowance, a few of us would take a crossing during a day off, paying just one pound.

After a few hours spent in the supermarket we would return loaded with beer, wine, French cheese, paté and bread. A party that evening inevitably followed. Due to the nature of the trade, Hoverlloyd had ensured a plentiful supply of pretty ladies, so company was never a problem!

The number of temporary or seasonal employees was usually over a hundred, and consequently the company had their own training routine, which took a week. I found it very thorough, and I have since wished that other shipping companies would practise something similar.

Foggy crossing

My training and ability was tested one foggy morning in mid-summer. We left at 0600 hours with zero visibility: the captain could only just see the concrete twenty-five feet below him. All the way over the conditions remained the same, but I picked our way through the traffic using the radar and closed Calais Hoverport without any problem from crossing ships. I advised the captain to reduce speed from 60 knots plus as we came closer and fine-tuned the radar until I could make out the shape of the terminal buildings on my scope. We kept reducing speed, the fog remaining as thick as ever, I picked out the waves gently breaking onto the concrete apron and advised the captain that we were no more than twenty feet to the left of the centre line. He picked up the three-foot-wide line visually just about where I said it should be, and still he could not see the buildings. We slowly edged up to the pad, and I remember giving a inaudible sigh of relief when he could make out the 'spot' and the indistinct shape of the terminal just ten feet ahead. When we went 'off cushion' I felt the need to leave my sticky seat so I made my excuses and wandered around the outside of the craft doing the external checks for the engineer – and taking plenty of deep breaths.

As is often the case with summer fog, by the time we set off on the return journey it had begun to lift, and on arrival at Ramsgate it was yet another sunny day.

'Poling'

Dennis Ford now and again had me swap seats with our engineer Ray, to give him some practice navigating and also to let me have a go at operating the throttles and 'poling' – controlling the craft by use of the aircraft-style yoke. This controlled the four pylons that held the variable-pitch propellers and the four fans that gave the lift air. Along with the foot pedals that operated the two large rudders on the stern, a combination of effects could be made and it was all rather complicated, in much the same way as a helicopter differs from a conventional aircraft.

In calm weather it was relatively easy to keep the beast on track, but in anything above wind force three, the entire pilot's skill and experience was required. Getting there was only half the battle. Avoiding the large holes in the ocean that suddenly appeared in front of you was more important.

The opposition

1978 saw the first flights of the ill-fated French Sedam N500, a much larger hovercraft that entered service for SNCF, the French Railways partner of Seaspeed, our British Rail opposition, which was based in Dover. Unfortunately the first of a pair had been burned out the previous year during building and the remaining craft, *Ingénieur Jean Bertin*, proved to be very unwieldy. They had major problems with skirt design and reliability that eventually caused the machine to be scrapped. As far as we were concerned, we endeavoured to keep well away when it was manoeuvring, as it rarely seemed to make the position allocated on the apron.

The stretched Super 4 introduced by Seaspeed from Dover the same year seemed to be a far better option, and it was considered that Hoverlloyd might convert their craft in a similar manner to take advantage of the increase in trade. This was not to be, however. Eventually, in late 1981, Hoverlloyd amalgamated with Seaspeed to form Hoverspeed, and the terminal in Pegwell Bay was closed down. A great pity, as it was obviously far better suited than the constricted new terminal built within the Western Docks at Dover.

The last day

The season tailed off by September, and it was a case of first in, first out. I had already been interviewed by Cunard Line and was to join the *QE2* on 18 September. So 10 September was to be my last day on the craft. We made one return crossing around lunch-time, had a two-hour break, then set out again at 1632 hours. The weather had taken a turn for the worse and there was a blow in the Channel, but not sufficient to be above normal craft limits. About ten minutes before arrival at the Calais hoverport we received a radio message from the port asking us to keep an eye open for a French yacht in distress.

We saw him shortly afterwards, and the craft commander, Captain Childs, attempted to close towards the boat, the sails of which were flapping madly in the wind. I made my way to the centre passenger door and, with the car-deck men behind, opened up and prepared to throw a line. From the elevated height of about fifteen feet above the sea I envisaged problems, and had no real idea how to overcome them. On the first pass the skipper of the yacht appeared dazed, and there was blood running down his face. He caught the line but was too slow in making it secure. The yacht continued into the murk.

We circled the hovercraft, and on the second attempt came down off cushion. The yacht approached again, and as it passed I jumped down into its cockpit, quickly taking a turn with the line on the nearest cleat, thus preventing my impend-ing departure in a boat which I was not in the least capable of navigating. I rushed forward and dropped the jib, then what remained of the mainsail – it looked as though the boom had swung wildly and hit the skipper on the head, thus causing his apparent inability. A frightened-looking woman emerged from the little cabin with a child in her arms. I manhandled them both up to the waiting arms of the car-deck crew and then shoved the man in the same direction.

By this time a large workboat had come out from Calais and landed clumsily alongside the hovercraft, rupturing the plenum chamber in the process, though we did not realise it at the time. They took the yacht in tow and I returned, dripping wet, to the control cabin, passing our wide-eyed passengers on the way. Captain Childs attempted to resume passage, but the external damage prevented the craft rising onto cushion, the fans being unable to push the water out from underneath. There was no danger of the craft sinking, as the inherent buoyancy from many sealed duralamin compartments guaranteed flotation. We eventually 'boated' into the hoverport, gushing great quantities of spray as we crossed onto the apron.

The casualties went ashore along with the passengers, and an external examination revealed two holes in the side of the hovercraft. The damage would have to have a temporary repair before a return crossing could be made, so the whole crew had to return as passengers on the next available flight. Some sight I must have looked, and it was an unusual end to a particularly interesting season. After 446 crossings of the English Channel in 1978, my official logbook finally ended in France.

Cunard

Queen Elizabeth 2

I joined the Cunard Line on 18 September 1978. After working for Hoverlloyd for over seven months as a seasonal second officer, I had applied to both P&O and Cunard on the off chance they might have vacancies on their passenger vessels. My enthusiasm for cargo ships had waned and I felt that, if I had to go to sea, I might as well do so in relative comfort.

The *Queen Elizabeth 2* looked very large as I walked down the Ocean Terminal in Southampton at seven in the morning. I had been advised by the office to be early, but they never told the ship, and consequently only the night security watch were around when I boarded. Soon my presence was announced and Roland Hasell, the chief officer, showed me the mate's office and some paperwork to read – not very imaginative.

I soon met the other deck officers, and then my introduction to the ship commenced. It truly is a huge ship to find your way around, and it takes months, not weeks or days, before you can really feel familiar with all the nooks and crannies one finds on a passenger ship.

My watch was to be the 12–4 (hardly surprising). Although the ship often travelled at 28 knots, I found that it was not particularly difficult to navigate. Being a lowly second officer, however, I was really a glorified 'gofer', so I put positions on the chart, logged the in and out telexes, and answered the phone. The most important responsibility I was given was looking after the uniform locker, a tedious task made worse by the fact the previous incumbent had made a complete mess of the inventory. After the responsibility of navigating a hovercraft it was all a bit of a comedown.

After I had been on board for a week or so, I went onto the bridge just before midnight to hear a big row going on in the 'barn', the space behind the bridge where the quartermaster and bridge boy sat when not required for look out duty. John Carroll, the Australian first officer, went to see what was happening and found himself accosted by a drunken and half-crazed quartermaster who was throwing furniture around. The QM shot off down below and Carroll followed him, leaving me to navigate on my own. Some five minutes later I heard over the walkie-talkie that the QM had barricaded himself into his cabin with the chief officer, whom he was holding at knifepoint.

This was, needless to say, not what I expected of Cunard Line staff, but anyway I was quite happy out of harm's way while the others were being heroes down below. A short while later, Alan Bennell, the staff captain, came to the bridge, no doubt to see whether I could handle the navigating 'on my own'. He was quite a character, and instructed me to go and get him a gin and tonic. I thought perhaps this was a little unusual, on the bridge of the *QE2* in the middle of the night, but I was prepared to play along and asked him if he wanted ice and lemon. Of course he did, and he was most upset when I said he had no ice left in his cabin. He sent me off to find some with the remark, 'Come on Rentell, how do you expect me to drink gin with no ice?' He soon realised that driving the *QE2* on my own was not beyond my capability,

QE2

so before long he left me to my own devices. Carroll appeared another hour or so later, after they had managed to sedate the sailor and lock him up.

I worked on board *QE2* for ten years, and there were many incidents of one sort or another. I experienced fires, grounding, bad weather, deaths – but I don't remember a birth.

Bad weather

I was on the 8–12 watch with Dan Robinson and we were approaching New York on a dark and very rainy night. The Nantucket light vessel was some miles behind us and the ship was steaming at close to 29 knots on a course of 270 degrees, due west. The radars were completely blocked out by the intensity of the rain but the visibility still appeared to be reasonable.

I was behind the chart table poring over some magazine or paperwork, and Dan was keeping the visual watch with the quartermaster. He called to me, saying that he thought he would have to alter course for a crossing ship. This was fairly unusual on this stretch, so I asked him to hold on while I tried to pick the other vessel up on radar. The screen was completely blotted out and no adjustment of the rain clutter control made any difference. I could see the faint red light of the ship fine on our starboard bow so I told Dan to alter the course on the autopilot.

We had a new adaptive autopilot under trial. Dan turned the dial and the ship began to change course, but then seemed to slow down, and the other vessel was getting close very quickly. The adaptive autopilot had the rate of turn set into it, and it wasn't fast enough! The visibility was obviously a lot less than we thought, and the oncoming ship must have been a lot closer than we first believed. Just at that moment, the staff captain phoned up and started to waffle on about a morning call. I was getting impatient to get over and change autopilots, and had to hurry him off the line.

I put the helm hard to starboard. The ship started to race around, taking a list to port, but the oncoming vessel still seemed to stay on the same bearing fine to starboard. Quickly the red light became several small lights and it was possible to see the shape of the other vessel, which was a cargo ship of about 3,000 gross tons. In a mere moment of time the hull of the other ship disappeared below our bow and, as we continued to turn, the masts and bridge of the ship raced past onto the port side, missing us by no more than twenty feet.

The final moments passed so quickly that it was almost a blur, but it had happened – and after I put the helm over the other way I was just in time to see the other ship disappear into the darkness. We were incredibly lucky not to have had a collision, and I can only presume that the watch on the other ship had not been very attentive, as they never attempted to alter course.

The end of the watch was only twenty minutes away, and I told Dan to leave any talking to me. I didn't really want some major enquiry going on if I could help it. Unfortunately quite a few people in the nightclub had seen the lights race past the window and we were barraged with questions. I told Captain Arnott next morning, but he showed little interest. No doubt he had been through similar experiences in his long career and knew that they happen now and again. He was that sort of chap, never ruffled, never got excited, never raised his voice – well respected by us all.

There were of course many occasions when the ship had bad weather, common on a transatlantic crossing in the autumn and winter. Freezing cold conditions were often experienced in New York around the Christmas period, when, on occasion, the Hudson would freeze around the ship. Those early mornings on the forecastle were a bitter experience, wrapped up to the nines, but the cold permeating every layer of clothing. I had to lay the anchor out one night when we went on a cruise to nowhere. Captain Ridley decided he wanted to use the spot we had used a few nights before and I was on the foredeck for over an hour in very strong wind conditions when the chill factor brought the temperature down to something like minus twenty. We tried to get whatever shelter we could behind the windlass machinery, and when I had to stand out on the platform overhanging the bow the wind actually went straight up my trouser leg. Never has an anchor been laid out so quickly – and Ridley, obviously feeling at least some pity, invited me up for a shot afterwards. I could not hold the glass as my hands, slowly thawing, were very painful.

Grounding

The first time I remember going aground was leaving Port Everglades at the start of the 1979 World Cruise. There was a strong wind coming up from the south, and as we crept through the channel I felt the ship lurch to starboard twice. The bosun's mate aft, where I was on stations, thought it had been a tug, but in fact we had bounced off the bank of the dredged channel on the port side. Captain Portet had of course kept his implacable cool and just increased speed to ensure we didn't become stuck. The damage was restricted to the port bilge keel, which had torn from the hull over thirty or forty feet. A weld had cracked, and one fuel tank became contaminated with seawater. The damage was eventually repaired at the next refit.

The second occasion was far more serious. Captain Jackson was in command as we approached San Juan, Puerto Rico, and there was again a strong wind blowing onto the beam. San Juan is not an easy approach as there is an almost ninety degree turn not long after the entrance and it is necessary to keep speed on to make the turn and counteract the drift effect of the wind. Unfortunately we probably had too much speed and we sideswiped the starboard-hand buoy, eventually coming to stop resting on the right-hand side of the channel with the buoy dangerously close to the propellers.

All the tugs came out to assist, but the ship was well stuck and the captain did not want to use the starboard engine in case of dragging the buoy and its chain into the prop. After some four or five hours a large dredger working in the harbour came and manoeuvred off our stern and took two of our steel mooring wires. The combined effort, plus a last-ditch effort with both propellers, pulled the ship off, breaking one of the wires at the same time.

We were pulled to the berth, towing the buoy and its chain in behind us. Divers were sent down and found that the buoy chain had actually become trapped, not around the propeller, but above the rudder close to the stock. The divers worked all night to release it and in fact had to take turns, sawing through the heavy chain with a hacksaw. Fortunately there was little other damage except to the underwater hull paintwork.

Only a few weeks later we went aground again, going into Barbados. I had set up the ship for the approach and handed over to Peter Jackson, explaining that I had about five degrees on to counteract the northerly set. The young pilot came onto the bridge, saw that we were apparently heading for the breakwater, and instructed the quartermaster to go hard a-port. He then realised his mistake and put opposite helm on, but it was too late. The ship set up to the left, and to miss the port-hand buoy he tried to bring the bow to port again. Of course, the captain could see we were fast running out of water in front and instructed the engines to be put astern. We lost steerage and landed gently onto the side of the channel, again with our stern perilously close to the buoy.

The ship remained stationary for an hour or so, rolling gently with the swell, but touching the bottom as she rolled to port. Captain Jackson eventually took the bit between his teeth and went full astern on both engines – and we gradually pulled off the bank, this time without the buoy.

After gaining sufficient space we made a new approach and docked without further incident, and again there was no damage except to the paintwork. For sure the *QE2* was a strongly built ship, designed to withstand the pounding from the north Atlantic and thus able to accept these minor excursions onto 'the putty'.

Fires

Within twelve months of my being on board we had the most serious fire that I experienced on the ship. In the middle of the night a crew member had gone into the galley of the Tables of the World restaurant, normally closed down at night, and had used one of the ranges to cook a meal. The range had been left on with a pan of fat left sitting on top. The fat eventually self-ignited and filled the galley with smoke.

The alarm was raised and two fire teams mustered. They entered the galley from forward and aft, but the smoke was so thick that it took them twenty minutes to find the source of the fire. Fortunately the flames had not taken hold inside the vent trunking, and the fire was extinguished relatively quickly with hoses and CO_2 gas. We discovered that there was a great deal of enthusiasm to use the fire equipment, and at one stage there must have been at least twelve sets of breathing apparatus in use – probably not a very coordinated use of resources, for we could not recharge the air bottles as fast as they were being used.

The galley was a mess, with smoke damage everywhere and all surfaces black and greasy. But the staff made a superb effort, and next morning breakfast was again being served.

Another fire was rather unusual as it was in a vacuum cleaner bag. The cleaner had most probably sucked up a still-burning cigarette and then been left on a crew stairwell. Late into the night a report of smoke was received from the crew galley two decks above and the sailors' night gang went into action. There was a tremendous amount of smoke, completely filling the stairwell, which covered about five decks. The smoke was seeping through the edges of fire doors on different levels and being recirculated around the air-conditioning system. When the cleaner was found it was soon extinguished.

Suicide

Sadly, we had one suicide while I was on board, a male passenger who was travelling alone in a penthouse cabin during a ten-day

Caribbean cruise from New York. The steward called our attention to the cabin, which had not been slept in and in which the tipping envelopes for the different staff had been carefully placed on the desk. Upon investigation it appeared that the gentleman, who was only in his thirties, had dined mostly in his cabin, and had befriended just one other couple, who had also dined with him on occasion.

He had for some obscure reason taken apart the lifejacket from the closet, removed the flotation polystyrene and stuffed the blocks into a drawer along with the cords for securing the lifejacket. The orange exterior material was missing. Also missing was one of the towelling robes placed in the cabin, as well as the cord from the spare one – he had always insisted that the steward provide two clean robes each day.

There was little we could do. It appeared that he had climbed out over his balcony some time during the night, clambered across the lifeboat which was opposite, and then just jumped into the water – a distance of at least sixty feet. After several hours of searching the ship, the captain decided that it would be fruitless to turn the vessel around, and a report was therefore made to the authorities. A mystery of the sea.

Captains

The first captain I sailed with on *QE2* was Captain Lawrence Portet. He was a very tall man, over six feet four, and perhaps the most eccentric of the lot. His manner was rather rigid, and he could not be considered a great conversationalist, and I was just a junior and therefore rated well down the scale when it came to social intercourse; even orders usually came through the senior watchkeeper. I got to know him a little better after he returned to the ship in the mid-eighties.

Captain Douglas Ridley was the staff captain who first did relieving voyages as master, a formidable man with an amazing IQ and memory – it was very unwise to cross him, or suggest that he might be incorrect. If an officer tried to hide a mistake he would soon know about it and a furious tirade would descend upon the unfortunate. He later became general manager and commodore and I became trusted by him, not because I was always right, but because I was fairly quick with the sums when he wanted an answer and because I was honest enough to tell him when I'd cocked up.

He sent me out to South America to investigate the ports of Valparaiso in Chile and Callao (Lima) in Peru, to ascertain whether the ship could berth and also whether they could supply the fresh water, fuel, stores and so forth that she might need to accomplish a voyage round South America. That was my first introduction into the world of ship management and planning, and I found it absolutely fascinating. I even took the initiative of flying down to Puerto Montt, an anchor port in the middle of Chile close to volcanoes and lakes. I felt great satisfaction when the ship made the voyage some two years later.

One particular incident remains in my memory. I was navigator of the ship, and Ridley phoned me up one evening to check the distance to the next island in the Caribbean. I quickly checked the course card and informed him, and he made the decision there and then to sail later that night. After checking again I realised I had made a mistake and had told him the course instead of the distance. Fortunately it was not going to be a problem, but even so I knew he would check for himself later and find out. The other guys on the bridge visibly winced when I told them my mistake. There was no way out – I had to go and tell him.

I found him in the chief officer's cabin with about ten other senior officers having a drink. I knocked, apologised for entering and told him my error. The other officers in the room went silent. Ridley's face was a picture, one of severity, but also I could see he was playing with numbers in his head. He asked me what time was sunrise the next day, obviously with a view to arriving at first light. This time I did not readily know so I phoned the bridge from the cabin and asked John Scott, one of the second officers, to check our prepared sunrise table. Being Australian and somewhat of a character, he immediately asked, 'What's the matter? Are you going to be shot at dawn?' This was quite audible to the other officers in the room, and they had one hell of a job to control their laughter. Meanwhile Ridley looked like thunder and I, red with embarrassment, just asked Scott to read the 'bloody table!'

Captain Peter Jackson came next, a short man who was an accomplished pianist. I liked him very much, not because he was just a total contrast to Lawrence Portet, but because he was very approachable and always seemed very humble. He trusted his officers, allowing them to 'have the ship' sooner and for longer, thus giving them more job satisfaction. Somehow I had the impression that, even though he was obviously a very experienced seaman, he held the QE2 in some sort of awe. Peter was the captain who took the ship down to the South Atlantic during the 1982 Falklands crisis. Regrettably I think he made his feelings known about the management style of the office in New York, and they in turn allowed him to retire from the ship with little ceremony when his time came, unusual for a captain of the QE2.

Next was Captain Robert Arnott, a tall, well-built man who lived near Blackpool. He was an incredibly popular captain, respected by passengers and crew alike – never visibly angry, unflappable, and obviously a great socialite who could keep people amused with his stories. He had a lovely northwest accent which belied his position as master of the world's most prestigious liner. He eventually retired in the mid-eighties and the company helicopter was flown onto the after deck to lift him off, a big public relations ploy, with his officers lined up to wish him well. In fact the helicopter took him to the local airport in Southampton, and Captain Bob came back by taxi to pick up his bags.

Lawrence Portet then returned, and stayed until the major refit in 1987. He could be one of the most pedantic of masters. Because of his height he always looked down at me, and his voice at times sounded rather condescending. On more than one occasion I felt he showed me up because I did not do exactly what he asked or because I tried to suggest a different way, but in the end I think he grudgingly respected my ability. By the time he was due to retire I had known him for almost ten years, on and off. I offered him my best wishes, and he looked at me and said, after considerable thought, 'Thank you, Rentell, for your good works over the years. It's been ... interesting!'

One his most memorable comments was apparently made during a World Cruise with the ship heading through the bay towards Yokohama. The Japanese pilot was rushing from one side of the bridge to the other, panicking because of the number of fishing boats that were blocking the way. Lawrence eventually had had enough of this and went off to the bridge wing, where he walked up and down outside seemingly oblivious to whatever was happening elsewhere. The chief officer came out and mentioned that the pilot was a bit of a worrier, to which Lawrence replied, pointing first to the medals on his blues uniform and then in towards the wheelhouse – 'I got these for killing those' – and continued walking.

Alan Bennell followed on from Lawrence, taking command not long after the ship had had a major refit – when the steam turbines had been removed and a diesel electric plant had been installed. He was another interesting character, quite a ladies' man, and a sad loss when he died with cancer just a year or so later.

I remember one occasion when the ship was alongside in Southampton during the night of the big storm of 1987. The wind was well in excess of 50 knots, blowing onto the starboard quarter and fortunately pushing the ship onto the dock. I came up to the bridge in the early hours, unable to sleep because of the noise. Alan and I spent most of the night up there waiting for the wind to veer and possibly push the ship off the dock as it went round to the port quarter. There would have been little we could have done except release the wire mooring lines before they broke and drop the anchor, and just hope it would not drag and allow the ship to go aground onto the bank on the other side of the river. No tugs were available, as they were attending a super-tanker that had broken from its moorings down at Fawley.

Fortunately the wind began to moderate without veering during the early daylight hours. We remained safe alongside, but a dockside crane had blown over and throughout southern England there was considerable damage to trees and buildings.

Alan's relief was Robin Woodall, who was to take over and stay until 1994, when he finally retired from the ship. Another very tall man, Robin was well liked, very approachable, experienced and happy to delegate in order to educate his subordinates.

Trivia

Amongst others, we had two rather famous names that I man-aged to meet – Larry Hagman, the famous J.R. from the TV series *Dallas*, and Loretta Swit, better known as Hot Lips Houlihan from the series *M*A*S*H*. I met them both at the officers' wardroom cocktail party, which was a regular event on each voyage. I arranged to show Larry Hagman the bridge the next day, after which I took him down for a drink – noting that he managed to get through many shots of Bacardi before leaving for lunch. Loretta Swit came up to the bridge with her chaperone, a man of much younger years. She did not appear so impressed but did ask if she could use the 'ladies' room'. She was pointed in the direction of the not so salu-brious bridge toilet, and came out after a few minutes or so. Being the type of chap I am, I asked if she would mind if we had a small plaque made and put up in the loo – 'Hot Lips Sat Here'. Funnily enough, she did not seem very amused.

There was at times a very good atmosphere on the ship, par-ticularly on world cruises. I used to organise, once a year, a special train party, the theme of which I'd learned from someone else some time before. The basic plan was that the party was based on a train timetable, with different cabins being different stations. At each station the train would stop for twenty minutes and a different cocktail would be served, with five minutes' travelling time between each station, and wherever possible passenger alleyways were not to be used. There was a driver, a conductor and a guard, and the timetable had to be rigidly adhered to. There would be no more than eight or nine stations, and no more than twenty or so staff, definitely no passengers. Needless to say, by the end of a train party there would be some very inebriated people, especially as it was almost a challenge to make the most outlandish cocktail. One of mine was 'After Eight Mints', a concoction of crème de menthe and kahlúa, with whipped cream on the top, quite foul really, especially if it's the ninth different one you've had. On one occasion the cream bowl ended up on my head and cream was flicked all round the room. Quite a smell the next day and one that lasted for weeks, even after constant cleaning.

I was not so stupid as to go to the full party, as I inevitably organised it when I was on the 8–12 watch and therefore joined in halfway through, after midnight. On one occasion, when Captain Jackson was in command, I learnt that he had heard of the event and was somewhat disappointed he was not invited. I quickly put him on the guest list and sent an invitation. He went to the first station, which apparently was a little slow to get going, and consequently caused a diversion to his quarters. I later saw him just before midnight, when he explained he had decided it was time to leave the party when he came across the 12–4 second officer playing the piano in the main deck rotunda with a great palm leaf sticking out of his ear.

The Falklands campaign

In 1982 the Argentine government landed troops on the British dependencies of South Georgia and the Falkland Islands, taking control of those remote South Atlantic Islands by force. The British government, in response, told the Argentines to leave or they would in turn send troops to recapture the territory. The Argentines did not voluntarily leave, so a task force was rapidly assembled and proceeded south.

Requisitioned

After the P&O liner *Canberra* had been requisitioned, it occurred to me one night on the bridge that *QE2* would be a logical next step for moving a large number of back-up troops to the Falklands. I did not particularly relish the thought of giving up our pleasant summer cruising schedule, in particular our Northern Capitals cruise in July, when I had planned an event in Geiranger Fjord with a Norwegian hot-air-balloon enthusiast who had come down to the ship on previous calls and launched his balloon, complete with me in the basket on two occasions, from the back end of the ship. This year we were to attempt something new, involving a hired float plane plus me and my skydiving sports parachute.

Going into the southern winter did not appeal either. Being at sea for seven months of the year makes the average 'jolly jack' appreciate our brief glimpses of the British seasons, particularly the spring, which I always feel cheated if I miss. However, I still had that childish irresponsible sense of adventure, and this appeared to be right up my street.

Second officer Paul Jowett and myself were responsible for the 8–12 bridge watch. The trip had been interesting, with a first-time call at Philadelphia, where we had stayed for three days to start off their festivities to mark the founding of the city two hundred years before. During our time in the port, over 12,000 guests had come aboard to tour the ship. The carefully organised programme had allowed for 500 coming for breakfast, 1,500 for lunch, 1,000 for afternoon cocktails and 2,000 for a dinner dance each evening.

After that, we were glad to return to the normality of driving the ship – which is, I suppose, much like piloting an aircraft. Once you get the 'meaty bits' of navigation out of the way, you appear to be doing nothing except looking out of the window. It's called 'execution and monitoring' by the Department of Transport. The result, however, is that at times I find myself wanting to get the brain to tick over a little faster by finding work for it to chew on. I

decided to do the sums necessary to get the ship to the Falklands
– approximately 8,000 miles by direct route from Southampton,
ten and a half days steaming at 27.5 knots, our economical top
speed. The ship has been known to do 30 knots at times, but this
would depend on displacement (weight), weather and another
factor not often realised by the layman, the sea temperature. The
warmer the sea, the harder it is to condense the recirculated distilled water, which is used to make steam to power the turbines –
and we would of course have to cross the Equator. We could just
about make it on 'one tank', but we wouldn't have very much
fuel left when we arrived. We would use just under 6,000 tonnes,
which at $180 per tonne would cost over a million dollars.

These scraps of useless information I passed onto Captain
Alex Hutcheson, the relieving captain of QE2, when he came up
to the bridge after dinner one evening. His only comment was,
'You two will have us down there ...!'

I believe he thought it most unlikely that such an event would
take place, but I think he was pleased to have the information at
hand a few days later when being quizzed by a radio reporter.

On Monday 3 May I was invited to one of the Penthouse passenger suites for a lunchtime drink, and it was on the way up
that one of the nurses, on passing a group of us, passed the news
that the BBC had just announced that the ship was to be requisitioned as a troop ship. We stood there almost in a state of shock.
Naturally we did the only thing possible in such a situation – we
had a drink. But the conversation was a little stilted and nervous. Little did I realise then that the very room in which we were
drinking champagne would be the one that General Moore, the
designated commander of the Falkland land forces, would be
moving into when we reached Ascension Island.

I had to go back to the bridge just before 1300 hours, and there
I found out that the report was true, and that Captain Hutcheson
had been phoned up by the BBC and asked whether he was
aware of the decision. He could only answer 'no'. It is a great pity
that Cunard Line could not have phoned the captain first. After

that we could only listen to the radio broadcasts, which were now easily received as we were rapidly closing the south coast of England and due to arrive in Southampton that evening. The atmosphere around the whole ship was somewhat stunned.

The takeover

In the morning of the following day I went up to the bridge before eight to find a Royal Navy lieutenant commander, in civilian clothes, poring over numerous plans of the ship, scrawling jottings down on paper and saying this was the third ship he had been given to put helicopter pads on. I walked around the open decks with him and the chief officer, Ron Warwick, and was slightly amazed to hear him say –

'Oh yes, I think we can chop this lot off here ...' and 'fill the pool full of cement to take the load of the flight deck supports.'

Certainly it was something I had never envisaged happening to any ship I worked on, yet alone the *Queen Elizabeth 2*, on which I had now served for over three and a half years and felt was a part of my life.

For some time during that day, while endless meetings were taking place, we knew nothing of what was going to happen to each of us. I was due to go on leave for three weeks, but I suggested to the staff captain that I was willing to change places if any of the married bridge officers wanted to stay at home.

Captain Douglas Ridley, then serving as executive captain on board (a slightly grandiose title for general manager), tracked me down after yet another hydraulic lunch and asked me which courses I had done in the Royal Naval Reserve. Only one in fact, the introductory course at Dartmouth a few months before, and I had only joined in a bout of enthusiasm some six months previously. Ridley wanted me to sail with the ship as liaison officer, both acting for Cunard Line and assisting the Royal Navy party which we would be carrying. I was later introduced to Captain 'Jimmy' James, who would be my new boss. He said he would like me in RNR uniform, and I was therefore allowed to plead for a few days' home leave to go and collect my gear.

I went home by train with a sort of satisfied feeling, believing that I was going to be involved in something useful. My father picked me up at the station and took me back to my parents' house. My mother was of course delighted to see me, but the nine o'clock news was showing on the TV and reports were just coming through that HMS *Sheffield* had been hit by an exocet missile, causing an unknown loss of life and the remaining crew to abandon ship. Suddenly everything was put into perspective. My mother was not really impressed to hear I was going with the ship, and even less so when I told her I had volunteered.

After a short four days of hectic leave (during which time I made a will for the very first time), I arrived back to the ship early on Sunday afternoon, to find that some bureaucratic cock-up had placed my new berth down in a 1 deck cruise staff cabin, which, although not in the pits, would not have been close enough to 'the boss'. Considering I was meant to be Jimmy's ADC, as it were, it would not have been particularly handy. A few words in his ear, and I shuffled off to meet Major Ron Cocking who, with his team of stalwarts, was in charge of the berthing arrangements. I ended up in 8101, a penthouse suite with a connecting staircase up to Jimmy's room. Never had I had such luxury – my only regret being that this trip was sure to be unaccompanied!

VIP visits
Needless to say, the next few days went extremely quickly, with total panic only being replaced by sheer desperation. The majority of the flight decks were in position, but a great deal of welding still had to take place. Workmen were scurrying around twenty-four hours a day, achieving in hours what would normally take days, or even weeks – funny what happens when there is a certain amount of incentive.

My duties were to achieve solutions to problems for the embarked Naval Party Number 1980. Problems concerning the ship I knew intimately, and of which they knew very little. The officers soon knew enough, however, to make sure they were well ensconced in the top penthouse suites before the remainder of our 'guests' arrived. The navy does have this propensity for ensuring that their own needs are met.

The one problem that was to add to our frustrations was that, on sailing day, Wednesday 12 May, just about every member of the top brass was going to drop down to see the ship. We had to sort out some sort of schedule for them, ensure they would be met, guide them around the ship, take them to see the captain if required, and so on. By this time Cunard's senior master, Captain Peter Jackson, had come back from leave and resumed command. I believe we had an admiral, four generals, including the Chief of the General Staff and followers, all arriving by helicopter. The large area on the other side of the customs shed, normally used for new cars in transit, was fast becoming Southampton's equivalent of Battersea Heliport.

They stayed for lunchtime cocktails with Captain Jackson in his cabin, along with Ralph Bahna, Cunard Line's New York president, and Victor Mathews, the head of Trafalgar House, the group that owned Cunard Line.

The biggest panic was caused by the arrival of John Nott, the Secretary of State for Defence, who turned up at 1430 hours in yet another helicopter, along with the now infamous Ministry of Defence spokesman, Ian MacDonald, who was far from the sombre person he appeared to be during his regular TV appearances. When I quizzed him on this he was quite worried to think he was being depressing, and in fact he had regularly caused great mirth in the officers' wardroom. He told me that he had been instructed to talk faster, but he was apparently speaking to members of the press from all over the world, some whom were not to brilliant with the English language, and therefore he did not wish to be misquoted.

The Navy and Army had planned a route around the ship for John Nott so that he would be able to speak to some of the already embarked troops, who numbered over three thousand.

However, I believe he had no intention of being caught out by any tricky questions, and therefore he moved as quickly as he thought reasonably possible. The route was soon covered, so I led him to the bridge, allowing my fellow navigators their moment of glory.

We then worked our way back to the midships lobby via the now crowded boat deck, with half an hour before our scheduled sailing time. It seemed that the total number of troops on board were hanging over the starboard side of the ship – and no wonder, for there was a rather agile-looking lady in some very interesting underwear delivering a singing telegram from the dockside, and yet another lady who decided to divest herself of some of her garments, much to the obvious pleasure of the lads.

The sailing

Down below in the engine room all was not well. Only one of the three massive boilers used to provide steam for the turbines was on-line. To make 29 knots the ship needed all three boilers; with two she could make about 21 knots, but with one we might make 5 or perhaps 7 knots, and the ship would be most difficult to handle. The load from one boiler was mostly taken by the electrical requirements for the hotel side of the vessel.

Captain Peter Driver, our pilot, was not a happy man. He knew the ship and understood the technical considerations which would affect the vessel's handling, but to add to his problems there was a force seven wind blowing, and *QE2* is greatly affected by the wind at slow speeds due to her high sides. The scheduled sailing time of 1600 hours rapidly approached, and literally the whole world was aware that the ship's departure from Southampton full of troops was imminent. Any delay would not only be embarrassing, but the country's ability to achieve the great task ahead might be put in question. We simply had to sail!

During the past few days it had been decided that the ship would sail on two boilers (a fairly normal procedure) and the third would be put on-line the next day. During the in port period one was in use to cover lighting, liquid pumping, galley and other hotel requirements, while the other two would undergo routine maintenance. The day before had seen a second boiler flashed up and made ready for sailing, but a massive reserve-feed distilled water leak was detected, a loss of nearly twenty tonnes per hour, which could not be made up by the ship's own distillation plant. The boiler feed water has to be exceedingly pure (less than four parts per million of contaminating solids are allowed), and therefore the water is continually recirculated, and after it has been turned into steam and its energy used, it is passed through a condenser which in turn is cooled by seawater.

The problem was first considered to be a fractured tube in one of the boilers, so this boiler was shut down for examination, a lengthy business which required allowing time for the boiler to cool down before the inspection could take place. No leak could be found and the loss was still continuing. The same process had to be repeated with the other on-line boiler, and still the leak could not be found. Consequently when we came to sail only one boiler was back on-line. The problem was not found until some time later – a forgotten valve had been opened and not closed.

A relatively minor problem such as lack of power was not going to change the minds of the powers that be, and by 1600 hours the tugs had been made fast. The ropes and wires were taken in and the band started to play as the ship was slowly hauled from the quayside and into the river.

A tricky operation at the best of times. Captain Driver swung the ship perfectly off the old Ocean Terminal and we were pulled past thousands of relatives. Never had I seen so many people on the quay, and never had I seen so many hanging over the ship's side, troops and crew everywhere, on the winches, by the rails, in the boats, on the penthouse balconies, even a couple on the forward crane. The engineers managed to give us sufficient power to make 6 knots with a tug pulling on the bow – a rather ignominious start, but only realised by a few in the know. All the tugs except one were let go when the ship picked up speed, and the final tug was not dismissed until we had navigated around the treacherous Brambles Bank, often the temporary resting place of large ships in the past.

Flying stations

We steamed slowly down the eastern Solent, leaving Cowes and the Isle of Wight to starboard. The ship was brought to 'flying stations' for the first time, and preparations were made to take on two Sea King helicopters of the newly formed 825 Squadron. They had come from the Royal Naval Air Station at Culdrose in Cornwall via RNAS Portland and were led by Lieutenant Commander Hugh Clark, who was later to be awarded for bravery in the rescue of personnel from the ill-fated *Sir Galahad*. Clark flew around the ship and then hovered to one side at the stern, 'exploring the envelope', I was told by Lieutenant Commander 'Tiger' Shaw, the officer in charge of flying for the embarked naval party. He was finding the areas around the flight deck that may be adversely affected by turbulence caused by the ship's superstructure and thus a hazard to pilots landing on board.

He landed his aircraft, number 595, with the precision expected of a squadron commander. Within minutes the second Sea King, number 597, came into view, followed a similar manoeuvre and landed on the number three spot. The forward flight deck under the bridge was the number one spot, while the landing area aft was divided into number two and three spots. After landing, the rotors were automatically folded back, the machines rolled into their allotted parking place and secured down to the deck with the practised efficiency of a well-run team.

Captain Driver was disembarked once we had reached open water and the decision was made to anchor the vessel until a second boiler could be brought on-line. We anchored at 2130 hours just three miles south of the Nab Tower off the east coast of the Isle of Wight. We often considered what the press would have made of the situation, had they found out. For the time being, however, we took to the wardroom bar to chat about the day's most unusual events.

Rendezvous

The next day brought a better turn of events for the engineers. They had found their valve, and just after 0900 hours *QE2* set sail again. We were to rendezvous, or RV as the Royal Navy says, with *Grey Rover*, a Royal Fleet Auxiliary tanker. A trial replenishment at sea (RAS) was to take place. One became accustomed to, if not totally familiar with, the endless abbreviations used by the Navy.

The afternoon became a busy one. As we made our way down the English Channel it was reported that we had a soldier on board with suspected appendicitis and it would be necessary to land him ashore. A little after five o'clock 'hands to flying stations' was piped. A little confusion became evident on the bridge as different messages were being received from the after deck. The patient was put on board the helicopter but it still did not take off. Eventually, after a further twenty minutes, with the rotors turning, another patient was put aboard. A doctor, a nurse and two patients left the ship at 1745 hours. Little Jane Yelland, one of our own nurses, came back a few hours later bubbling over as a result of her unexpected flight.

QE2 began to reduce speed for the RV, then *Grey Rover* came up our starboard side from astern and a rocket line was fired across. To this was attached a heaving line, followed by another heavier line called a messenger. The two ships took up station about 150 feet apart and a distance line was secured between the two forecastles, with *Grey Rover* acting as the station keeper.

Approximately a hundred soldiers waited on 2 deck, by a door normally used for baggage that had become our RAS point. The men took up the slack in the messenger and commenced heaving in the eight-inch flexible hose slung from the derricks of the tanker. With tremendous effort the end was brought aboard and coupled to a new bunker line which had been installed from the door, across the passenger alleyway, down the forward engine room escape and into the fuel reception tank. A few tonnes were pumped to test the line, and the line was then 'blown through' with compressed air to clear any oil residue, and disconnected. The operation proved a success, proving that we could go south and refuel at sea if the need arose. The situation is an unusual one for most navigators. The pressures involved between two ships in close proximity can quickly result in collision if sufficient concentration is not kept, and the manoeuvre is therefore one we do not, as a rule, practise.

Grey Rover retrieved her hose, and the two ships separated with the sound of three long blasts on the whistle, the sailor's salute.

In the meantime helicopter 595 was sitting at Trelisk Hospital near Truro in Cornwall. Apparently the doctor and nurse were causing minor chaos by attempting to purloin the daily papers. They finally returned just after 2000 hours, and the ship turned towards the Bay of Biscay two hours later. The business of getting our troops to their destination was now our priority.

Drill!

The *QE2* headed for Freetown in Sierra Leone, a voyage of almost 3,000 miles, and during the next few days we settled into the routine of being at sea. The normal shipping lanes were avoided to prevent visual detection. The Navy expected Soviet surveillance of one type or another but to our knowledge none came, although we were buzzed by a French Atlantic class reconnaissance plane, whose pilot came over the radio and wished us well.

The first emergency drill for the troops was on the Thursday, a 'find your way round drill'. Friday's was to be more comprehensive. First Officer Bob Hayward and I had a lengthy conversation as to how we should run the drill, and there were many problems to overcome. The twenty lifeboats could not take all crew and passengers so extra life rafts had been put on board. We first intended that the normal procedure of passengers following the coloured arrows to their muster stations as indicated in their cabins should occur, but the sheer volume of troops at each muster station was staggering. Cabins intended for two now housed three or four, with men using collapsible camp beds.

I had explained to Regimental Sergeant Major Hunt, a little man with a big voice, our plan to get the men to their stations and divide them into groups of twenty-five. Confusion reigned the first day, but gradually things became sorted. Each muster station had an officer or NCO in charge, and each group of twenty-five had a designated leader. Four of the ship's deck officers went around on Friday and spoke to each muster station in turn, explaining what we expected of them and that should an emergency arise, each group would be led either to a boat or to a raft, which would already have been swung out into the embarkation position by the ship's crew.

All were quite receptive, and the troops organised themselves well. It had been my intention to take the onus from us and put it into their own hands, as in a real emergency we might be busy elsewhere. The Gurkhas, the soldiers from Nepal, were the best, disciplining themselves to form tight groups, sitting down cross-legged and silent when all were present. The officers were quite amusing, seeming to stand uneasily at their muster point, waiting for leadership – which Sergeant Major Cocking soon gave! One young captain thought it would be better if he mustered with his 'boys'. I respectfully pointed out to him that we would not be holding hands when we got into the lifeboats.

The drills soon worked well, and over the next few days we took the group leaders and gave them instruction on the techniques required to launch the boats and rafts, as well as basic lessons in survival. Not surprisingly, they were very attentive.

Daily routines

The army devised an impressive timetable to cope with the 3,000-plus troops, divided so that small groups of men could be seen anywhere at any time, in alleyways, lounges, recesses, stairwells, etc, learning to take their firearms apart and put them back together – blindfolded. There was also first aid and enemy aircraft recognition. Some would be jogging around the boat deck, later with full kit and backpack with firearms, and sometimes carrying each other. PT was a regular occurrence on the outside decks. The swimming pools were used on a rota basis throughout the day.

The Gurkhas amazed us on Saturday morning. They had been allocated cabins on 5 deck, as these were low down in the ship and thought to be more suitable, as the men were known to be prone to seasickness. These cabins were furthest from the boat stations, and their British officers decided that the troops should practise their escape blindfolded, which might simulate the effect should the power fail and the lighting be extinguished. Consequently odd groups of ten or twenty could be seen at various times of the day groping around passageways and up the stairs. A certain amount of amusement was guaranteed when one of them got lost and was found staggering around the tables in the restaurant.

Firearms practice commenced from the flight decks, with the considerable amount of 'ready use' ammunition we had loaded for this purpose. An officer was posted on the bridge to ensure firing was halted should we come within range of other vessels. There was a large variety of weapons being carried, including submachine guns, self-loading rifles, shoulder-held anti-tank weapons and 'blow pipe' anti-aircraft missiles. Needless to say, some of the watchkeepers found it difficult to sleep with the staccato sound of firing being heard at odd times during the day. Target practice often meant firing at bags of rubbish deliberately thrown over the side, and frequently the nets surrounding the flight deck were shot away. The ship still had a stanchion on the forecastle with a shell hole many years later.

Flying practice
Flying practice took place in earnest from Friday onwards for two or three hours a day. The Navy were still unaware of how or where the troops would be taken off the ship, although it

was anticipated that they might have to be transferred by helicopter while the ship was under way. Many of the young pilots had never flown on or off a ship before and consequently they needed to practise the manoeuvres involved, to find the areas around the ship to avoid and the correct angle of approach.

In the event of a two-spot operation taking place at the after flight deck, the pilots would have to fly on and off the forward spot, number two, in an athwartships direction while the after spot, number three, would involve flying fore and aft, or in the direction of the ship's travel. To land on a heaving deck in rough rainy weather on a ship making 25 knots is difficult enough; landing sideways takes considerable skill. The pilot has to approach the ship using part of the vessel as a fixed visual reference, his eyes telling his brain that the ship is stationary and it is the water below that is moving. He must be flying sideways at 25 knots, and it is the thrust given by the tail rotor which is the deciding factor as to whether he can maintain his direction and position.

During these flying operations the bridge was a busy place and the 'yes' or 'no' for landings and take-offs was given by Tiger Shaw. He was fed information direct from the flight-deck officer, Roger Bevan, via a rating stationed with a talkback system on the port side of the wheelhouse, and also from a naval petty officer who sat at one of the ship's radars, adapted to receive signals from the helicopter transponder. He was also in direct communication with both helicopters via VHF radio. The business was very intense, and there was little time for our sometimes frivolous comments regarding their 'paraffin pigeons'.

Throughout all their operations the Navy had great respect for our ship and at all times showed courtesy and professionalism.

Freetown

On Tuesday 18 May, at 0800 hours, the bridge gave the engine room one and a half hours' notice for our arrival at Freetown. The call was made solely for the purpose of replenishing our tanks with fuel and water, and it would be the last time the ship would be secured alongside till our return to Southampton over three weeks later. I had been to Freetown several times before during my employment with Palm Line, most recently almost five years previously while serving on the *Matadi Palm*.

Two harbour pilots boarded at the fairway buoy and assisted the captain with their local knowledge. They appeared highly qualified, as they had more gold braid on their shoulders than most of the other officers on the bridge, although on one of them this air of respectability was somewhat dulled by his sickly green shoes with enormous heels, the latter presumably fitted so that he could see over the bridge dodger. It was a sight that kept us amused for some time.

By 1145 hours the ship had been secured to the Queen Elizabeth II quay. We had travelled 2,956 miles in a little over five days, making an average speed of 24.35 knots and consuming 1,919 tonnes of heavy oil fuel. Shore leave was not granted, and only the agent came aboard. A few people came inquisitively around the dock, and one or two expatriates came past in their speed boats, Union Jacks patriotically flying. The usual 'bum' boats came and sent their lines aboard to peddle their wares. We were also passed by a Soviet trawler, which seemed to have one or two aerials too many. We had been expecting sooner or later to be detected by one of their spy trawlers, known as alien intelligence gatherers (AIG).

Ascension Island

A film was being shown on deck as we pulled away from Freetown around 2300 hours, with only a few people on the dock to witness our departure. A total of 1,867 tonnes of fuel had been pumped on board. The pilots disembarked before midnight, and the vessel set a course for the island of Ascension, the small outcrop of British sovereignty deep in the South Atlantic near the Equator.

The Admiralty had informed Captain James not to go within twenty-five miles of the island, we presumed to avoid any unnecessary detection and reporting to the 'other side' of our intentions or whereabouts. It was much to Captain James's annoyance, therefore, when a Soviet AIG approached on Thursday morning. The small ship took a good look and then departed.

We made a rendezvous with HMS *Dumbarton Castle*, the navy's latest patrol craft designed for North Sea oil protection duties. One of our Sea Kings was launched at 1330 hours and despatched towards the island, and less than an hour later a yellow Sea King of the RAF headed towards the ship, looking rather out of place away from the UK coast, where its prime duties were those of air–sea rescue. By 1500 hours the Sea Kings were operating a shuttle service between the *QE2* and the warship, which by now was keeping station off our starboard side, transferring stores and personnel. By 1600 hours flying was completed for the day, but we had to keep within the area in readiness for the arrival of General Moore and his command staff, who were flying out from the UK that night. This was the night of 20 May and, unknown to us, the next day was to be the occasion when British troops would land at San Carlos on East Falkland.

Flying commenced in earnest early the next day to transfer stores and mail destined for other ships in the task force, including the STUFT ships – 'ships taken up from trade'. Three Sea Kings, two Wessex and one Chinook helicopter were used to carry underslung loads and more troops, including General Moore. The general was allocated what was normally the most expensive accommodation on board, the Queen Mary Suite.

Some very impressive flying was seen that day, with, at times, up to three 'helos' stacked up astern waiting to come in and drop their load. Over 200 tonnes of stores were loaded. The forward spot in front of the bridge, number one, was also used at times, but only by the RAF Sea King pilot, who seemed to be unconcerned by the fact that as he hovered athwartships just above the deck, there was 67,000 gross tons of ocean splendour rushing towards him at 18 knots. From the bridge we could look down directly into his cockpit. He also showed great skill in coming down aft and putting the underslung load onto the after deck as the ship was skidding around in a 180-degree turn.

The pilot of the large twin-rotored Chinook also showed us his impressive flying prowess at the end of the day by hovering level with the port bridge wing for several minutes, while his crew poked their heads out of every window, plus the tailgate, taking photographs. He turned his aircraft through 90 degrees and flew sideways facing the bridge, and matched our forward speed for a few minutes before he left. We continued our southerly progress.

After General Moore and his officers boarded we became tight on space. I was the only officer other than 'Jimmy' James with a single cabin. Needless to say I had to move, and I found myself in suite 8002, sharing with Tiger Shaw and Roger Bevan. The room had two beds that folded away during the day, so it was not really an inconvenience, but I received a certain amount of ribbing from my fellow officers in the wardroom.

We did have a few laughs together. Every evening before going to take a shower Roger would imitate Major Hugh Afleck-Graves, whose voice was almost as 'far back' as his name. Afleck-Graves was responsible for coordinating the troop disembarkation, and would muster the men by announcing, 'Assault stations, assault stations, groups so-and-so proceed to assault station now.' After a while this broadcast would send everyone into fits of laughter, and Roger would announce to the cabin before he went to take a shower, 'Ablution stations, ablution stations, stand by to ablute!'

Throughout the voyage south we were following the *Baltic Ferry* and her sister ship *Nordic Ferry*, who were a day or so ahead. Behind was the *Atlantic Causeway*, sister ship to the ill-fated *Atlantic Conveyor*. All these ships had equipment belonging to our passengers, the 5th Infantry Brigade, as well as more helicopters and pilots of 825 Squadron. We did send a helicopter over to *Causeway* the day after we left Ascension to pick up important equipment, and on that afternoon a Wessex helicopter arrived unexpectedly with further stores.

Blackout

Captain James was under instruction to black the ship out, and preparations were made after we left Freetown. I was given the task of supervising the operation. We had to change *QE2* from being 'the brightest star on the ocean to the darkest,' said Jimmy when he addressed the crew. There are of course many hundreds of portholes and windows on the ship. Bill Bailey and his team of four carpenters cut out templates for the different sizes, and I think thousands of pieces of black plastic were cut. Each deck became the responsibility of one or two army officers, and the troops were given large amounts of masking tape to complete the job. The large windows in the ship's side were given to fatigue parties, and the whole exercise was completed in three days.

In the tropics the sun caused the black plastic to heat up and crinkle, and it also resulted in the ship becoming much warmer.

I was able to take a helicopter trip one evening when the flight crews were commencing their night flying exercises. From a mile away it was difficult to spot the ship, even though the blackout was not fully complete. Except for a few areas not yet covered, only the navigation lights were visible, and these were not used after we left Ascension. The effect was rather ghostly and surreal – most impressive.

We darkened ship at sunset, and checked as best we could from the overhanging bridge wings and also by clambering around the lifeboats to check some of the penthouse suites – whose occupants were at times a little forgetful.

The blackout routine spoilt the party Brigadier Tony Wilson intended to have on deck. Instead he transferred the venue to the Q4 Room, the ship's nightclub, and continued with the entertainment, which included ten minutes of Gurkha bagpipes, followed by the pipes and drums of the Welsh Guards and the bagpipe band of the Scots Guards. Very entertaining, but somewhat hard on the ears in that relatively small room.

Reports of attacks

Captain James and Brigadier Wilson gave a brief lecture to the ship's crew in the theatre in order to pass on what information was possible regarding the task ahead. They explained the problems and dangers and thanked the crew, as they were the only ones on board who had actually volunteered to take the voyage.

There was much interest shown in the broadcasts made by the World Service of the BBC. Unconfirmed reports were made on the evening of the 22nd that a landing had been made at San Carlos. These were confirmed shortly after by information coming into the military satellite equipment which had been set up on board. Most disturbing was the news that the Argentine Air Force were making successful bombing attacks on our ships, and of the loss of HMS *Ardent* and HMS *Antelope*.

Then came news of the attacks on HMS *Coventry* and *Atlantic Conveyor*. The latter was a ship belonging to the cargo division of Cunard, and it was particularly bad news for those who had either worked on board or knew men there. We also considered the effect this information would have on our families at home, who would be party to less information regarding our wellbeing than we knew ourselves.

The days of sailing south continued, flying operations carried on, blackout was enforced and extra lookouts were posted with machine guns. Large Bren guns were mounted on platforms on either bride wing, and test firing was carried out with their five-inch ammunition – very noisy! The watertight doors were closed at night, as the Navy considered a submarine attack possible. Radios and radars were kept switched off to prevent our position being obtained by their transmission.

On the 26th we commenced evasive steering. The weather was deteriorating as we sailed further into the southern winter. With visibility reduced, on the morning of the 27th First Officer Bob Hayward decided it would be more prudent to have the radar on – a fortuitous decision. The ship had entered a field of large glacial icebergs, and the radar showed them both behind and ahead. Captain Jackson took over the con, and for the next six hours the ship was navigated with caution, deviating from its intended course to avoid the large bergs. When dawn broke we were rewarded with the spectacular sight of huge bergs visible above the mists, the sunrise creating wonderful shades of red, orange and yellow reflected from the normal blue-white ice.

We passed one berg which we calculated to be over a mile long and three hundred feet high. As we altered course to give it a wide berth, the mists came down and enveloped it like a shroud, its ghostly shape hardly visible beneath.

HMS *Antrim*

Captain James received instruction to rendezvous with HMS *Antrim*. General Moore and his staff of about forty were to be transferred so that he could quickly catch up with Admiral Sandy Woodward and the British troops who had landed and were now setting up defensive positions at base camp near San Carlos Water. *Antrim* had been having similar problems with ice, but the rendezvous went ahead on schedule. They had known our position from the moment our radars had been switched on.

The decision had been made to transfer most of the men by our own Harding launches, as the sea conditions were slight except for a fairly large swell. General Moore went over by helicopter and, even though the Sea King was considered normally too large to land on that deck, the pilot managed it by landing at 45 degrees, thus enabling all three sets of wheels to touch – a difficult operation in the swell.

The swell also made the boat transfer more hazardous than expected, and several attempts had to be made before all had embarked onto *Antrim*. One junior army officer, however, was not quite agile enough: as he jumped for the rope ladder hanging from the warship he was caught between the two as the swell lifted the launch and trapped his leg. He was lifted to the deck, diagnosed and immediately put on the helicopter to be returned to *QE2*, where our hospital took care of him.

Antrim had already seen action, in both South Georgia and East Falkland. The evidence was visible by her somewhat weatherbeaten exterior, but also by the line of shell holes down her side. Her Seacat missile launcher was out of action as the result of an unexploded bomb that had lodged itself in the magazine and had fortunately been defused before it could explode and remove the stern of the vessel.

South Georgia

By 1330 hours we were on our way, with instructions to make for South Georgia. The fog was still present and we could see nothing when 'stand by' was rung at 1745 hours. I made my way forward to supervise the letting-go of the anchor. Because of the new flight deck, just getting forward was a little precarious, and I had to virtually swing over the ship's side to get there. The two carpenters who operated the controls of the anchor windlass were all but hidden from me by the tons of steel, and we had to communicate by walkie-talkie – or bellow at the top of our voices.

Captain Jackson brought the ship into Cumberland Bay, navigating through the fog by radar. On the forecastle we walked the anchor back to two shackles in the water, 180 feet of the chain below the surface. The bay was very deep, and if we had let go 'from the pipe', the anchor and cable would have raced down to the ocean floor and the momentum would have brought the remainder out of the cable locker, probably causing considerable damage.

I peered through the murk at the water, black as the blackest night. I could see nothing except the gentlest ripple as the stem cut through the waterway below me as we crept gently into the bay. The bridge was invisible behind me, a rather unnerving experience considering the circumstances of our position. When the captain had decided on his anchor position the engines were put astern, and then I could not detect the ship's forward momentum through the water, just feel a slight vibration under my feet as the propellers brought the 67,000 tons to a halt.

The wash made by the astern movement gradually came

forward, and I could see the discharged water from the galleys coming towards the bow. When the order was given the carpenters opened the brake of the windlass and the anchor cable dropped away with increasing speed, the anchor hitting the bottom as the fifth shackle raced over the gypsy. The carpenters struggled with the brake, trying to slow the progress of the cable, which was now jumping along the rollers and down the hawse pipe bringing mud, rust and sparks up from the chain locker. I darted for the port side in an attempt to miss the 'bitter end' should it part from its securing point in the locker, but to my great relief they brought the rushing chain to a halt with only two shackles left on board.

QE2 anchored at 1922 hours, approximately one mile from the old whaling station at Grytviken. The passage from Freetown, a distance of 5,035 miles, had taken eight days, twenty hours and twelve minutes, and had consumed 3,570 tonnes of fuel and at an average speed of 23.9 knots.

The ferry *Norland* and the P&O liner *Canberra* were already at anchor, and a meeting took place soon after our arrival with the senior naval officers and Captain Barker from HMS *Endurance*, which was also anchored in the bay. The troops were to disembark immediately into requisitioned trawlers, to be transferred to *Norland* and *Canberra*. The delay in transferring troops would therefore be minimal, but the discharge of stores and ammunition would be more time-consuming. These would be transferred to the Fleet Auxiliary ship *Stromness*, which would be arriving the next day with the survivors of HMS *Coventry*.

Disembarkation
HMS *Leeds Castle*, sister to *Dumbarton Castle*, was the first vessel to try and come alongside in the late-evening darkness, her lights only becoming visible as she closed to one hundred feet. Her mast hit our bridge wing extensions as she tried to manoeuvre under number one hatch, and she had to move away.

The *Cordella* then was the first to secure alongside. She was one of five North Sea trawlers that had been taken up from trade, and she and the others, *Northella, Farnella, Junella* and *Pict*, made up the newly formed 11th Mine Countermeasures Squadron. They were manned by Royal Navy officers and ratings to act as mine sweepers in the waters off the Falkland Islands. Except for paintwork, and a ship's pontoon that should not have been down, very little damage was done in bringing these large vessels alongside, their new commanders showing considerable skill.

The transfer went on throughout the night, the trawlers making repeated journeys over to *Canberra* or unloading stores from number one hatch forward. The Admiralty salvage tug *Typhoon* was also utilised to take troops to the *Norland*.

The following morning I woke to see a hive of activity. The fog had become very patchy, and one of the most remarkable vistas in my experience was visible. South Georgia is a land of tall rugged mountains reaching up towards 10,000 feet, and in every valley there appears to be a glacier, Hamberg, Harker and Nordenfjold Glaciers could all be seen from our anchorage. Nestling between these barren peaks was Grytviken, a deserted whaling station of rusted iron and dilapidated wooden buildings. Through the binoculars the conning tower of the crippled Argentine submarine *Santa Fe* could be made out lying at an angle against the old wooden jetty. The wreck of an Argentinian helicopter was on the hillside above King Edward Cove.

In the foreground lay *Canberra*, looking slightly the worse for wear with rust streaking her side. She had already been in the firing line at San Carlos. *Norland* lay astern of us, looking very far away from home in the North Sea. Flying commenced a little after eight, as soon as the fog lifted sufficiently for us to be able to see the other ships, then went on throughout the day with stores being lifted from our forward flight deck. The Wasp helicopter from *Endurance* flew on with their captain, and a number of conferences seemed to take place. On board *QE2* Lieutenant Commander David Poole, our executive officer, took charge of the transfer operation, assisted by the navigator from *Endurance*.

During the morning it became evident that we might not get all the troops off within the prepared schedule, and a worried-looking officer from the 7th Gurkha asked if we could use one or two of the ship's own Harding launches to transfer his men. I assisted by starting to load up just before midday. Most of the Gurkhas were tiny, and in some cases their equipment appeared more than the man could physically carry. Upon reaching *Norland* we realised that they had no pontoon for us to come alongside, only a shell door opening some eight feet above the water, normally used for the loading and discharge of vehicles. The Gurkhas could not even see over it let alone climb through it, but we brought the boat alongside and by using the roof of the boat's cab plus a good shove from behind we managed to safely embark them all. I was sorry to see them go, for the Gurkhas had been courteous, obedient and efficient.

The chief officer of *Norland* dropped down onto the boat and talked of his recent experiences with the ship at San Carlos Water, the area now referred to as 'Bomb Alley'. He told me that he had been on the port bridge wing when an Argentine Mirage fighter had flown past beneath him and a Skyhawk had been shot down by soldiers lying on their backs using their submachine guns. Another Skyhawk was 'splashed' by a British missile, hit over their heads, parts of plane falling all around them. There was a line of canon shell holes along one section of the side, similar to those we had seen in HMS *Antrim*.

On our return journey to *QE2* we carried some of the survivors of HMS *Ardent*. They looked a pathetic sight, as few of them had their own clothing, and what they wore was mostly borrowed, with their few personal belongings in plastic bags. Even though they looked a shambles, they did not look defeated – but there was no light-hearted banter.

By 1655 hours, when darkness had returned, all flying had ceased and our two helicopters with their crew were embarked onto *Canberra*. The troops had gone, and by the next morning so had *Canberra* and *Norland*.

The weather had remained settled, with only light airs and a temperature of 0–3.1 °C. The overcast skies had ensured that we were not visible from above, and consequently our greatest hazard could have come from one of the few German-built submarines which the Navy knew the Argentinians had in service. QE2 would have presented an admirable target while at anchor at the head of the bay, and this was possibly the most dangerous period of our voyage.

Ashore in Grytviken

Throughout Friday night stores were continually being transferred into the trawlers. These were stores for which *Canberra* could not be held back, and they were therefore later loaded onto *Stromness*.

Afleck-Graves had been liaising with the commanding officer ashore where approximately one hundred troops were now based in the British Antarctic Survey base, close to the old whaling station. On Saturday morning one of our boats was put down and thirty of our people headed for the shore. The closer we came, the more desperate the landscape looked, and this dilapidated, forgotten little cluster of buildings appeared more like a Wild West ghost town than anything I had seen before.

The temperature was colder inshore as the boat pushed its way through the brash ice, and the mountains looked daunting in their numerous shades of sombre grey and black, flecked with the white of snowdrifts and hanging mist.

We were met by one of the army officers who had been with the troops who had retaken the island a few weeks before. He had the cold hard look of the SAS professional, a serious man whom I don't recall smiling throughout our visit. Our landing was at the old wooden pier near the submarine *Santa Fe*, and he advised us not to poke around on our own, as there was a possibility of Argentine booby traps as yet undiscovered.

We passed the submarine, with its conning tower lying at an angle away from the jetty, and a message crudely painted

Philip Rentell

Grytviken, South Georgia

on the side in large white letters – 'Keep Off, by order of the Commanding Officer *Endurance*' – as though coach-loads of tourists would appear at any moment – or perhaps it was meant for the more light-fingered, souvenir-hunting soldier based at the camp. Two whalers lay partly sunken in shallow water close by, just abandoned when the last men left in the early 1960s. The fresh snow lay on the rotting jetty, where odd boards were broken or missing. The impression was that we were the first people to arrive for twenty years.

The other buildings around were factory units, offices, dormitories and even a church, all made from timber and looking similar to the houses found in the Norwegian countryside, except that the paintwork was faded and chipped, doors were ajar, windows were dirty and broken. The steelwork and galvanised iron sheeting of the working areas had rusted and collapsed over the years, giving an air of decay.

We followed in the officer's footsteps, passing two soldiers about to start a week's patrol. The garrison was split roughly into two, with half on patrol for a week, sleeping in bivouacs, while the others were back at base. They were equipped with the usual sort of armaments, and they also had VHF radios with headsets around their helmets. We went around the factory with its whale-oil tanks, part of the processing plant.

Paul Guest, the ship's photographer, and I held back to take a few photographs while the others proceeded into an old wooden church, complete with steeple. Quite suddenly we were surprised to hear the sound of an organ coming from the white building. We followed inside to find that one the second officers, Chris Haughton, had found a wonderful old organ on the inside balcony. With some little persuasion and hefty pumping he managed to play the first few bars of Bach's *Toccata and Fugue in D Minor*. The church was not in fact as dilapidated as the other buildings, and had been in regular use by the Antarctic Survey and latterly by the army.

We continued our trek through the old whaling station, seeing old tools, lathes and other machinery, which all looked as though they had been left one Friday night prior to a weekend off. One old whaler was still afloat at another jetty, and, except for its rusty and unused appearance, it looked as though it could be made seaworthy.

Our path took us out of town, past the derelict hulk of an old sailing ship long since beached and with only one mast remaining in place, to a tiny cemetery where about thirty graves could be identified. Here lies the grave of Sir Ernest Shackleton, the Antarctic explorer whose perilous journey across the Southern Ocean to South Georgia is recalled in Frank Worsley's *Shackleton's Boat Journey*. Worsley was his captain on the *Endurance*.

There was also a new grave in the cemetery, that of Victorio Artuso, the Argentine submariner who was unfortunately killed after the island was recaptured. The story we were told was that as the submarine was being moved to the jetty under escort, Artuso was shot when he reached up to adjust a ballast valve, the guard believing an act of sabotage was about to take place. His grave was marked with a simple polished wooden cross with his name and the date.

We made our way back to the launch, some of the lads picking up old whalebones and harpoon heads for souvenirs. In the distance *QE2* looked surreal in the mists. Another boat followed us back, full of troops from the base, coming out to sample briefly the comparative luxury of the ship.

Departure Grytviken

During that afternoon stores continued to be discharged, but the weather was changing quickly, with the barometer falling and the wind picking up. The sea was being whipped up, and the increasing swell coming through the entrance of the bay was causing the ship to yaw uncomfortably – which in turn made the trawlers alongside heave unpredictably.

Captain James had a report that the tanker *British Wye* was being bombed by an unidentified aircraft just four hundred miles to the north. He assumed the Argentines could therefore reach our position and decided that we should leave, even though munitions were still in the hold.

All the survivors from the attacked warships *Ardent*, *Antelope* and *Coventry* were safely aboard, and at 1727 hours the anchor was raised and we steamed out of the bay, increasing speed to 18 knots and heading east. By 1930 hours we were back in the ice field and Captain Jackson manoeuvred his ship through the many bergs which in the darkness could only be seen on the radar, assuming the ice would also make detection difficult for the Argentinian forces. By 2200 we had cleared the ice field, and speed was increased to 25 knots and the course to 045 degrees.

Journey north

The following morning Captain James chaired his usual nine o'clock meeting with two of the executive officers from the warships – the third had not survived his ship's attack, and his place

▲ Where it all started: the training ship *Worcester* at Greenhithe, Kent, seen here in the 1950s.

◄ *Reina del Mar* in Montevideo, 1973.

Third officer in the chartroom of *Reina del Mar*, 1973.
▼

▲ PR (centre) as second officer
of the freighter *Ikeja Palm*.

◄ At work as navigator on a Hoverlloyd
SRN4 hovercraft, 1978.

►
Flagship of the Cunard
fleet: *QE2* anchored off
Moorea in the Pacific.

◄ Second officer in *QE2*, 1979.

► First officer in *QE2*.

Troops clambering over *QE2*'s lifeboats at Southampton to get a better view of family and friends on the quayside before sailing for the Falklands in 1982. A volunteer crew of 650 sailed with over 3,500 troops of 5 Infantry Brigade.

▲ Sailing south to war: soldiers and sailors bound for the Falklands watch the Sea King helicopters on the helipad fitted to *QE2*'s afterdeck.

▶ Taking on supplies
off Ascension.

QE2 in the Southern Ocean,
taken from a helicopter
during a twilight flight to
check blackout procedures.
▼

QE2 at anchor
with trawlers
at Grytviken,
South Georgia.
▼

◀ RFA *Bayleaf* Refuelling *QE2* at sea.

▶ Homeward bound in *QE2* after the war: troops and crew relaxing in and around the jury-rigged pool during the crossing-the-line ceremony.

▼ The Queen Mother's visit during the *QE2*'s refit after our return to the UK.

▲ *QE2* attended by tugs in New York harbour. Her new grey livery was not kept for long, as it showed up the inevitable rust marks from North Atlantic crossings.

Cunard Princess in Alaska. ▶

My first command. On the bridge wing of *Scandinavian Saga* , preparing to sail from St Petersburg, Florida, in 1990. In the background is *Scandinavian Song*, later renamed *The Empress*. ▼

Philip Renz

With the crew of *Fantasy World*, 1993.

Bob Curtis

The Brixham pilot boat, *Brenda M.*

Green Ridge, which I piloted through the Channel and North Sea, laden with ammunition.

Military Sealift Command

The murder ship:
Coral Princess,
alias *Cora Princess*.

▲ *The Empress*, 1994.

◀ Bow damage to
The Empress, 1994.

In the Singapore
repair yard.

was taken by another officer. All three were not comfortable and were obviously still suffering some degree of shock from their experience under fire. They did seem, however, to be attempting to give the impression of a brave front and continue life as normal. Discipline and ship routine continued while they on board *QE2*, with each of the vessels treating itself as a separate unit.

I raised the matter of boat drill, and explained that this would occur for the survivors during the morning. There were only approximately 650 men, so the routine should be that much simpler than before, but I was questioned in great detail about our procedures. They were very anxious, as experience had taught them that plans prepared on paper do not always follow the expected path in practice. One of the men believed that the crews should muster below the level of the lowest aluminium deck, as it had been proved that aluminium burns extremely well after being hit by an Exocet missile. I had to point out that in a ship of our size this would be extremely impractical, and that at least they should try our well-proven method. The drill was practised and found to be satisfactory, except that I found the Navy ratings seemed a little less disciplined than the men of the army – a holiday mood had set in.

After leaving the bumpy waters of South Georgia the weather gradually improved, and as we proceeded northwards the sun appeared and the pensive mood on board began to lift. The blackout procedure and radio silence continued, although messages via the satellite equipment could still be sent and received.

Rendezvous with *Bayleaf*

Only 886 tonnes of fuel remained on board by Tuesday 1 June, enough only for another day and a half steaming. A rendezvous was scheduled with the new Fleet Auxiliary ship *Bayleaf*, and by late afternoon we had reduced speed to keep station with the oiler. But the sea was considered too rough, the wind was force eight from the west-north-west and *QE2* was rolling moderately to a rough sea and heavy swell.

The weather had moderated only slightly by the next morning, but the refuelling had to proceed. *Bayleaf* approached up our starboard side and a fuel line was connected just after 0900 hours. The ships were only 150 feet apart and the sea between was being whipped up as both vessels rolled in the heavy swell. *Bayleaf* was shipping spray over her foredeck and rolling through 40 degrees or more. Captain Jackson watched apprehensively from the bridge wing as the operation continued and the oiler kept station with *QE2*, a role reversal for the Royal Fleet Auxiliary. We continued on a course of 300 degrees, and all the time the pipeline heaved and fell, at times looking as though it would part, as awful grating noises could be heard coming from the shell door recess where the hose was connected.

Bunkering was finally completed shortly after 1830 hours, and the pipelines were disconnected, possibly only just in time, as the joining shackle which supported the block which in turn supported the fuel-oil hose was found to be almost worn through from the constant chafing – it could have parted at any time.

Bayleaf cleared away by 1850 hours. We had been steaming in tandem for almost ten hours and bunkered 3,834 tonnes of fuel, a remarkable achievement and a creditable performance by all the navy men involved.

Entertainment

The continued involvement of *QE2* in this war was still uncertain, but we expected our passengers to disembark at Ascension Island and that the ship would proceed south again. The Navy decided to put on a show, and in a few short days managed to find more 'acts' than they could cope with. The performance was extremely funny, most professional, and of course quite crude at times, as can be expected from sailors. Our ladies from the laundry, who had replaced the normal laundrymen on board, were given front-row seats and enjoyed every minute. The Double Down Show Room was alive with the spirit of these brave men who had come from the very front of battle, and when at the end they sang *God*

Save the Queen the atmosphere was one of great emotion.

A few nights later, on 3 June, a naval mess dinner was given in the Princess Grill by the officers of the sunken ships and Naval Party 1980 for the officers from the wardroom of *QE2*. There were a couple of patriotic speeches, but the dinner was unusual in that the survivors were wearing a hodgepodge of borrowed shirts, epaulettes and other clothing, not the blue 'mess' that the navy normally wore for these formal occasions.

The spirit and fervour was maintained after dinner by returning to the Queen's Grill Bar, where 'traditional mess games' were to take place. In my capacity as liaison officer I felt it my duty to provide whatever accompaniments were deemed necessary, and these included two-dozen empty wine bottles and a dozen broom handles. Balancing on an upturned wine bottle and attempting to dismount your similarly handicapped opponent using a broomstick is a tricky and dangerous operation – the shins suffering the most from repeated blows.

Tug of war using a broomstick in place of a rope is another popular 'pastime' on these occasions, with both teams squatting on the deck holding onto each other. The game is equally uncivilised, the aim being to win by fair means or foul.

New orders

Our new orders arrived. It had been decided that *QE2* would return to Southampton via Ascension and not return to the south. Many of us initially felt disappointed because compared to *Canberra* we had done very little so far, but we came to realise that much had in fact been achieved, and that transporting the troops would prove to be invaluable in shortening the process of war in the Falklands.

On Friday 4 June we were to rendezvous again with *Dumbarton Castle* off Ascension Island to transfer stores and personnel, including two casualties and six SAS men, the survivors of the helicopter crash that killed nineteen of their comrades. They were a very private group who kept themselves to themselves and wanted to be lifted off the ship before we reached Southampton and thus avoid any publicity or welcoming committee. One of the injured was the helicopter pilot, he had broken his foot in pushing his way out through the nearest window after the helicopter had crashed into the sea and turned over. His action had saved the lives of those who would otherwise have died, but he was at first uncomfortable with his memories. We managed to bring him around during the remainder of the voyage by including him in our more sociable activities – plus generous quantities of alcohol.

The transfer was complete within four hours, and by 1830 we were back up to full speed and heading a course for the United Kingdom.

The return

The final days passed quickly as preparations were made to return to Southampton. A reception committee was expected, and we would pass the Royal Yacht *Britannia* on our way up the Solent. A decision was made to re-kit the navy survivors before arrival, so on the afternoon of Thursday 10 June 'hands to flying stations' was piped again. Helicopters from RNAS Culdrose flew out to meet us off Mounts Bay, bringing stores and a few important people, one of whom was to tell us what we could and could not say to the press. The SAS men left, and overnight we proceeded up the Channel at slow speed.

The timetable for Friday had been carefully planned, with our arrival at the Needles pilot station around 0845 hours. Earlier in the morning Admiral Sir John Fieldhouse was to join by helicopter, accompanied by Lord Matthews. They went around the ship talking to the sailors before holding a press conference in the Q4 Room, which I had to introduce and give my version of events, with the forty media that had also arrived by 'chopper' off Portland.

Captain Driver boarded at 0848 hours, and we proceeded up the Needles Channel, past the western end of the Isle of Wight.

The survivors lined up on the starboard side of the flight decks on this beautiful June morning, and as we slowly passed the Royal Yacht they gave three cheers to the Queen Mother, who waved from the after deck of *Britannia*. She sent this telegram to Captain Jackson:

> I am pleased to welcome you back as QE2 returns to home waters after your tour of duty in the South Atlantic. The exploits of your own ship's company and the deeds of valour of those who served in Antelope, Coventry and Ardent have been acclaimed throughout the land and I am proud to add my personal tribute.

We proceeded up Southampton Water surrounded by dozens of small boats, while helicopters and planes flew overhead, and as we passed the oil refinery at Fawley each ship lying alongside signalled a salute and filled the air with a cacophony of whistles. On the dock hundreds of people were visible, all waving flags and banners.

The ship turned off the berth, and by the time we approached the quay the cheering and shouts were even louder than the marine band playing in front of the terminal. Everywhere there seemed to be cameras and press, and when I went through the wardroom I saw that the whole spectacle was being shown live on TV.

A red carpet had been prepared, and as soon as the gangway was in position the survivors were ushered ashore to be met by a host of senior naval officers and local dignitaries applauding. Each of them was given a red rose. They were, I'm sure, surprised by the reception, and perhaps a little bemused by it all, but the main intention was to reunite them with the families as soon as possible, and a secluded area in the terminal had been set aside, away from the prying eyes of public and media.

The crew of *QE2* meanwhile started to file ashore from the forward gangway. It soon became almost impossible to move, with hundreds of emotional but happy relatives all gathered around. A very special day for us all.

Postscript

The conversion of the ship back to its original condition took considerably longer than its conversion to a troop ship. When the helicopter decks were removed Cunard took the opportunity to complete much other work, including changing the Q4 Room into the Club Lido, one of the inside pool areas into a spa with Jacuzzis, and repainting the dark blue hull a light grey. Survey work intended to be completed at the next scheduled refit was finished, and the ship eventually left Southampton on 14 August, making her way to New York, where a huge welcome awaited her.

Queen Elizabeth 2 achieved a new following by being at the forefront of the world news, and the relatively short period 'at war' ensured her continued success as the most famous ocean liner in service.

From the *Daily Mail*, 20 May 1982, by Ross Mark in Washington:

> The Soviet Union has deployed two spy satellites to pinpoint the *Queen Elizabeth 2* for air and submarine attack, according to the authoritative *Aerospace Daily*.
>
> American intelligence sources confirm that at least some of the twelve Soviet radar, photographic and communication satellites are being used in the hunt for the liner.
>
> Former American Chief of Naval Operations, Admiral Elmo Zumwalt said in a television interview he expected Argentina to make an effort to destroy the *QE2* by air and submarine attacks. 'It is one big fat target,' the Admiral said.

From 5th Infantry Brigade *QE2 News*, 20 May 1982, on board:

> Gurkha soldiers have difficulty saying 'General Galtieri'. Instead they have come up with the name 'General Galti Gare'. As well as being easier to say, this name is actually most appropriate. It means 'the General who made a mistake'.

From 5th Infantry Brigade *QE2 News*, 26 May 1982, on board:

A message from the Commander, M J A Wilson, Brigadier – very shortly we shall all transfer to other ships off South Georgia and start the last phase of our move to the Falkland Islands. It looks as if the Brigade will be there about 1st June, that is early next week.

Once there, we shall join 3 Commando Brigade. We shall sort ourselves out; and then start joint operations to recapture the Islands.

Orders will be given out on landing; it is too early yet to issue a detailed plan, for it would be bound to change over the course of the next five days.

This is the final issue of this newspaper, and to the Master and ship's company of *QE2* I would say 'Thank you for the way you have looked after us on this voyage. We have come to know you well, we admire you, and we shall always be proud that we sailed with you in your magnificent ship.'

To the Brigade I would say simply this, 'We shall start earning our pay as a team shortly; and we are in this game to win'.

Captain Peter Jackson, *Southern Evening Echo*, 12 June 1982:

It's been a most worrying trip for me.

The important thing was that we concealed ourselves at all times by our speed, by the route we took and with the assistance of the weather. The *QE2* is so fast that you can disappear. To the best of my knowledge we were only sighted by one ship all the way down on the outward voyage.

I have never seen so many icebergs in my life before. I was very thankful for a very fine radar.

Editorial comment, *Daily Mail*, 13 June 1982:

Yesterday, at Southampton, Britain's greatest passenger liner, the *QE2*, returned with the survivors and wounded of the Royal Navy ships, *Coventry*, *Antelope* and *Ardent*. The tumultuous welcome of the huge crowd ashore reflected the feelings of gratitude of the whole nation to those who have fought bravely and endured so much for us all.

The cheers also echoed the universal sense of relief that this great ship, which sailed so swiftly with 3,000 troops down to the South Atlantic where it was a prime target for the Argentines, has returned unharmed.

It was a wonderful achievement to take this 67,000 ton vessel with her precious complement of men and material, to keep her out of danger from enemy aircraft and submarines, but in waters thick with icebergs, transfer them to troop carriers and then return with the crews of ships which went down gallantly fighting the enemy.

We bid both the *QE2* and all those who have returned in her a prosperous voyage into the future.

Driving the new hotel, 1987

After the exciting interlude sailing to the South Atlantic in 1982, and a very long refit that followed in order to prepare the ship for her return to passenger service, life returned to some degree of normality. I gradually climbed the ladder of seniority, and became engaged and then married to Helen, the dance captain for the superb Peter Gordeno, our resident 'top of the bill'.

Cunard decided, some time in the mid-1980s, to replace the fuel-guzzling steam turbine propulsion system with a modern diesel electric plant. The intention was to lengthen the life span of the ship and also to reduce the ever-increasing fuel costs. The six-month refit took place in Germany, and we emerged in the spring of 1987 with a ship that could maintain over 29 knots, but with a fuel consumption reduced by over one-third to around 350 tonnes a day at full speed.

I was asked by Douglas Ward, a colleague I had first sailed with in 1973, to write a brief article for his cruise newspaper, Cruise Digest, *giving a navigator's perspective on how the ship handled with the new power plant. This is what I wrote.*

In the almost forgotten days of the steam turbine, slowing down the *QE2* from full sea speed of 29 knots would often cause the first officer on the bridge some heart-stopping moments. Because of the need to reduce speed gradually and therefore allow the turbines to cool evenly (in normal operation!) it was common to allow as much as fifty miles in the last two and a half hours prior to picking up the pilot. This necessitated the officer of the watch to constantly monitor the ship's position and the rate of reduction in speed, to ensure the ship was at the pilot station with the engines ready to manoeuvre.

Naturally, because the engines were slowed down 'manually' by the engineer on watch, the rate of slowing down often varied depending on who the engineer was. Some of the younger chaps were more 'ambitious' than the experienced hands, which on more than one occasion resulted in the ship being ready to receive the pilot, i.e. at a speed of approximately 8 knots, ten miles before the pilot boat! This was of course more acceptable than the other option, which occasionally required the first officer to make a 'dogleg', or alternatively to go steaming past the boat, leaving the pilot behind shouting nautically flavoured language over the VHF telephone, and the captain staring stonily over the bridge wing, no doubt wishing he or preferably his OOW were on leave, or on any other ship but his.

Those days have gone. We now have the largest marine diesel electric plant in the world, with a control system adaptable to even the most unpredictable navigators. Instead of fifty miles in two hours we take about eight miles in the last half an hour, and even this is possibly the worst scenario. During our protracted sea trials one of the many manoeuvres we made was the 'crash stop'. This required the stopping distance to be measured from a speed of 30 knots. Not only did QE2 stop in 0.75 of a nautical mile, but in a time of three minutes and forty-two seconds, surely a feat to impress even the most sceptical of our critics, and one to reassure those of us whose task it is to embark pilots at the right place at the correct time.

This ability to stop easily whenever we wish, without undue stress or fatigue on the machinery, can be mainly attributed to the controllable-pitch propellers. Prior to the major refit we had two six-bladed propellers, the blades of which were fixed. To go astern the shafts had to be first slowed and then reversed. Now the shafts rotate in one direction all the time, and at a speed of 142 RPM whilst we are 'deep sea', although this is reduced to 70 RPM as we enter pilotage waters. The ship's speed and direction is changed by adjusting the 'angle of attack' of the propeller blades. Instead of the old wheelhouse telegraphs we have 'combinators', two short levers which act very much like an accelerator on a car. Of course the levers are not coupled direct to the engines: there is a very sophisticated 'power management unit' which controls the rate of change of the pitch angle and thus the speed of the ship, particularly at high shaft RPM, so there is still a certain amount of thinking ahead to be done and of course the prudent navigator will always remember that machines are only human! Things can occasionally go wrong.

When we wish to slow down, the combinators, or pitch control levers, are brought slowly back from the full forward position. This changes the pitch angle of the propeller blades and consequently the load to drive the ship at her full sea speed, now approximately 31 knots, which requires all of our nine diesels to be running and providing electricity to power the large electric motors directly coupled to the propeller shafts. As the load decreases, diesels are shut down automatically but remain available for immediate start-up should conditions warrant. During times of 'harbour steaming' the PMU is on combinator mode, which maintains a certain number of diesels on-line and gives the pilot almost instantaneous control of the ship's speed and direction. In fact the pitch control is capable, when being handled by the more dextrous of navigators, of moving the ship as little as one or two feet up the quay.

Naturally the march of progress dictates the ever-increasing use of computers, but it is reassuring to know that through the initial teething troubles that *QE2* experienced with her new heart, our friends the engineers were quite capable of stepping in, taking control and sorting out the gremlins which inevitably occur with a sophisticated plant such as ours. From an operational point of view, it is indeed a rare privilege to be given the responsibility of driving what may be the last of the great superliners and the flagship of the British merchant navy. May she continue, as the Cunard Line would wish, to sail on and into the twenty-first century.

Cunard Princess –
a week down Mexico way

After almost ten years serving on QE2, *I was offered the carrot of promotion and was promptly despatched to the* Cunard Princess, *one of our smaller cruise ships serving Florida, into the Caribbean and up as far as Los Angeles on the west coast. During the winter months we plied our trade up and down the coast of California and Mexico, a regular run which, although not exactly a bus route, became very familiar to those of us tasked with navigating. I wrote an article describing a typical seven days, which was published in the British shipping enthusiasts' magazine* Ships Monthly *in November 1989.*

I'm fairly certain that it was the tourists who were following the whales originally, these days I'm not so sure. The cruise ships start their migration from Alaska by early October and a majority end up on the Mexican run, jockeying for berths and anchorages wherever they go. The whales reach the fun just before Christmas, and what a spectacle it is! Cabo San Lucas, that most southerly tip of Lower California, is a small bay renowned on the west coast for its sport fishing, where one ship in the anchorage looks significant, two looks busy and four ridiculous.

Four thousand souls are ejected by tender for four hours on terra firma, giving just enough time for the taxi drivers to use a couple of gallons of petrol in exchange for a couple of months' wages, the shopkeepers to lighten their endless load of sombreros – never to be worn again after another week, and the barkeepers to drain yet another vat of tequila, distilled no doubt next door.

The 813-mile run down from Los Angeles takes just a day and a half, enough time for passengers to find their cabin, the restaurant and the Showboat Lounge, plus of course the outdoor café, where that raging hunger that occurs between breakfast, lunch, dinner and the midnight buffet can be suitably quashed with the ubiquitous burger, hot dog or healthy salad – with plenty of dressing. Scenery is intermittent and dependent on visibility, but the approach to Cabo, with the sandy barren slopes of Cabo Falso, is not dissimilar to an Arabian image. Marine life abounds, dolphins chase the bow wave, whales proceed at their sedentary pace, sighted by their spray and occasionally by their tails reaching out as they dive for deeper water, even seals lie on their backs with their flippers spread wide to take the sun. All this causes feverish activity amongst some, indigestion with others, and judging by what my sailors have to scrub off the decks, at least a few bottles of 'tropical tan' to go flying. But the schedule is relentless – no lazy Sunday ramble this.

Getting 800 passengers ashore and back aboard in four hours using ship's launches is not easily achieved. Organisation created by experience creates a thinly disguised disciplined operation – if only the passengers would do what's asked of them. Complaints are regular and expected, and everyone wants to step ashore as soon as the anchor touches the bottom. Each launch takes fifty, loading takes ten minutes, the ride-in five, unloading another five. Simple arithmetic leads to a ready understanding of the logistical problem – unless you've paid $499 for the holiday of a lifetime, are easily misled and, dare I say it, American. I can only assume that people expect that TV series to be 'like it is'!

I often take a launch in, partly to say I've been ashore, but also to have first-hand experience of the current problems, satisfy myself the operation is running as smoothly as we can hope for, and watch the folks enjoy their first taste of freedom for

Tony Davis

almost two days. It's quite surprising how difficult some people find trying to relax. When all the cares and worries are taken away, the little things are magnified to extreme. For example, leaving the sunglasses in the cabin drawer can become a major issue between husband and wife. 'Do we have to get another launch ticket if we go back aboard?' – 'Why do we stay such a short time here?' – 'What happens if we miss the last launch back?' – for the twenty-eighth time. Patience is not a virtue, it is an absolute godsend.

And then, suddenly it seems, the traffic between the ships thins out, a windlass cranks, chains rumble and crash to a pile in the locker, the anchor emerges, 'sighted and clear' from the fo'c'sle. First the little *Polaris* takes a slow arc close by the rocks and out of the bay, *Bermuda Star* backs out from a gap between *Dawn Princess* and *Cunard Princess* – it seems the captain with the most nerve, or the most skill, gets the better 'hole', and being first doesn't mean the best position. Just like your local car park – there's always someone who'll get into the spot you thought was too tight, but then necessity is the mother of invention.

193 miles across the Baha to Mazatlán, probably Mexico's biggest port on the Pacific, but today not big enough for all and the *Dawn* finds herself anchoring again – another day of tender

operations when all deck work ceases while the ABs drive the boats. The *Star* takes the remaining cargo berth and we, fortunately, turn and 'park' alongside the passenger quay – between the ferry terminal and the oil terminal. I'm happy, reasonable water pressure on the dock and water trucks at $31 each will mean we'll leave full of fresh water tonight – just another of the mate's worries.

Mazatlán is boat drill day, known to us all as Board of Trade Sports – well, at least to that minority on board this Bahamian registered vessel who look back to the days of sailing under the red duster. Still, fun and games – and in my exalted status as overlord I enjoy the developing drama from my vantage point on the boat deck. The chief officer's bark is worse than his bite and this is the day it shows. No doubt the effigies and the voodoo will be out in the crew accommodation tonight. The practice, however, means that when we do a drill in front of the US Coast Guard they will be suitably impressed. How can it be that with a ship of thirty-seven different nationalities we manage to get our act together? I know why.

The other mates have the bridge visit in the afternoon – if they haven't suffered enough already today. For those who've never seen our office before, it can appear awesome, especially when you explain there is only one officer on duty at a time, 'Wow!, all these dials and buttons, how do you know which one to press?' – sometimes I ask myself that question.

By six we are ready to sail, with all crew and passengers hopefully on the right ship – 'Señor Frogs' margaritas cause havoc among the unwary – still, all the ships will be in Puerto Vallarta tomorrow. By the time we have crossed another 182 sea miles the *Dawn Princess* has raced ahead, not to be outdone yet again. The *Tropical*, however, has taken the only alongside berth, and the *Dawn* anchors, much to our consternation, on the leading marks. There is only one slot left in the tiny harbour, just big enough for our 17,495 tons. The captain deftly manoeuvres our ship round the stern of the *Dawn*, does a 180-degree turn and creeps stern-first towards the entrance. Meanwhile the pilot, now on his third ship of the morning, attempts to anchor the *Dawn* again. He boards our ship, after the bow has passed the entrance buoys, and too late to be of any real assistance, but his boat will be used to run our stern lines to the shore. As we pass the *Tropical* the stern is swung to port (thank heavens for calm winds and a good bow thruster), until we are parallel. First the port anchor and then the starboard anchor are let go, the fo'c'sle officer jumps from one side to another, two shackles, three, brake open, hold on, anchors in gear, heave on both, tightening the stern lines until the ship is in position a mere 150 feet from that other recent addition to the floating condominium frater- nity – who said seamanship was dead?

0730 hours, we're in position, moored, the pontoon is down and ready to board our first shore-bound revellers. Few takers, however. The clocks went forward one hour last night and that innocent enthusiasm has lapsed after only two days – Mexico, been there! But come they eventually do, squinting as they emerge from the shell door into bright sunlight. By this time the 150-foot gap is a mass of boats of all sizes, eager to pick up their organised excursions, deep-sea fishing, snorkelling, island tours, booze cruises. The *Star* has arrived and anchored out- side, and a newcomer to the area, the four-masted *Sea Cloud*, has dignified the surroundings with her presence. She too has to search the shelf outside for a ledge shallow enough to place her anchor.

By noon the ship is quiet, and for a few precious hours we feel just a little relaxed and I take the opportunity to escape. Permission is granted to step back in time, the bosun runs number seven boat outside the harbour and drops me off at the foot of the *Sea Cloud*'s gangway. This prestigious barque, built for Marjorie Merriweather Post on her marriage to E F Hutton in 1931, had been rescued from dereliction in 1978 by a group of eight German shipowners and industrialists. From lying forlorn in Cristobal, she is today a wonderful example of a ship that is lovingly cared for by everyone who works on board, the varnish work is superb, the brass shining, the wooden decks sea-white. Captain Shannon, her unassuming and pleasant American master was the master of US Coast Guard sail training ship *Eagle* for ten years. The two hours I spent on board were a porthole into the past which, no doubt, her sixty or so passengers will only appreciate after they return to their busy twentieth-century lives.

After brief conversations on my hand-held VHF (what did we do before radios?), the bosun returns in number seven with a few gallons of black paint, fair payment I think, and I'm speedily removed from the scene. We pick up a few stragglers on the quayside and return to the ship, the boats are hoisted, the pontoon stowed, stations called. The operation of departing is no less fraught as the wind on the beam is now brisk, and as soon as the ropes are let go aft the stern has to be carefully held up with dextrous use of the twin screws while the anchors are heaved home and we power out of the harbour, three long blasts as we go.

The return voyage commences, and the passengers try to take advantage of the sun to finish off that tan, but it quickly gets cooler. A deep low has passed over Los Angeles and we're feeling the effects already. The following morning we pass close to Cabo yet again, where *Stardancer* and *Pacific Princess* are making their four-hour call – they too will soon be following us north. Thursday, 1700 hours, and we are passing the island of Santa Margarita. The late afternoon gives a golden hue to the hills which rise 1,800 feet from the rocky barren foreshore. The lighthouse on Cape San Lazaro looks like some long-forgotten fort from *Beau Geste*.

As we emerge from the lee of Cedros Island on Friday morning the weather deteriorates even further. We're pitching now, and spray is passing level with the bridge wings. This is not usual around here at this time of year. A northwesterly wind, force five, plus the ship's speed of 17 knots can cause a certain amount of 'mal de mer' – not the best of endings for a holiday. Fortuitously we have some speed in hand and can afford to come down to three engines, 14.5 knots, in the late afternoon, consequently the motion eases – too late for some.

Night arrives and with it sleep. Tomorrow is another day, another cruise. Our cargo walks off a little browner, a little heavier and a little poorer. For us life continues with our very own version of 'the daily grind'. Our grass, though, is certainly greener on this side of the hill.

CERTIFICATE OF COMPETENCY

AS

MASTER

OF A FOREIGN-GOING SHIP

No. 4050

To ——— Philip Rentell ———

WHEREAS you have been found duly qualified to fulfil the duties of Master of a Foreign-going Ship in the Merchant Navy, the Secretary of State in exercise of his powers under the Merchant Shipping Acts and of all other powers enabling him in that behalf hereby grants you this Certificate of Competency.

Dated this **9th** day of **September** 1980

Countersigned

Assistant Registrar General

P L. Gregson

An Under Secretary of the Department of Trade

REGISTERED AT THE OFFICE OF THE REGISTRAR GENERAL OF SHIPPING AND SEAMEN

Command

Scandinavian Saga: first command

During the early part of 1990 I was at long last offered the chance of command, when a position as master with a Florida-based company whose vessels specialised in the one-day cruise market became available; I had obtained my foreign-going master's ticket back in 1980, during my second year with Cunard. The decision to leave Cunard, where I had been employed for twelve years and had risen to the position of chief officer, was not an easy one. I realised that another ten years could pass before I might attain that most honourable of maritime positions if I were to stay, a prospect I found both daunting and depressing. The cruise industry, although expanding overall, was stagnant with respect to British officers being employed on British ships.

I left England at the end of August, spending a day in Miami visiting the head office of SeaEscape and suffering the inevitable medical. Within a week I had sailed for a few days on the *Scandinavian Sun*, had a day on board the *Scandinavian Dawn* (ex Sealink *St George*), which was completing a refit in Freeport, Bahamas, and finally joined the *Scandinavian Saga* for familiarisation and ship-handling experience.

The company had at that time three vessels operating one-day cruises out of Port Everglades, Miami and St Petersburg, Florida. The *Dawn* was converting and two more ships were in the pipeline. With this amount of activity, manning arrangements needed to be somewhat flexible, and consequently I never returned to the *Dawn*, where I had been expecting to relieve the master for his vacation. After a few days on the *Saga* I took over the staff captain's position to learn the new role in which I found myself – for better or for worse! The duties were much the same as those of chief officer on my previous ships. Captain Glan Phillips, an expatriate Welshman, took me under his wing and had to suffer the heart-stopping surges of adrenaline which any master has to deal with when handing over the controls of his only source of income to a perfect stranger.

I look back with sincere gratitude for those few weeks of initial training. Initially my dockings were traumatic but relatively controlled, although for no apparent reason the ship would sometimes do quite the opposite of what might be expected – so my confidence would rise, only to be shattered a few days later. Double rings astern on both engine-room telegraphs were not unknown. Just one day before I was due to take over command a close call with dock was just avoided by Glan's appreciation of the situation. I learnt that 'small speeds mean small dents', and to 'always have room to make one more ahead movement with the engines'. Sound advice.

The *Scandinavian Saga* had been built in Greece in 1974 as the *Castalia* for Hellenic Mediterranean Lines. Gross tonnage was 7,768, length 433 feet, twin screws and a bow thruster, originally operating as a car ferry between Italy and Greece. Unlike my previous vessels she was not fitted with bridge control or controllable-pitch propellers. When docking the ship the master shouted his engine orders into the wheelhouse from the wings, the steering and thruster being controlled from outside. A somewhat disjointed way of putting a ship alongside the dock – imagine trying to park your car with the passenger operating the foot pedals.

At that time the ship was operating four days a week to Freeport from Miami and three days to the island of Bimini, where she would anchor, the passengers being ferried ashore for a two-hour 'beach bash'. Weather had been excellent, with calm seas and temperatures in the 90s. Winter was approaching, however, and on 9 October, my first day in command, it arrived.

We left on schedule a little after 0830 hours, and set off across the Florida Straits, where the warm ocean current of the Gulf Stream flows north at 3 or 4 knots. A cold front was approaching and the wind was gusting up to force seven, the net effect being a short steep sea and swell reaching fifteen feet, which, needless to say, was causing a certain amount of discomfort among the passengers. The average 'day cruiser', if there is such an animal, is not known for his ability to retain the contents of his stomach, much of which was hastily transferred to that necessity of sea travel, the 'barf bag' – a quaint American expression unfamiliar to me before this time.

Our speed was reduced from 16 knots to 13 as a result of the head seas and high exhaust temperatures on the main engines. Wind gusts of over 60 knots were showing on the anemometer, so our arrival at the Freeport pilot station was delayed by over an hour. The pilots were concerned about the weather and recommended two tugs, a suggestion to which I of course prudently agreed. But the wind reduced in strength to 20 knots and berthing was not the problem we had anticipated, the tugs in fact being more of a hindrance with their heavy towing wires. After only a few short hours we departed, without mishap or assistance. It is always much easier to take off than to land!

The return voyage was not the 'event' of the morning: seas had moderated and winds were following. I remember that the boarding of the pilot off Miami was decidedly dangerous – for him, not for us – and in my diary I read that the docking was 'interesting but satisfactory' – an understatement, I suspect. Strong winds onto the dock can result in difficulty keeping the ship from landing heavily. The *Saga* had, I discovered, a limit of about 20 knots of crosswind to successfully dock without the assistance of a tug.

The bad weather continued for a few more days, emanating from tropical storm Marco, which passed to the south of Florida and into the Gulf of Mexico. Our next two trips to Bimini were cancelled, there being insufficient sheltered water off the island. With the wind blowing from any direction other than east, launch operations could be hazardous, and even the slightest swell resulted in horrifying gaps between ship and tender, punctuated by frightening crunching noises as the two vessels came back together, bending the railings, buckling gangways and scaring old ladies.

The company was going through a rescheduling phase, so I was instructed to leave Miami on Saturday morning at 0400 hours and take the vessel to St Petersburg in Tampa Bay. Consequently, Friday 12 October saw us take one last trip across the Straits to Bimini, return to Miami for two hours, then sail again with a thousand passengers on a 'party cruise', returning at 0300. At 0425 I sailed again, an engine problem causing the slight delay. The four-hundred-mile journey around the southern tip of Florida took just over twenty hours. I picked the pilot up at 0600 on Sunday and arrived alongside at 0900. Over three hundred passengers were waiting to embark, and we sailed again at 1000 on a cruise to 'nowhere', returning at 2030. There was barely sufficient time to take water and fuel bunkers for the next voyage, a three-day cruise to Mexico – we left at midnight. No doubt some mariners would consider the one-day cruise market a 'soft option' or an easy way of going to sea, but I believe the schedule speaks for itself.

My first undocking at St Petersburg turned out to be yet another event. The pilot, who had the unfortunate name of Cropper, was quite happy for me to back the ship around out of the relatively small basin and into the channel. As we came off the berth we lost the port engine, I continued manoeuvring on one engine and the bow thruster but found I was turning too short. It was then that the chief engineer phoned and said he had lost most of the engine starting air. Again, imagine yourself trying to remove your car from a parking space when some misguided fool has hemmed you in during your absence – with wheels that will only turn in one direction. I was informed we had just one engine start left, and I was backing myself into an even smaller hole. Not to be outdone, I used the one start to stop any further astern movement, but by now the ship was moving ahead, with insufficient room to swing the bow or the stern.

It is perhaps at times like this, when all the experience in the world tells you that you are not going to get away without mishap, that a certain resignation starts to set in. Yet I find that my seemingly endless years of training and watching stimulates, not panic, but a quiet determination to persevere. I tried to get one more engine start, got it, then dropped the port anchor – the ship swung gradually out of the hole of my own making. For all the dockings I've watched other masters make, there is no substitute for doing the job yourself, having things go wrong, and getting out of the situation using your own skill and experience. It isn't really scientific, it's certainly not computerised, it's just using what you've got to your advantage – the machinery, the elements and in the early stages almost the 'seat of your pants'.

The cruise to Cozumel in Mexico is used primarily for the purpose of revalidating the United States visas of the foreign crew on board the vessel. The ship has to go 'foreign' once a month to satisfy a quirk of the US Immigration Service, but the trip is a pleasant interlude from the daily routine and, with cabins for just over three hundred passengers, the ship is like a small select club for a very few days. The usual shipboard activities prevail, and I even host a captain's cocktail party, not quite so dressy as in my Cunard days, but entertaining nonetheless. A friendly atmosphere, enlivened this particular trip by a large group of Savannah Georgia 'Shaggers' who all but took over. The 'shag' in question, I am reliably informed, is a particular style of American country dancing.

Three days soon pass, Cozumel for eight hours is just an interlude, and we soon return to our daily schedule – 1000 hours departure, 2030 return, with two cruises on Friday and Saturday before we finally dock at 0230. A certain degree of tedium can set in if it is not fought off with enthusiasm and the satisfaction of seeing the schedule maintained, and the appearance of the ship both inside and out kept up to the standards one might

Pride of San Diego, formerly *Scandinavian Saga*

expect. Inspections of crew quarters, galleys, storerooms etc, are carried out routinely, safety drills come around like clockwork, and every three months they are witnessed by the United States Coast Guard, who verify that our weekly drills and procedures are up to internationally recognised standards. Perhaps most importantly, the staff are encouraged in their work. A smile and a 'good morning' from the captain goes a long way, I find.

The short cruise 'experience' must be one of activity, friendliness and informality. There must be good entertainment, good food and good service, but most of all there must be that quantity which the first-time cruiser expects, but which is unknown – and not realised until the voyage is over and looked back upon. The customers are our best advertisement, and our best hope for future business.

To comply with the local regulations we had to travel 'three leagues' from the mainland before we could open the ship's casino, which of course is a big money earner on board a one-day ship. Gambling, which includes slot machines, is allowed in only a very few places in the USA – Las Vegas and Atlantic City being well-known examples. To reach the required distance meant a thirty-five mile journey around Tampa Bay, and this necessitated taking a local pilot who would stay on board all day, resting for the few hours the ship was anchored outside territorial waters.

Some of these seamen were characters. Walter Egan, seventy-two years old, remembered going to sea on the *Leviathan*. He told me many stories in the hours we spent on the bridge together. An expatriate Australian called Cahill, or the 'Roo', was engaged to a female second mate from an American tanker. He drank lager and tomato juice mixed. There was an ex tug skipper from Texas, who spoke in a Southern drawl and regularly lost more than his daily earnings in the casino, and Fred Smith, who invariably brought a box of doughnuts to keep the bridge team happy. All interesting and individual men who had served their time at sea and opted for the satisfying work of driving ships every day but spending life always close to home.

In seven weeks we carried close to twenty-two thousand passengers, and I made one hundred and seventy dockings and undockings, happily without mishap. There were some of course that were more difficult than others, and I also encountered the problems of training someone else. I allowed the staff captain to manoeuvre the ship on several occasions when I believed the conditions to be suitable. I found myself reflexing much the same way as a husband might when he teaches his wife to drive! There is a fine line between stepping in to correct a developing situation and at the same time trying to avoid destroying the confidence of the trainee – and in judging where to draw that line you discover yet another facet of your character.

In early December we sailed away from the Bay and made for Mobile, Alabama, to complete the bottom and annual surveys required by the Classification Society, along with other maintenance work which could not be carried out afloat or with the ship in service. Another of the company vessels had taken over the St Petersburg service, and my ship was bound eventually for California, a charterer intending starting a new service from San Diego to Ensenada in Mexico. I took a short vacation, rejoining the ship a few days before the inaugural voyage.

I completed another three months with *Scandinavian Saga*, under her new name *Pride of San Diego*. The charter was unfortunately not a success, one of the reasons being strong competition from a Greek shipowner who had managed to start a service a few weeks before. The charterer lost money, ceased trading, and SeaEscape were left with a ship on their hands just at the time they were also in financial difficulty. I could see the writing on the wall, and during my next leave I managed to secure another master's position out in the Far East. My first command had been an interesting period professionally. I had become a ship handler as well as a master. It was to be the start of a new phase in my life.

Sembawang Johnson Management

Cora Princess

In March 1991 I was offered command of the *Cora Princess*. This old lady, built in 1963 as *Princesa Leopoldina*, was best known as Swire's *Coral Princess*, operating cruises in the Far East for many years before being sold to Hong Kong owners Universal Boss in late 1990.

I was not quite sure what to expect, the ship being managed by a Singapore company but on charter to Indonesian interests. Effectively I could have been working for three groups. I was unaware of its trading activity other than that it was on a four-day round trip, Singapore to Jakarta, which did not sound too unpleasant.

My initial flight was cancelled as a result of bad weather, so I arrived in Singapore on the morning of 22 May, had a brief interview with the operations manager, Mr James Seah, and the managing director, Mr Lars Sjogren, then down to the ship, which had arrived that morning at berth M19, a cargo wharf near the container terminal. Fortunately I was to sail for a round voyage with the incumbent master, another Englishman, Captain

Andrew Wilson, who was to explain the rudiments of the business. Apparently, although there was a cruise aspect, the main revenue was generated in the casino – and in fact the operation was financially the biggest floating casino worldwide.

I took a few days to familiarise myself with the ship and staff. There was nothing complicated or strenuous about the run, departing from the two ports around 1800 hours and arriving, after a day and two nights at sea, at 0830 hours. The route followed was via Bangka Strait, thus giving calm waters for most of the voyage, these waters being sheltered from the prevailing monsoon. This was in fact very necessary, as our mainly Indonesian Chinese clientele were very susceptible to the slightest motion and the casino, which was open all the time the vessel was in international waters, would abruptly clear if the ship started to roll.

The ship was rather cumbersome to manoeuvre, having twin screws but only one rudder and no bow thruster. Consequently two tugs were usually taken during berthing operations. In the port of Singapore the pilots and tugs are generally very good, the pilots hopping from one ship to another in a port where I was told there are over 7,000 piloted movements a month. The port of Jakarta is Tanjung Priok, and here it was sometimes difficult to understand the way the pilot's mind was working – and similarly, the tugs did not appear to be on our wavelength. English was not widely spoken or understood, so the operation of docking was often carried out with nods and grunts of semi-understanding. Having said that, I was fortunate and there was never any mishap or accident. Delays were of course inevitable, both arriving and leaving, but as our schedule was unhurried it never seemed to matter.

During the holiday periods of Singapore we sometimes carried up to a hundred Singaporeans, who either sailed out and returned home by air after a few days in Indonesia, or made the round trip on the vessel. The players in the casino, however, usually only travelled for two days, sometimes flying back to Jakarta

Cora Princess, alias *Coral Princess*

only to rejoin a few days later. They were known as 'junket', and those designated to organise them were the junket leaders. I use the term 'organise' loosely, as most of the time there seemed to be little organisation. In the so-called passenger terminal in Tanjung Priok the boarding arrangements appeared chaotic, and I was told money often changed hands for one favour or another. The junket themselves would sit in little groups while their leaders scurried about the place with handfuls of passports, getting stamps for this and paying a tax for that – most confusing.

I don't recall ever sailing on time. We usually had to wait for one or two VIPs – big players – who of course had their entourage. I was also informed that the junket didn't actually pay for their cabins, but guaranteed to deposit up to US$10,000 at the casino cashier's desk, which was in turn exchanged for non-redeemable chips – in other words they had to be played, and if the player won he would then be given chips that he could cash. Hundreds of thousands of dollars could be won or lost during a two-day voyage.

I remained with the ship for three months, during which time the charterers started becoming increasingly careful about their expenditure. They had no previous experience of operating a large passenger vessel, nor were they aware of the expenses involved. Before I left, the charterers' representatives took over the purchasing of all food stores, and at one stage appeared on the ship with Indonesian food previously cooked ashore and put into plastic dustbins, telling our chef he would only have to reheat before serving! I would not accept it – my years of experience with US port health regulations told me to be sceptical of cost savings made this way and the possible health complications that could arise as a result. I did not think the authorities would be too impressed if I took a ship into their port with two or three hundred cases of gastroenteritis on board.

On 29 June I had possibly my saddest and hardest decision to make. Sometime during the previous night, crew member Hla U Min, a Burmese utility hand, jumped overboard. He had only been with the ship a few weeks, and during the ensuing investigation I discovered that he had been unhappy and possibly of unsound mind. His absence was reported to me after breakfast, and a search of the ship revealed no sign of his whereabouts. It seems he must have left his cabin in the very early hours and not returned. The ship had been following the channels off Singkep Island in the Berhala Strait, and by the morning we were some considerable distance ahead. I had an urgency message passed to the local authorities and advised all vessels in the area to keep a sharp lookout, but I decided against turning around because I considered the time involved and the uncertainty of the hour he went overboard would make the chance of finding him most unlikely.

He was, to my knowledge, never found, and the tragic consequences, both for himself and for the family who loved him and needed his support, will always be somewhere in the back of my memory. It only takes a look at a man's meagre remaining possessions to put a scar into your own optimistic belief that all's well that ends well.

Orient Sun

The previous master returned in mid-August, and I took my vacation back home in the UK, eventually being recalled by Sembawang Johnson to join the *Orient Sun*. She was previously the *Orient Express/Eurosun* and originally the *Bore Star*, a Baltic ferry built in 1975. Her more recent career had been as a cruising vessel for Sea Containers in the Mediterranean. The charterers were the same as for *Cora Princess*, and my troubles were about to begin in earnest.

After a brief few days' handover I took command on 13 November. That very day I had to delay sailing from Singapore as no machinery lubricating oil had been delivered. The charterers had taken over the technical purchasing but had no idea how to go about it. Because they had no credit facility, large bags of money had to be taken to buy such things as fuel supplies!

The new cruise liner terminal in Singapore had just been opened, and we were one of the first ships to use it. There were three berths connected to the World Trade Center, a large complex of shops and offices, and far more interesting than the old cargo berth we had previously been allocated. The berth we were to use most regularly was designated CC3, an as yet unfinished dock alongside what was going to be a large exhibition hall.

The new berth was the cause of some interesting manoeuvres for me, and fortunately *Orient Sun* had twin controllable-pitch propellers, twin rudders and a powerful bow thruster. With 24,000 ship's horsepower I could almost make the ship walk sideways. The berth was tucked into a corner, and the T pier, with CC1 and CC2 on the inside, had to be passed to get into

Orient Sun

it. If there was a ship on CC1 there was little room left for error – and with a strong flood tide setting you down, some interesting moments were had! One particular occasion comes to mind when I decided to let the pilot berth the ship, as the bow thruster was not available. He overcompensated when the flood set the bow down, and then the tug aft applied too much weight to his line, which broke under the strain. I had to use plenty of 'screwing' action to swing the stern away from the *Royal Odyssey*, then more power to prevent the ship coming up against the end of the basin. I found the pilots to be very competent, provided they had tugs fast at either end.

At first I used to turn the ship before the Cruise Center and back down into CC3, but the harbour authorities accused the vessel of causing disturbance to their new breakwater foundations with the propeller wash, so a forward berthing was required. I preferred on occasion going stern-first into a berth, as there is always more power available from the engines to push you out of trouble if required, or the rudder to swing the stern away from danger.

We shuttled back and forth to Jakarta every four days, and there always seemed to be some problem with the charterers, invariably as a result of non-delivery of stores or fuel. Berthing in Tanjung Priok was less complicated, as we didn't require tugs and the pilots just stood and watched, telling me when the ship was finally in position alongside, by which time I already knew anyway. Leaving was even easier, and several times the pilot boarded, had his paper signed and left before the ship had moved off the berth. Of course we never sailed on time, but the ship had plenty of speed in reserve so we were never late at the other end.

On one occasion in Singapore the charterers' representative, Madame Koo, and her sidekick, Serena Yeo, came aboard just over an hour before the scheduled sailing time and told me not to sail as the casino concession had not paid them. This was, I thought, a turn-up for the books, as I knew the concession, Ace

Casindo, had in fact been supplying cash direct to keep the ship going. It was all political, of course, but I refused to take any notice of these two clowns until I had received formal instructions from the charterers in writing. A flurry of activity occurred with Madame Koo using her two portable phones to talk to Jakarta and Hong Kong simultaneously. One was thrust into my face but I just reiterated my decision. It was a Sunday, with no one at our office, so I phoned the managing director at home. He duly appeared some thirty minutes later, still in his sailing gear and looking most irate.

He slammed his fist on the table and repeated my instructions. By this time the passengers had boarded and a port regulation required us to leave the berth by 1830 hours, as it was not ready for nighttime operation. A fax came at 1825 hours authorising me to remain alongside and put the passengers ashore, but sufficient time was no longer available for the passengers to disembark, and I took the ship to the anchorage. There was much rumour and speculation on board as we lay there, but around 2130 I received another fax instructing me to sail for Jakarta – and that was the last I heard of that little escapade. It was, however, just a taste of what was to come.

The entertainment on board was superior to that on *Cora Princess*, but in the main consisted of Chinese acts that would come on for one or two trips. The cruise director, Morgan Kent, stayed for a few weeks but was offered I presume a more lucrative position working on board the *Royal Pacific*, a Greek ship which had been chartered by Ace Casindo for the same run – and which was to sink in August 1992 after a collision with a Taiwanese fishing boat. I was sorry to loose Morgan, as he was an excellent ship's entertainer.

The Yugoslav chief engineer, Nick, went home to an embattled Croatia and was replaced by a Swede, 'Pe Pe', who along with his staff chief Kristian proved to be invaluable for their technical ability – and for keeping me informed of their own troubles down below.

Things became gradually worse with regard to technical spares, and I faxed a letter to the charterers stressing the need for them to re-stock the vessel as per the charter agreement. Eventually we had to stop one of the four main Pielstick engines as there were no spare exhaust gas valves with which to replace the ones that had burnt out. I sent another fax.

As we arrived back in Singapore on 20 December, a turbo-charger blew on another engine, so I was down to one engine on each shaft, with suspect exhaust gas valves on the other two. I therefore decided that I should refuse to sail the vessel that evening, as I believed it both unsafe and unwise. I faxed the charterers again.

My managing director was delighted. Madame Koo was not. She arrived down with her entourage of lawyers and technical experts, to whom I thrust a bookful of unfulfilled technical stores orders covering the previous three months. They looked down, and I knew they agreed with me. Hasty measures were made to deliver the necessary parts. In the meantime, I took the ship out to anchor and also informed the Classification Society and the Singapore Marine Department, with whom the ship was registered, and I'm pleased to say they both supported my actions and issued preconditions before the ship would be allowed to sail.

The ship remained alongside overnight, but the following morning, 21 December, I was given instruction to proceed to Singapore's Eastern Working Anchorage. Here we remained until the early hours of the 24th, by which time all four main engines were in good working order and one or two other items had been rectified to my satisfaction. The charterers were furious, but there was nothing they could do. And I found out where the buck stopped – at my door.

The whole business had of course left a bad taste in my mouth. The charterers, either through ignorance or by pure conniving, had pushed just a little too far. I heard later from my MD that their first reaction was to 'sack the captain'.

We continued in service over the Christmas period with no

further mention of this last episode, but gradually, over the 'galley radio', I heard reports that the casino concession were intending to pull out. This rumour became very strong by 6 January, and on arrival Singapore the following morning I discovered that Ace Casindo intended removing all their machines, tables and associated equipment. The charterers told us nothing.

The casino was stripped, even down to the lights above the gaming tables, their staff left with their belongings not really knowing where they were to end up. Fuel for the next voyage was not delivered, and therefore, as I had not been informed the voyage was to be cancelled, I faxed the charterers' representative a message advising her I could not sail without fuel. The whole business was a political game between the casino concession and the charterers – we were in the middle.

The following morning I took the vessel out to the anchorage, and I heard from my management around eleven o'clock that the charterers had cancelled the charter and that the future employment of the vessel was now uncertain. I presumed it would be for the courts to decide on compensation to the owner.

Over the next week, many of the ship's crew were repatriated, which was extreme bad luck as they relied on their ten-month contract and meagre wages to support their families in the Philippines, Burma, Malaysia and the other Eastern countries from which they came and where good work is hard to find.

The intention of the management company was to transfer me to the *Shangri-La-World* when Captain Larsen returned from his vacation on 23 January. This was the second time he had relieved me on a vessel where the charter had turned bad. I left the ship on the 24th, still at anchor in the Eastern, where she was to stay for another month before being repositioned to the Baltic and new owners. The spell in the anchorage not had been without incident, as we had a fire one night in a passenger cabin, apparently caused by a smouldering cigarette carelessly left by a person unknown. Fortunately the problem was dealt with quickly, but there was damage to the area and the officer who should have been on the bridge was dismissed for being absent and thus not being aware of the automatic fire alarm.

Shangri-La-World / Asean World

On 27 January 1992 I joined *Shangri-La-World*, the ex-Norwegian Cruise Line *Skyward*, which was working for different charterers but on a similar trade. Originally intended for the Jakarta–Singapore run, there had been many problems from the start when the authorities in Jakarta had refused the entry permission after an alleged gambling rule infraction. In fact it had again been a political nonsense between different groups, and it seemed ours didn't have as much 'clout' as the other – or at least were not prepared to pay as much 'back hand' money as was expected. Great efforts were made to have the ban lifted, even going as far as changing the ship's name to *Asean World*. Nothing worked, so we continued on four-day round-trip voyages to Phuket, the holiday island on the west coast of Thailand. The island is very pleasant, and gave much pleasure to the crew. The berth was originally built for the export of tin; although not big, it was of ample size for our vessel. The weather was fine and I rarely used a tug. The pilot boarded on arrival but always watched the departure from the quayside – most civilised.

Asean World, named after the five countries of the Association of Southeast Asian Nations, was more of a luxury vessel than either *Cora Princess* or *Orient Sun*, and the service on board tried to reflect that. I stayed two months, and in that time we had none of the problems previously experienced. Many of the regular 'players' would fly from Jakarta to Singapore to take the vessel, and one in particular I remember, referred to only as Mr Wong, came about every eight days and usually left in Phuket two million dollars lighter! One of the charterers, Mr La Tief, would sail with him, and several times I was asked to expedite the docking to ensure that this little ensemble reached the airport in time to catch their flights. This proved interesting on one occasion, when the port engine was not available for docking due to a turbocharger failure, but fortunately the weather was fair, the tug was available and I had become sufficiently confident not to be too worried.

I left the ship after being out of the UK for four months, and went up to Trinity House in London to sit the examination for deep-sea pilot, after which I was fortunate enough to work for the Hutchinson agency. I was not to return to the Far East for almost a year, when I was once more to join *Asean World* – by which time it had been renamed yet again as *Fantasy World*, her third change but not the last, as in due course I would also be aboard her as *Continental World* and *Leisure World*. Only the charterers, who also changed, really knew the reason behind all the different names, but this ship must surely hold the record for the greatest number of names in such a short interval of time.

North Sea pilotage

I had for some time considered taking the licence to become a deep-sea pilot. These men board ships to take them up the English Channel and on to the North Sea ports of the United Kingdom and the rest of Europe, offering inexperienced or overworked masters the benefit of a competent licensed seaman to assist with the navigation in the sometimes hazardous waters around our coasts.

The Corporation of Trinity House is the body delegated by our government to examine and license deep-sea pilots. Their London headquarters are at Tower Hill in an imposing building opposite the Tower of London, and it was here I ventured in the early part on 1992 with the intention of obtaining this most respected of nautical qualifications.

I had studied the charts and prepared a bridge book for one of the 'Elder Brothers' to inspect, and I expected a tough time during the examination, which is an oral one only, as I had not actually been up the Channel for five years, the last time being on the *QE2*. Only officers who have been master for at least one year's sea time may apply for the examination, and it is necessary for you to prove you can safely navigate any vessel through the Channel at any time.

The examination in fact was not particularly difficult, even though the conference table had been set out with many charts, Admiralty Pilots, tide tables, etc. For sure I did not know all the courses and distances around the Channel in my head, but I had most of them down in my bridge book, a large tome of information gathered in an A4 looseleaf file. I proved my courses by taking out my own charts, and obviously satisfied the Elder Brother as to my knowledge. He issued me initially with a limited-draught licence. I had to carry out six pilotage acts with vessels below thirty-eight foot draught before I could be let loose on the largest supertanker.

I was never to reach anywhere near that draught during my piloting time, but I was lucky enough to be taken on by Deep Sea and Coastal Pilots as soon as I let the elderly Captain Hutchinson know I had a licence. Within a few days he sent me off to join the Indian cargo vessel *State of Orissa*, and what a state it was in. Boarding off Brixham by pilot boat, I climbed the ladder and was introduced to the master and shown my cabin, a small drab room with no carpet and only painted bulkheads to look at. The small shower room looked decidedly seedy, and I later learnt that the toilet did not flush (bucket handily provided) and the shower only ran cold.

The run up to Antwerp was routine and completed in reasonable weather. Apart from stopping the chief officer from going the wrong side of a buoy, my services were hardly required. After arrival I had to prepare myself for the return voyage and keep myself occupied during the interval. As with all my pilotage trips, it was this interval of waiting that was the most frustrating – a good book is only part of the answer to alleviating the boredom. After what seemed an interminable time, but was in reality only about four days, the ship left and sailed over to Teesport,

Deep Sea Pilotage Certificate

TO ALL WHOM THESE PRESENTS SHALL COME, WE
THE CORPORATION OF TRINITY HOUSE OF DEPTFORD STROND, LONDON

Send Greeting. Know Ye that in pursuance and by virtue of Section 23 of the Pilotage Act 1987 we being an authorised body recognised for the granting of Deep Sea Pilotage Certificates, have duly examined

Captain Philip Rendell Master Mariner

of _Truro - Cornwall_ and

having upon such examination found the said mariner whose personal description is endorsed on the reverse hereof, to be a fit and competent person to act as a Deep Sea Pilot for the purpose of conducting ships sailing, navigating and passing on the seas and channels within the areas hereinafter specified.

DO BY THIS CERTIFICATE APPROVE

the said mariner to act as a DEEP SEA PILOT within the following sea areas, as detailed on the reverse hereof, as are outside any Pilotage District. Provided always that this Certificate shall not authorise, entitle or empower the holder to supersede any other person as Pilot of a ship.

SEA AREAS _1, 2, 3 & 4_

This Certificate _(if the same shall not be revoked or suspended in the meantime)_ is to continue in force up to and including _27 - 4 - 99_ after which time the same shall be of no force or effect unless renewed either by endorsement on the reverse hereof or by issue of a new certificate until such further time as shall be specified.

GIVEN UNDER OUR COMMON SEAL

on the _15th_ day of _July_ in the year _1992_

_____ Deputy Master

_____ Secretary

3155

where I was glad to depart and take the long train ride down to my home in Cornwall.

Over the next ten months I piloted eleven different vessels, some more than once. The *Green Ridge* was an American cargo vessel of 9,514 tons on charter to the US Defense Department, her cargo was ammunition, and I went aboard three times, always going up to Nordenham on the River Weser in Germany. The permanent master was a man in his forties but still with an appearance one would associate with a 1960s hippie – a long beard and long thinning hair in a ponytail. A relaxed atmosphere on board made the first trip interesting, and there seemed to be little concern about the nature of their cargo.

The second trip I made on the ship was rather protracted, as I remained on board during their stay in Germany. I had been without work for a while, and as I was only paid for the jobs I did, money was becoming rather short – so I needed the trip back down the channel to Brixham, which was worth over £450. I must have watched most of their videos during my stay in Germany, and life was a little dull. The relief master was a rather overweight man in his early thirties, somewhat nervous with his first command. The ship discharged some of its cargo and then commenced loading everything from shells to missiles, which I presume had reached their shelf expiry date and had to be returned to the States for reprocessing. There were the usual delays, but finally the last of the cargo, which was in containers, was placed on deck and off we went down the river.

The weather deteriorated as we passed through the North Sea and down into the English Channel, until as we were passing the Kent coast visibility was down to a mile and there was a fair amount of traffic. An RAF Sea King helicopter from the Manston base could be seen flying around conducting exercises. It came quite close and hovered alongside a few hundred yards off. The side door opened and the winchman gesticulated to us as we stared from the bridge wing. I went inside, and the helicopter pilot was calling us up on the radio. I assumed he was just letting us know that he was conducting exercises and I said fine – it had been difficult to hear exactly what he said as the noise from the machine was very loud. The captain, showing signs of nervousness, said that he hoped the helicopter would come no closer. I reassured him, but then realised that not only was he coming closer, he was lowering the winch wire with a man attached down onto the after deck. The old man almost had a fit.

The captain went off the bridge to meet the intrepid aviator, but he must have gone one way while the airman came up by another, and I was greeted with a big smile, as he no doubt thought I was the captain. He quickly outlined the purpose of the exercise and suggested that he be winched off the foredeck. I explained the captain's concern, that a hovering helicopter above a ship full of explosives was perhaps not such a good idea. At this point the captain came back in through the bridge door looking as though he was about to explode. I quickly explained the situation and sent the RAF chap on his way.

The situation soon calmed down, and the helicopter went off to play on the next ship following us down the Channel. The captain slowly regained his composure and my embarrassment soon disappeared, but I was quite pleased to take to the pilot ladder later in the day off Brixham.

Amongst the vessels I piloted there were car carriers, refrigerated cargo ships (reefers), and one tanker carrying phosphoric acid, the *Sabarimala*, an Indian vessel of 21,035 gross tons. This last vessel I took from Brixham to Rotterdam and back in late November, early December. The weather was reasonable on the way up, and as the ship was only six months old I expected few problems. The discharge of the cargo went quickly enough and we were soon back on our way southwest, crossing the traffic lanes to pass down the English side of the Channel. The sea conditions were picking up, with a strong wind blowing from the southwest as we cleared Dover and I, having completed over eleven hours on the bridge, went off to put my head down for a few hours. I woke up before midday, took a shower, and was getting dressed when the young Indian third mate came knocking on my door with a request to come onto the bridge as soon as possible. I found the master somewhat excited, and he told me that the port anchor had run out on its own and we were now anchored some twenty miles off Portsmouth

Apparently the ship had been slamming into the head seas and the windlass brake must have been sufficiently loose to allow a little movement of the anchor, which had become worse until the brake held no longer – and down it went! Fortunately the old man had the presence of mind to pull back on the engine control, and the ship was stopped before all the cable could be dragged out of the chain locker. Even so, the depth of water was well over twenty metres and most of the cable was outside the ship. The master asked me to stay on the bridge while he went off with the mate to the forecastle to see what could be done to retrieve the errant chain.

Unfortunately something mechanical had become bent or broken inside the windlass, and even though I was taking the weight off the chain by using the engine, it could not be hoisted. We went on for about four hours like this until finally a very large hammer was found and, in true heavy-engineering style, a few well-directed blows solved the problem and the chain was returned to the locker. The light was just going so it was fortunate that they succeeded when they did, but even so it meant a late arrival for me off Brixham, and I missed the last train of the day back to Cornwall.

I never really had very bad weather when I was piloting, but even so there were a few uncomfortable moments boarding and disembarking from ships, and having to climb the ladder up or down onto the pilot boat, which would be riding the seas some way below the deck. The secret to disembarking in bad weather was to make sure you gave the boat a good lee, in other words to place the ship in such a position that it sheltered the pilot boat if only for a few minutes. Of course this was not always easy to do in rough weather, when if you slowed down too soon or turned

A flotilla of pilot boats off Brixham

too early the ship would start to roll, leaving the pilot boat to rise and fall perhaps more than twenty feet by the time it was alongside. Judging the speed just right, it was possible to get close up to the land, swing the ship towards its new course, call the pilot boat in and take a run down through the accommodation, onto the deck and down the ladder, waving a glad goodbye to the luckless captain and his crew, who had to press on into no doubt increasing seas in the Western Approaches.

The large car carriers were the most awkward ships to handle, but fortunately in the main I had plenty of sea room in which to carry out my manoeuvres. I piloted five of them in all, culminating with the Japanese-owned *Fuji*. By the end of 1992 I had had so few ships that I was becoming a little desperate. I was the extra man and not on the divided 'pool' money of the other regular pilots, only being paid for the ships I worked, and then the agent took 15% – which left me with not a lot if I'd only been away for a few days.

I anticipated having to work over Christmas, and, needless to say, I received a call to join the 47,751 gross ton *Fuji* in Avonmouth on 23 December. The ship was on charter to NYK Line and was bringing vehicles in from Japan. The captain and chief engineer were Japanese, just about all the other crew were Filipino, and when I boarded I realised that my Christmas was going to be non-existent.

From Avonmouth we sailed to Cherbourg, Antwerp, Sheerness, Rotterdam, Bremerhaven, Zeebrugge, Southampton, Le Havre and finally back past Brixham, where I disembarked on 5 January. Not only was it the busiest pilotage trip I had encountered, but also the longest. We just about missed any port delay due to public holidays, as we were at sea on Christmas Day and New Year's Day. There were no celebrations on board, in fact because of the hectic schedule there was really no time to celebrate, but I think perhaps after I left them the crew would have been able to relax a little. The captain looked exhausted by the time I left, even though I had hardly seen him on the bridge during the sea passages. It was a good example of the reason for ensuring sea pilots are available, to help overworked masters whose officers and crew lack local knowledge on these very tiring coastal passages.

The *Fuji* was my last ship as a sea pilot. I had not had sufficient work to keep our bank balance in the black and Sembawang Johnson wanted me back out in Singapore. It was a bitter blow to my family, who had begun to think that I would be based at home for good, and that the long periods of enforced absence were over. Over the next few years I kept my licence up to date by returning to Trinity House every January, being interviewed and paying my hundred pounds. But there was still no offer of a place on the pool, Hutchinson retired, and the company that took over appeared to lose some of their regular business. Hammonds in Dover, the other deep-sea pilotage agency, kept my name on file, but it seemed the shipping business was again in recession, and one of the first things companies could drop was non-compulsory pilotage. When eventually Hammonds phoned in early 1996 suggesting a place might be available in April I asked what the average pilot's wage had been for the previous year, and learnt that it had been not much more than half of the salary I had received as master on the *Carousel*. We could not afford to take such a reduction, so I declined the offer, and turned my back on the idea of a future in pilotage.

Coral Princess: a murder

I sailed on board *Coral Princess* between 26 August and 12 November 1993, and my relatively short stay proved tragically eventful.

I can remember vividly saying goodbye to Helen and my son Richard, who had been born in 1991, at the airport. Helen had prompted him, and he said 'Bye bye, Daddy' – not really understanding the reason why, of course, but it was the first time for me to feel the real pain of leaving the one you've brought into the world when he had started to become a 'real person'. If there had been some way for me to turn around then, and support my family in some other way, I would have jumped at the opportunity. My heart and eyes were full. But life goes on – I had to go.

The *Cora Princess*, after I had left in 1991, changed to another management company. I presume there had been problems between owner and charterer until she eventually returned to Hong Kong. After many months, Sembawang Johnson were again awarded the management contract. A great deal of work had to be done to get the ship back into a seaworthy condition. It was never going to be a luxury liner, as it had been let go over the years and the investment required would never be recouped. The ship was put under the Panama flag, reverted to its previous name, and Jan Larson took over command. I was to relieve Captain Larson.

The operation
The ship was chartered to Malaysian interests, and she began service operating out of Port Klang, the port for Kuala Lumpur, running overnight cruises to nowhere, down to Singapore and the odd trip up to Phuket or Langkawi. The passengers were in the main Malaysian Chinese, some regular cruise or holiday-makers plus a large proportion of Malaysian Chinese junket.

Indications were good at the start of the operation, with

regular passenger bookings of over two hundred every day. Some trips were oversubscribed, and occasionally passengers had to be turned away. Very soon I realised that the marketing for cruise passengers was separate from the junket side, and it seemed there was very little liaison between the two. On most days there was overbooking in cabins, as many as eight in a four-berth. Passengers would come on board and quite naturally would be upset to find they had no bed. There was often a scene at the purser's desk, and the charterer's representative was of little help.

On board we had a new hotel manager, George Lam, who came from Penang and had never been on a ship before. His experience had been on shore with Malaysian hotels on the food and beverage side, and consequently he was very 'green' to shipboard life – and junket operations in particular. Initially he was not helped in the correct way by the charterer's representative and was often overruled. I made sure that George came to me with his problems when he needed advice, particularly with shipboard matters, and I would like to believe I gained his confidence. By the time I left he was certainly very open and relaxed, even to the point of being 'laid back'.

Problems

Very soon I wrote a letter to the charterer indicating what I considered could and could not be done with regard to the passenger occupancy. I made it known that even though the ship's stated allowed passenger total on the Passenger Safety Certificate was not exceeded, I considered that to have passengers on board without a berth was effectively breaking the spirit of the law and might be deemed so in a court if there was an enquiry after an accident. My intention was for the charterer to get organised in a professional way, in line with what might be expected within the rest of the cruise industry. In retrospect a far too optimistic hope.

I heard rumours that Eric Yeap, the charterer's representative, wanted to have the captain sacked, along with the hotel manager. He was naive enough to mention this in front of the other staff, who quite naturally came and told me. Apparently empty threats from a man whose way of dealing with a problem seemed to be to shout and wave his hands in the air. A conversation with Eric was like listening to a long tape that could not be silenced: two-way communication was hardly possible, constructive dialogue seemed out of the question.

Within a few weeks, a meeting was held in my room during one of our brief calls at Singapore. Our new managing director, Kjell Smitterborg, listened to my exchange of conversation with the senior representative from the charterer, Stanley Tham. I reiterated my thoughts on the passenger over-berthing problem, and Kjell finally stated the maximum passenger number on board would be 438, only some eight persons below the allowed figure. We discussed and agreed to my handing out a safety memo to those without a berth, instructing them where to go in an emergency, where they should collect their lifejackets, etc. I was told these would only be junket, who did not need to sleep and if necessary would 'hot bunk' it.

You have to be flexible sometimes, particularly where your livelihood could be at stake. So I backed off a little, but said I would monitor the situation. Needless to say it did not improve. The organisation was still lacking, and overbooking was done as a matter of course. I wrote a confidential letter to Kjell a few weeks before I left the ship, as I considered the reputation of the managers could be at stake in the event of an accident. The response was somewhat overshadowed by other events.

Day to day
Staff Captain John Simpson returned to the ship shortly after I joined. We had worked well together before, both on *Cora* and on *Orient Sun*. Along with a new Swedish chief engineer, Nils Stromberg, we made a good little team, intent on doing the best we could on a ship which really would be more suited as an Indonesian ferry or on a short voyage to a Taiwanese scrap

yard. The feeling amongst the crew did not appear to be as happy as when I had been in command before, uniform was in short supply, hours were long and the schedule arduous. The charterer's lack of professionalism and his representative's constant presence, tended to wear the staff down, particularly the pursers and the bar people. Rumour and speculation seemed almost to be a form of entertainment. The hotel team were affected by a lack of leadership, which was a direct result of Eric's interference.

The ship itself seemed to struggle on with a continual flow of defects of one sort or another cropping up. We had no telephones for about three months while we waited for a replacement exchange, and all communication within the ship was done by walkie-talkie. Motors kept burning out and had to be landed for rewinding, one of them being the windlass motor. If an occasion had arisen where I had been forced to drop an anchor, it would not have been possible to pick it up again. Air conditioning always seemed to be on the verge of total failure, and having a cup of coffee would bring me out in a sweat.

We struggled on, and the days went by. Problems with the charterer and our new catering concession were, to a certain extent, laughed off – and our opinion as to their ability was confirmed

Murder!
Then, on the morning of 29 October, our humdrum routine took a rather unexpected and gruesome turn. John Simpson came into my room at 0730 hours, just as I was waking up with a cup of tea at my desk, and said, 'I think we have had a murder.'

This short statement, said quietly and without melodrama, brought me quickly to my senses. A feeling of disbelief was probably my initial reaction. Murder, on my ship? John filled me in with the sparse details as we proceeded down to the crew accommodation, and I remember seeing crew members standing around as we approached the cabin, all in varying states of shock. On the starboard side of B deck crew accommodation, in cabin PB5, we found the body of Ricardo B Gawat, an engine fitter. He was lying on his bunk with his left leg bent, and around the top of his chest and just covering the bottom of his face was a towel, almost completely soaked in blood, which had started to go a very dark red, almost black. The head was lying to the left and most of the area around the temple was covered in blood, his black hair was matted where the blood had dried. The man was obviously dead.

I looked around, and saw blood covering the bulkheads either side of his head. It was as though a hose had burst under pressure and sprayed the area. The dried blood covered the photographs of a girlfriend he had met in Hong Kong – I remembered having seen them on one of my previous cabin inspections.

I was uncertain as to what my reaction would be on seeing a dead person for the first time, particularly under these circumstances. I had entered the cabin with John not knowing quite what to expect, and my heart must have been racing. In a few short seconds, as I took in the scene, my brain must have searched for an explanation, but I did not feel sick or in any way nauseated, even though the situation was most unpleasant. We backed out of the room into the corridor – and I asked myself what should I do? What was I expected to do? Looking back, I realise now that I knew there was nothing we could do for the dead man: he had gone and there was no way on earth he could be brought back to life.

The doctor had been called and was taking his time about getting there. The cabin had to be locked and the body left until we returned to port so that the proper authorities could examine the scene. Doctor Robert came and confirmed the death. I asked him when it had happened, and he thought within the previous two to four hours. The safety officer came up with the Polaroid camera and both John and I went back in, and I think it must have been then that I saw that the wound to the head was not just a gash, but his skull around the temple had caved in – the indentation must have been over an inch deep and as big as a fist. He had been hit by a large and heavy object that had just crushed the skull and had obviously caused instant death.

The doctor had been on *Fantasy World* as second radio officer. He was Burmese, and had taken that professional track because doctors' jobs in Burma were very badly paid. When a vacancy for a doctor had come up with Sembawang Johnson he was eager and pleased to accept a new contract, although he had been away from his country for over a year. I think this incident was perhaps more of a shock for him than for me. He looked grey and very shocked, but as there was nothing more he could do I sent him away to prepare a statement.

We sealed up the cabin and posted a man outside. The crew who were still milling around in the vicinity I told to muster in the crew mess. I suppose I was conscious of the effect the news might have on the passengers, as well as the remaining crew, who were as yet unaware of the situation. I firmly believe that whenever possible the crew should be told what is happening. I told them. I also asked for assistance or information, but more than anything else I told them to try and keep the news of this incident to themselves and not to gossip. To my surprise, my request must have had some effect, as even after we had returned to Port Klang it seemed that the passengers were unaware of the situation. I had instructed the hotel manager to have an announcement made saying we had to return urgently to land a sick crew member.

Investigations

I returned to my cabin with the staff captain to decide the next steps we should make. The safety officer was told to round up those crew members who lived either side of the dead man's cabin and any one else who was known to have been up late, along with the fire patrol, the crew members who patrol the whole ship twenty-four hours a day – they must have seen or heard something.

My hand phone could fortunately pick up the shore telephone signal, so I dialled the home numbers of the senior company men in Singapore. But it was just after eight and they were all on their way to work. I phoned the office, and Michelle, one of the personnel ladies, had already arrived. I passed on the grim news and asked her to get Kjell Smitterborg, our managing director, to phone me back when he arrived in the office.

The officer of the watch was instructed to make speed for the pilot station at the northern entrance to Port Klang, and advise me of our expected arrival time. I knew that we must return as soon as possible and try and convince the authorities to take over the investigation, which might be difficult, as the dead man was a Filipino, the ship was registered in Panama, and we had been in international waters at the time of the incident. Who was officially recognised as the authority empowered to conduct an investigation?

I returned to my cabin and ignored the piece of toast my steward habitually brought for my breakfast. Jessy Cabrera, the safety officer I had worked with on *Leisure World*, had gathered a few crew outside the bridge ready for me to start interviewing. Looking back, it is hard for me to remember whom I spoke to first, but gradually a story began to evolve concerning a small group of crew who had been left to carry on drinking well after midnight when the crew bar should officially have been closed by the bosun. Only one of the men, the fourth engineer Leo Aguilar, who was on the 8–12 watch, appeared in any way nervous or apprehensive.

I started to come up against a wall, not of silence, but of lack of knowledge. The occupants of the cabin on either side of Gawat had heard nothing during the night, the fire patrol had seen nothing, and I had great difficulty in ascertaining any hard evidence at all. I did discover that the cabin door had been left slightly open, but I did not know for how long. The engine wiper who discovered the body when he went to call him for his morning duty said the door was slightly ajar and the light was off. That was about 0715 hours.

The bridge, however, had received a strange phone call around seven saying that something terrible had happened – though this call was later denied. The deck fitter whose bunk pillow was on the other side of the bulkhead from the dead man, a distance of no more than two feet through half an inch of wallboard, didn't remember hearing anything.

I had the distinct impression that the Filipino crew had closed ranks and were going to admit nothing.

The managing director called and I passed on the information. He started the ball rolling by informing the authorities and advising the Klang agents of our earlier return.

Arrival

I continued to interview for several hours until I had to return to the bridge in preparation for our arrival. The berth was occupied by another vessel, but after some discussion the port allocated berth 3 in South Port. We picked up our pilot around 1100 hours and docked a little after midday.

The immigration and customs boarded with the agent, but I had to wait around half an hour for the first police officers. They were shown to my cabin and I briefed them as to the situation, also adding that I did not consider that any passenger would have been involved and that I wished that they could be allowed to leave as soon as possible. Their response was at first favourable, but they backed off when they decided they should first see the body.

I think the sight must have been a little unexpected, as they immediately called for assistance from a higher authority. Another twenty minutes or so passed, more police arrived, checked the body again, and again called for a higher authority. My cabin was beginning to look like a doctor's waiting room, police coming and going, two of the manager's Singapore office team who'd been sent to assist, the company's insurance representative, the charterer's representative – all vying for the four chairs in the room.

Eventually a senior police official, a tall gentleman with a turban, arrived on board and, along with numerous hangers-on, visited the scene of the crime. John Simpson told me that at one stage there must have been ten people trying to squeeze into the single cabin of the dead man – so much for protecting evidence.

I managed to get a few private words with the official, expressing my concern for the welfare of the passengers. They were still not aware of the real reason for our early return, and quite naturally some of them were getting rather irate.

We had to prepare tables so that as the passengers left they could pass on their names and addresses. Only then did I inform them that a member of the crew had died and that they would shortly be allowed to leave. In the meantime, the body was taken down to the lower ship's side door and landed, without dignity, ashore into the back of a police Land Rover. Many of the crew and passengers looked on as, I'm told, the vehicle drove off with the end of the corpse protruding through the tailgate.

As the passengers were questioned on their way off the ship, a large group of crew were gathered together in a public room ready to be interviewed. The police prepared themselves by having a meal sent into the small conference room. In this part of the world, no food, no work!

Both the charterer and I were concerned for the next sailing. I did not want to sail with the murderer on board, while the charterer did not want to lose the revenue. He had friends in high places. I did not.

The afternoon ground on with no obvious breakthrough. I tried to keep abreast of the latest news, but there was little. No crew could leave the ship, so there was a great deal of sitting around, but I think the opinion was that someone would soon be apprehended and we would sail away with everything sorted out, another incident in a busy schedule to forget with the passing of time.

The inspector built on the information I had given him by interviewing the six crew we knew to have been drinking in the crew bar till 0300 hours, but of course no one admitted to the crime and suspects seemed thin on the ground. Eventually, after many phone calls, the inspector said he would take the six ashore for further questioning. He could understand my concern, however, and he received permission for six of his men to travel on board for the next trip to Phuket and back. I knew he was under a certain amount of pressure from a higher authority as the charterer had contacts at government level. He told me in confidence that if he had had his way the ship would have been kept alongside for a week if necessary.

The men were taken ashore and the passengers came on board completely unaware of the events of the day. I was told that the police who were to travel would not be down until after midnight. There was some sort of police function on that night, although that was not actually given as the reason for the delay.

Sailing

We waited until well after 0200 hours, and finally sailed just after 0230 hours, and even that was an event. The tide was strong and the pilot dismissed the tugs too early, and as he went to make the turn the old ship just carried straight on, towards the fishing boats anchored in shallow water. I actually thought the rudder might have been sabotaged by some crew member who did not want the ship to sail – it would have been a relatively easy job to remove the pin which connected the normal steering gear to the emergency system, provided you knew which one to pull, and it was an engineer who had died.

Plenty of astern power solved the problem, and as we reached deeper water the ship became more responsive. The system was checked by the chief engineer and found to be quite normal. I was tired and my brain had been working overtime, I had to try and think of all the possibilities, all eventualities – no one knew whether the murderer was ashore or aboard.

Even when I left the bridge, around 0500 hours, I could not stop my brain running through the events of the last twenty-four hours. I think I even interviewed a few more crew then.

I lay down eventually, still mulling things over. The murdered crew member had not been well liked by everyone, when he had a few drinks inside him he had managed to upset a few people by being hostile, and a few weeks before he had pulled a knife and stuck it into the crew-bar pool table. The reason behind his anger I could not discover, but certainly he had been antagonistic towards three crew who regularly played there, an assistant cook, Recto Restituto, a baker, Ely Dequina, and a *chef de partie*, Job San Buenaventura. These three seemed to be a clique and were three of the six known to be drinking late the previous night. In fact I ascertained that Restituto and Gawat had been seen staring angrily at each other earlier in the evening.

There had been no row or fight, however, nor anything else that anyone would admit. The last person we knew to have seen Gawat was Leo Aguilar, the fourth engineer who, around 0020 hours, returned the camera Gawat had left in the crew bar. A few other whispers came my way, including one from the 12–4 bridge quartermaster, who was in the lavatory outside cabin PB5 around 0015 hours. He heard Job talking to Gawat outside the door, Gawat sounded intoxicated and Job appeared to be calming him down, but the cabin door soon closed and Job was seen a few minutes later talking to Ely the baker.

I was sure this was not the time of the murder, but no one admitted to seeing Gawat after this time, and it looked as though this was when he had gone to turn in.

There appeared to be no real motive for the crime. The crew members seemed to have been having a few drinks and playing pool quite happily before midnight, and Gawat was even taking photographs of the group. There is something about a closed community like a ship, however:. Relations look to be fine on the surface, but discontent is often suppressed, with feelings held in check to prevent trouble. Alcohol is often the catalyst that causes emotions to surface, and that is why we try to restrict the amount that is available.

I heard another whisper that the reason Job took Gawat back

to his cabin could have been to find out exactly which room he was allocated, in preparation for an attack later, and that there was more than one person involved. I knew Job and Ely from my inspections of the galley, and it seemed so unlikely that they could have been the perpetrators.

I can vaguely remember seeing flashes of the victim's face before I fell asleep – even though, as is possible on a passenger ship with a large crew, I knew him only slightly as our paths had crossed just once or twice.

The next morning

I was awake, up and about before nine. We were going to the island of Phuket in Thailand and due to arrive the following morning. I had my initial reports to write and I wanted to see the senior police inspector, Rahmat Bin Ariffin. Jessy the safety officer had already started to assist the police, and I discussed with Ariffin his intentions and also that I wanted to interview some engineer ratings who were known to have been involved in a fight a few weeks previously, one in which Gawat was also implicated.

During the day, after talking to those involved in the fight, plus their cabin mates. I discovered there had been yet another little conflict of personalities and I believed the wiper, Padernal Resurrection, was no great friend of Gawat. Another crew member, Florita Villaver, a motorman whom Gawat went to assist in the engine-room fight, also seemed to be someone with something to hide – or perhaps it was just his personality. I was getting confused. There just seemed to be insufficient motive for killing someone.

I passed on my findings to the police, and they also interviewed the engineer ratings. They started to take finger prints, but I think that was just at my request, as they indicated that they were not expecting them to be of any use, which didn't really surprise me after the way they had all piled into the cabin the previous day.

I began to feel that the killing was an accident, that a group of crew had gone into the cabin to teach Gawat a painful lesson, but that it had all gone wrong. Perhaps Gawat had struggled, and to keep him down one of them had picked up the barbell that Gawat used for exercise, and brought it down on his head, not realising that it would inflict such damage. Certainly it had to be a very heavy object, for the skull had been crushed by a single blow like a nut between nutcrackers.

The blood had even sprayed onto the carpet in front of the bed, so the perpetrators must have got some on their clothing. Looking back now I realise it would have been quite easy to throw bloodied clothing over the side without being seen, but the police officers conducted another search of crew cabins. A T-shirt was found in Ely's cabin with a spot of blood on, and also they found a bloody fingerprint on his locker. Damning evidence perhaps, but only if the forensic people could connect the two with the deceased.

Another little twist was that we kept finding possible murder weapons – two chipping hammers in the toilet opposite Job and Ely's cabin, a metal paint scraper in the spare drawer in their cabin and another hammer under the washing machines in the laundry room. All these were, I'm sure, planted after the initial search, so someone seemed to be trying to implicate Job and Ely, or to confuse things even more, or was even getting some warped sense of satisfaction by leading the investigation up the wrong path.

All day and into the evening I kept talking to different crew members, but was really getting nowhere, I liaised with Rahmat and came to the conclusion they had found nothing significant or he was just not telling me everything. They continued 'grilling' some of the engine crew, and both the chief engineer and the staff captain were not happy about their methods, putting the man in the middle of a circle of police officers and focusing a spotlight down onto his face – it sounded to me like something from a spy novel, but not totally unwarranted, I thought, bearing in mind the nature of the crime. However, we still had a ship to run, and our crew were getting both smaller in number and very jittery.

Yet again I went to bed late, tired but still with an active brain. I wanted to be mentally alert the next day in case of a problem with berthing in Phuket, but little did I expect that the events of the next day would give me an adrenaline kick I really didn't need.

Phuket

The following morning saw us making our approach to the port. Depending on the tidal strength, it can be tricky allowing the correct amount of set, as the tide just disappears as the ship enters the channel and the peninsula to the left blocks the tidal stream setting at right angles to the track. We picked up the pilot and officials outside and I made for the entrance.

Maggie, the chief purser, came over the walkie-talkie about this time calling for the safety officer – another body had been found! The pilot was taking a back seat and I could not afford to lose my concentration, but my immediate thought was 'not again!'

By the time we had navigated safely into the sheltered waters of the small harbour Jessy had advised us that a passenger had been found dead in his bed. The doctor had of course been called and diagnosed a heart attack, not such a rare occurrence on passenger ships which carry a large number of older people. The man had apparently lost $3000 in the casino, but was also known to have had a heart complaint.

Needless to say his death did nothing to improve the atmosphere on board. I spoke with the agent and had him arrange for the body to be landed, as we had no morgue on board. This also turned out to be unusual, as the agent just used his pickup truck to take the body to the local hospital, most undignified.

The Malaysian police had asked me to keep all crew on board, I presume because the murderer, if still on board, might decide to do a runner. In the meantime the charterer decided to take the police off on a conducted tour of the island. They did not return till just before we sailed, so investigations did not continue until later in the evening.

I was curious as to how the investigation was progressing back in Port Klang, and I had the ship follow a course that took us closer to Malaysia, so that Rahmat could use his portable telephone to call the police station. He was unable to make connection, however, and consequently we arrived back in port the following afternoon still unaware of developments.

Return to Port Klang

After our arrival I was informed that as yet none of those crew already detained had been charged, nor was any other information forthcoming. The police left, taking with them Villaver and Resurrection, and it was agreed that normal operations could resume with regard to crew shore leave, so in all respects life could return to normal. There was great disappointment on my part, as there appeared to be no progress, but perhaps this was just their way of operating. I knew the rest of the crew would have liked to have seen a result.

We sailed again on another cruise to nowhere and returned the following afternoon. Still no news. The agent said he had tried to visit the men but was not allowed by the police. All we knew was that the police could hold them for up to fourteen days without bringing a charge.

By this time the crew remaining on board were getting restless, rumours were spreading, and I felt it was time I should make a statement. My policy has always been to try and pass on to the crew whatever information I might have, even if it amounts to very little. I called a meeting in the crew mess for 2230 hours, and when I arrived I found the room packed, so full in fact that some were sitting on the floor, jammed by the door and standing in the alleyway. The officers were behind me and I don't think there could have been anyone off duty who was not there.

I asked for silence, and the noise dropped to nothing, I could literally have heard a pin drop. I'm sure they all expected the name of the murderer to be announced. I was a little nervous and no doubt repeated myself a few times, but I told them the little I knew. I talked for at least fifteen minutes, asking them to give me any more information they might have. I told them that I believed there were some crew amongst them who knew more, to consider their inaction and what it might mean to those held by the police should they be innocent, to think about their religious beliefs and to do the 'right thing'.

I talked of many different things, some of which I can no longer remember, but I finished by saying that, whatever the outcome, we had a ship to run, passengers to think about and our own lives to lead. 'Life is for the living – live!'

As I left the room, still in silence, I felt emotionally drained. I certainly had never had to speak to an audience like that before. I returned to my room and poured a large vodka and tonic, and sat in my big chair to recuperate, Nils the chief engineer passed by and said, 'That was good' – and that was all I needed to settle my own thoughts and make me aware that I hadn't made a complete fool of myself.

Superstition
The days passed by, and still we received no further information. On the sixth day it was brought to my attention that the purser's girls were sharing the same room at night, scared. Maggie talked to me, to explain how frightened they all were, and how superstitious. There had been a crew raffle a few evenings before, and I had gone down to lend a hand with the draw and to try and spread some goodwill. I pulled out the three winning numbers. The third prize number was the number of Gawat's cabin; the second prize number was the cabin number of the deceased passenger; and the first prize was won by the ticket which had been allocated to Gawat, but he had failed to pay his money so it had been resold to Danny the barman, who was one of those ashore at the police station. All this, of course, was coincidence, but it did not help to calm the nerves of our crew.

I had permission from the police to clean out Gawat's cabin.

His remaining belongings had to be collected and itemised ready for landing before being returned to his wife. The complete utility gang went to clean the cabin together – for moral support, I guess. Whatever furnishings remained I instructed to be taken to the garbage room, including the blood-soaked mattress, carpet and curtains. Photographs of the girlfriend were disposed of, and all other items were cleaned to make sure no blood remained on them. The cabin was scrubbed out more than once and then repainted till there was no trace of the violent act that had happened within. I didn't really expect anyone to want to use the cabin, but in fact less than two weeks later it had been allocated by the hotel manager to a new Burmese fitter, who was obviously unaware as to why his cabin was so clean, but pleased no doubt to have a cabin on his own. I wasn't told whether his attitude changed after he finally heard the story.

The following night was the seventh after the murder, and for the Chinese this is very significant, for the more superstitious believe that on this day the spirit of someone who has died violently will return. The charterer arranged for a medium to come and clear the cabin of any evil spirit. I think they were more worried about possible effects on their casino business than our crew.

My own suggestion was that the junket would think that the ship was unlucky and that therefore they, the players, would be lucky on the tables, and thus there was a likelihood the passenger carry would increase.

Maggie and her girls were still frightened, so I let them be together for one more night, but I spoke to her the following day. They had to brave their superstitions, and as officers they should set an example to the other crew. If they couldn't, then they should put their resignations on my desk. A little hard perhaps, but it worked.

Friday and Sunday saw the ship back in Singapore. I discussed with the office my thoughts as to who I believed should leave the ship if the murderers were not charged; also I suggested that after such an event it would be better to 'clear the decks' where possible. Until most of the crew who had been on board at the time had finally left the ship, there would always be talk, rumour and bad feeling.

The outcome

On Monday morning, on our way back to Port Klang, I received a telex advising me that the eight crew members had been released from police custody and would be coming on board later in the day to pick up their belongings before being repatriated to the Philippines the next day. I was shocked and amazed.

After discussing the news with the staff captain and the hotel manager I decided to refuse to let them on board. I thought that once the crew realised that they had been released then perhaps there might be some retribution. I was quite sure that the crew really believed that Job and his friends were the culprits. I also didn't want them on board talking about their interrogation – stories get embellished, and many things that really should not be talked about could come out.

We docked, the agent arranged for their belongings to be taken to their hotel, and I tried to get information from the police station. Rahmat came to the phone but said he had been on leave and had just returned that day. He would try and let me know on the following Wednesday what had transpired.

One of the hotel officers, a friend of Leo Aguilar, heard the news and went to the hotel to return some jewellery which he had looked after. When I spoke to him later he told me that Leo believed the killer to be still on board, Job and Restituto had been beaten every day but had not confessed, and all of them were apparently looking forlorn and hungry. Prison had been no holiday, which I'd anticipated, but I had seen no alternative.

Looking back, it is hard to believe that the police could not have found the culprits. All possible suspects were on board, they could not leave, the evidence was there for all to see – surely with modern crime-solving techniques it should have been a relatively simple matter. We were not originally impressed with the performance of the police, but I am not a policeman. The original cabin search had been cursory, their questioning seemed to have been without direction – and all the crew that were taken ashore were the names that I had given the police.

I waited for further information from the police, but none came. I now consider that perhaps, because the ship was not Malaysian, was not in Malaysian waters at the time of the murder, and the victim was not Malaysian, the case was quietly dropped. They had insufficient evidence and no confession. I also wonder if the police were under pressure from a higher authority, contacts in the government which the charterers had in their palm, a greasy and wealthy palm which lubricated the wheels of authority to ensure their business continued unhindered by the bad publicity which would surely have been generated by a conviction.

I had just five days to go before I was to be relieved by Captain Larson. All I could do was complete the paperwork and pack my bags.

There is a sad conclusion to the story. After the eight men were sent back to Manila and allowed to escape from any possible justice, the wife of Gawat sent a telex to Sembawang Johnson asking the company to do all they could to ensure the perpetrators of the crime were caught and punished, as some small justice for her and her four children. She believed the company to be honourable and the Malaysian criminal system to be fair, she believed in the righteousness of God. I think she would soon come to believe in man's inhumanity to man, and without the income of her husband she would have to rely on the generosity of her relatives to support her family through the long years ahead. In a country where poverty is a way of life and the chance to rise above the masses is just a tenuous thread, hers had been broken.

Empress Katerina

Checking my discharge book, I find I was assigned to the steamship *Empress Katerina* from 23 February to 23 March 1994, just a month, the last week of which was spent in a hotel in Singapore. Kjell Smitterborg had 'invited' me out to join the ship in the yard prior to it re-entering service for a Malaysian charterer whom I had previously met. He expected I would have to 'get my hands dirty' – and that turned out to be an understatement. The ship was an unmitigated disaster.

The vessel had originally been built in about 1951 as the *Patricia* for Swedish Lloyd and their service between Sweden and London. There is no doubt that when she entered service she must have been a lovely and delightful ship to sail on, and much of the original panelling and decorations within the ship were still in situ, including a stone fireplace that would have been more in keeping with some baronial hall. Of course the decor was looking more than just a little 'tired'. The ship was of 6,542 gross tons and had classic lines, although the shape of the funnel had been changed some years previously to give a more modern image.

There had been several owners and many names over the years. She had spent many years with the Greek Chandris Line, who had finally sold her about five years previously to a Greek Cypriot. It would appear that he had started a short cruise operation between Cyprus and the Near East, but this had obviously not been a remarkable success as she later made her way to Vietnam to 'star' in a film called *The Lover*. The ship had been there for quite some time before the owner sailed her over to anchor in Singapore roads, which is where the charterer, Irene Ng, had first seen her.

Arrival
The day I turned up, the ship had just been put into the Jurong dry dock, and the view from the dockside was not encouraging. Years of neglect were evident, and the growth of weed on the

underwater hull looked like something from a reef formation. Some of the fan coral was over a foot in length, the grass even longer, and the thousands of barnacles seemed to be cemented in place.

I boarded in the early afternoon after a direct flight out from London followed by a briefing in the office and lunch with Kjell. There were between twenty and thirty Sembawang Johnson staff now living on board, plus a further twenty or so of the owner's staff, a mixed bunch of Poles and Burmese, with an Egyptian cook thrown in. The accommodation was, to say the least, dismal, old, dirty and small. I was given a passenger suite room – sounds good, but with no air conditioning and no hot water (not that you needed it, given the ambient temperature) it was no palace.

I saw a few familiar faces and met our staff captain, Martin Johnson. He had been in town for over two months, going out to the ship whilst it was at the anchorage, making out defect lists, stores required lists, etc, etc. He showed me around and told me his tales of doom and gloom – not very encouraging, but I had an open mind and was determined to give it a chance. I was soon to be disillusioned by the attitude of the owner, who apparently was living in a top hotel in town and coming down to the ship to monitor the refit. According to the charter party, the owner was responsible for getting the ship back into class while the charterer had agreed to get the passenger ship safety certificate. I learned that the owner had no money and could only pay for repairs, by drawing down on the escrow account which the charterer had set up with the bank; she had even paid off the creditors, who had had the ship arrested because of unpaid bills.

The representative from the P&I (protection and indemnity) club, Swedish Club, was on board to ascertain whether it was in their club's interests to insure the vessel. A meeting in the ship's dining room, which became our general office and meeting place, ended up with a certain amount of acrimony between the various parties. The surveyor wanted to see all records pertaining to the vessel and the report from GL (Germanischer Lloyd

Classification Society), but the owner, Nicholas Patias, was reluctant to release anything. The charterer, Irene Ng, arrived and tried to smooth over the waters, even suggesting to me that there was a special way to deal with this man to avoid hurting his pride – I thought we'd come to get a ship back into service!

Inspections

From the brief inspection I made the first day I realised that there were major defects, with large steel repairs to be made in the trim tanks. These looked like they had been 'doubled' by ship's crew using plastic steel instead of weld metal. In other words, repairs had been made which were purely cosmetic to get the ship through survey, hoping that a conscientious surveyor was not asked to check.

On my second day the underwater hull area was inspected. Scraping of the whole area was taking place and was to take two days. Intake and water chest grids were removed and the propeller scraped. Two blades were found to have serious cracks that would necessitate repair, the rudder pintle clearances were taken and one was found to be zero. By this time the owner's technical representative was starting to get more than just a little agitated, not only with the owner's 'secretive attitude' but also with the fact that the yard had still been given no order to carry out steelwork repairs. In the meantime, grit blasting of the hull commenced in the late afternoon.

On the third day, when priming was started on the hull, I found more than just one or two defects outside: loose rivets, deep pits in the steel and a cracked weld by a void space. I made notes and passed them on to the yard. Steel repairs were finally ordered by the owner for the tanks.

Our men started making up other defect lists within the ship: crew cabins – which were a mess – galley, lifeboats, bridge, radio room, and so on. Much needed to be repaired or replaced. More of our own hotel crew were arriving on board to start the clean-up and begin painting out their accommodation.

I found several holes through the hull shell plating over the next few days, from the engine room and also the butcher's shop. We checked the anchor cable, and found many studs were loose and needed welding. On the following Sunday (27 February) the propeller was finally taken ashore for repair, and the hull painting was coming on well – this was probably due to the fact that the charterer was paying for it. Outside, a vast improvement could be seen, but great problems were being experienced inside in the way of the steel repairs to the tanks. 'Grey' water was leaking onto the tanktops, which prevented welding taking place. The owner was blaming the charterer for putting too many crew on board and thus overloading the sanitary tanks, but this was not strictly true. The flushing water had been switched off and toilets were being flushed using buckets – and as the large sewage tanks filled it became more and more apparent that they were rotten and leaking like a sieve.

We kept our own spirits up, mainly by cleaning up in the evening and drinking 'one or three Tiger beers' – our favourite Singapore brew. The ship was so hot inside that all day the boiler suits we wore just stuck to our skin, and taking a shower provided only momentary respite because the sweat came back before drying-off had been completed. Sleeping was only possible by lying out without clothes or a sheet – I was one of the fortunate few who had a fan! But the food was good: our own chefs did a great job in the grotty galley and came up with some pretty good results.

By Wednesday 2 March, the underwater painting had been completed except for repairs to holes, trim-tank repairs were continuing slowly and superintendent Maw arrived. Irene had insisted Sembawang Johnson should appoint a technical representative to monitor the progress. On the Friday the owner employed a new superintendent when the first had thrown his hand in, obviously totally discouraged. We continued to find evidence of much steel wastage in other areas, around the stern frame, above the double bottoms 1 and 2, in the void spaces behind the reefer boxes. The underwater steel had been repaired, and the propeller refitted. The owner was asked to confirm the stability for the vessel when it lifted off the blocks. We knew he couldn't, and we knew the stability was below the required criterion because his crew had been playing around with the tanks to accommodate the cleaning of fuel tanks near the void spaces, which had to be emptied and cleaned to allow burning and welding to take place.

Undocking

On Saturday 5 March the dry dock was flooded and we were towed out. There had been some serious discussions beforehand, and I refused to take any responsibility for the stability. In the end the list was only 5 degrees to port – enough to get a few people worried. A leak was discovered in the hull down in the machinery shaft tunnel. There was an oil-covered cement box (a temporary repair) there, and water was coming in at about the rate of a normal tap flow. The interesting thing was that this cement box was within a few feet of where the GL surveyor must have stood to examine the water pressure test on the repair to one of the shell holes. No action was taken, but the Jurong yard insisted the ship had to leave the yard. They were fed up with the attitude of the owner and his prevaricating when it came to work orders.

The ship was towed about five miles to the Atlantis shipyard, where we tied up to a large pontoon in the late afternoon. Kjell and Irene arrived and we tried to impress on them the severity of the defects we had found and the lack of progress with the owner's repairs. Our crew had been living in poor conditions for a week and I decided to try and get some of the auxiliary plant operational, even though it really wasn't our responsibility I felt we had to move forward, or we would never meet the charterer's intended schedule. We had to find out everything that didn't work – and it was no use relying on the owner's word that everything was fine and dandy! I knew it would take more than just the few days he promised to get all the ship's services operational.

Flood

On Sunday the 6th I asked our own Indian chief engineer, Prem Singh, to see if he could get the sanitary water on-line. By the afternoon he had managed to get about 50 per cent of the system operating at a relatively low pressure. All seemed to be coming together fine, with a gradual reintroduction of ship services – but my initial misgivings were soon to be justified.

I think it was about 1930 hours, and we were sitting around chatting about the lack of progress on the owner's side with steelwork repairs, drinking yet another Tiger, when the chief had a sort of panicky call over his walkie-talkie from our junior engineer standing watch in the machinery spaces. I decided to accompany Prem down below, where, as we got closer, we could hear the intermittent but rapid sounds of water falling around the forward area.

On closer examination we found that the port sanitary tank drain line had collapsed, and the pump used to empty the tank to the sea was cutting in and out when the float switch was being operated, first by the sanitary pump filling the tank and then again as the level dropped when the tank contents deposited themselves onto the double-bottom tank top below. Basically, the ship was trying to sink itself from the inside. I ordered the sanitary pump stopped while we took stock of the situation.

Prem, Martin and I started climbing around behind the port auxiliary boiler, into the void space around the sewage tank. Here the water was rushing down and disappearing through an unwelded seam in the steel plates, which were part of the repair to the stabilising flume tanks. As the port tank filled it would have eventually flooded over to the starboard side if left unchecked.

Meanwhile on the starboard side I discovered something even more alarming. The starboard sewage tank was leaking out into the surrounding void space also, and here it could be seen that the fluid level had reached a certain level above the double-bottom tank top before the sewage pump had cut in and started pumping out both the tank and the void space. The ship started to take a starboard list and the void space fluid disappeared to the shipside as the water found its natural level. Then I noticed water bubbling up through the tank top, the top of the double-bottom tank below the void space.

What this effectively meant was that all the tanks and spaces in this area of the ship were connected by holes or corroded steel, and there was no way of isolating a particular double-bottom tank, void space or even sewage tank. In my estimate, assuming this was indicative of the steel condition throughout the vessel, hundreds of tons of new steel would need to be brought in, thousands of man hours would be involved, and surely the cost would be astronomical. This could only mean further delays to the date set for cruising, and quite possibly an abandonment of all initial plans.

In the meantime we were back to buckets, and the engine-room tank tops were covered with a large quantity of oily brown water. The latter was obviously of no particular importance to the owner's engineer, as he promptly pumped the whole lot into the dock, leaving a large slick to slowly disappear into the darkness with the tide.

Fire
The next day saw a meeting between owner, charterer and manager, at which the owner promised to provide a schedule as to when we could expect the ship's services to be reinstated, but little work was being carried out on his side and the general frustration level was high.

On Tuesday 8 March we had our fire. The yard, who had been reluctant to start further work until the owner had given some money on account, had just a few men working in the void space behind the main fridges. Access to the space was limited, and burning tools had to be passed through a large lightening hole behind a passenger-cabin bulkhead. The void space itself was about thirty feet long and six feet high but only two feet wide, and many of the steel web frames were corroded and bent in way of the ship's side. These needed cutting out and replacing.

A worker had been using burning and welding equipment in the space, and it would appear that he put the tool down when he went off for his afternoon break and did not switch off the electric current. Consequently the electrode, which was lying near some water, caused the wood and cork insulation of the fridge, exposed by the corroded steel, to catch alight.

By the time we were alerted the smoke was getting quite thick in the area. I instructed our crew to get everyone not required to leave the ship, and to get out what breathing apparatus (BA) we had. Martin took one set and went for the fridge entrance; I took another and made for the lightening hole to the void space.

As fires go it was not yet serious, but access to the seat of the fire was difficult. Fortunately the smoke was not too bad outside in the cabin where I was preparing to enter the void space with a hose, with crew members assisting and trying to couple up the hose, nozzle and water supply while I donned the BA set. I soon discovered I could not get through the hole with the BA on my back, so I slipped it off, indicating for the guys to hold it while I climbed through. They thought the set was to be removed and proceeded to try and drag it away, but of course the mask was still attached to my face by the air tube and I was breathing from the set. For a few moments there were scenes reminiscent of a comic opera while I gesticulated furiously from inside the space to pass the set back through so I could put it back on. The mask virtually prevents you having a conversation with anyone more than two feet away, and when you are trying to communicate with crew members who have a limited grasp of English all you get in return is looks of complete incomprehension!

The hose was passed through and the water was switched on. This had to come all the way from the shore, so there was no instant reaction to my command of switching it back off again when I found the connection of nozzle to hose was not tight and thus depositing more water on my shoes than in the general direction of the fire, which I could see smouldering about six feet away. In the end some normality came back to the situation, the visible fire was extinguished and I backed out from the void space.

I just about managed to communicate with Martin via our walkie-talkies. He had seen the fire from the inside of one freezer room, flooded it with water and come out, closing the door behind. We discussed the situation, and I decided to see what he'd been up to, so we donned our BAs and re-entered the room. I felt around the stainless steel cladding, behind which was cork insulation. There were still hot spots, and they seemed to be getting larger, so we ripped some of the cladding from its supports and tried to feed the hose behind. We had a modicum of success – the smoke certainly seemed to die down.

By this time the yard had galvanised themselves into action and all sorts of people started to turn up. We had a discussion with their fire people, who then proceeded to dismantle the cladding and rip out the cork insulation and the wooden joists supporting. One or two of these had burnt through, and the fire had been progressively working its way along inside the insulation.

I went down onto the floating pontoon where the crew and Irene were waiting, happily chatting and without any apparent concern. She asked me why I was so wet when she thought it was supposed to be a fire.

Martin and I both talked about it afterwards and realised that none of the owner's crew had bothered to assist in any way. In fact the owner, who had been on board, was seen to have gone off ashore some time during the episode, and he did not return until a day or so later. We both wondered why we had actually bothered – it wasn't even our ship! In fact the only thanks we got were from the shipyard, who realised that without our intervention the fire could have become very serious, which not only would have cost them a considerable amount of money, but they could have had a burnt-out wreck on their doorstep to contend with.

Out to anchor

There was still no further work given to the yard the next day by the owner, and it was quite obvious to me that they were most frustrated, as the owner already owed a considerable amount. We saw his superintendent come on board with one or two people, and we began to realise his intentions. He believed the yard was charging too much and intended to take the ship to the anchorage and have the work completed by subcontractors.

I considered it was unsafe for all our crew to be on a ship at anchor with inadequate lifesaving equipment, in which none of the lifeboats had been down in the water for possibly years, in which there was no way we could be sure of putting out a fire using the ship's pumps and fire main, and in which even the emergency generator was out of commission because of a cracked cylinder head. I informed Sembawang Johnson of my concerns. I was told to try and test the boats.

On Saturday the 12th we finally managed to get number 1 lifeboat on the starboard side into the water. The davit arms had stuck through lack of use and maintenance, but we greased, pushed and generally cajoled the boat down. There were a few minor leaks, which we remedied, and I believe we even got the engine to run – our engineers had been trying to overhaul them as best they could. But we found holes had corroded through the steel davit arms close to the support for one of the rollers. This would definitely necessitate new davit arms if a surveyor saw the corrosion, and the boat would not be available for use until repairs had been completed.

I was despondent because of the degree of neglect – but also quite cheerful, because I thought now surely our management could not expect us to live on board.

In the early evening Kjell came on board with Kanawati, another chap from the office. When he walked into the dining room the ship had about a four-degree port list, but as we sat down to talk the ship rolled slowly through about eight degrees and settled with a starboard list. This was nothing new to us – we had been complaining about the lack of stability for days – and I knew that it was not too serious, at least for the time being. Kanawati, however, looked like he was about to wet himself. 'It's, it's still going!' he said, as Kjell looked on – and I slowly smiled.

I think only then Kjell realised that what we had been saying all along was true and not a gross exaggeration. I took him up to show him the davit. He looked at it, and the rest of the mess, and said he would phone Irene.

I think this was really the beginning of the end of the *Empress Katerina* for us. Kjell came back and said that many of our crew would be flying back to the Philippines as soon as possible and the remainder would stay with the ship for the moment. I was to try and check the situation with the remaining boats.

On Sunday morning forty of our crew disembarked and the ship was towed out of the yard to the West Jurong anchorage, where we arrived around 1030 hours. The owner's crew still remained, along with a few shore cleaners to prepare the area around the trim tanks for welding (though the government chemist sent to issue the 'gas-free' certificate had not yet passed the space fit to burn and weld). The remainder of the Sembawang Johnson crew left the ship by 1730 hours. I left four on board to keep a security watch and to monitor what the owner's crew were doing, while the rest of us were taken to the Great Eastern Hotel in town. Initially it was Kjell's intention to return to the ship during daylight hours to continue with our work, but to have the security, and comfort, of a shore hotel at night.

The last week
From that time on we spent every night at the hotel, commuting by coach and boat every day, a tedious journey which took almost one and a half hours in each direction.

Subcontractors for the owner came out and proceeded to do

yet more cleaning around the void spaces and removing of asbestos insulation in the machinery spaces. This was to access the area for burning, but I noticed that virtually no protection was being used to ensure the very dangerous asbestos dust was contained, even though I advised the chargehand. The subcontractors finally left the ship on the Tuesday, after the chemist still refused to grant a gas-free certificate.

In the meantime we attempted to get number 2 lifeboat into the water for testing. Many precautions were taken to prevent a mishap, but when we tried to lower the boat the friction brake just collapsed, corroded away around the brake lining. The boat dropped at an increasing speed, and I had visions of losing the thing altogether. The davit winch, none of which had worked when we first came on board, was applied as the boat fell, but unfortunately the winch motor had been rewired the wrong way round, so instead of lifting the boat it tried to increase the speed of its downward momentum. The extra lashings held, just. The winch wiring was quickly corrected, the switch was activated, and the boat started to climb slowly back to the stowed position.

The lashings had started to part by this time, but as soon as it reached the top the harbour pins were rammed home into the davits and the boat came back to rest, safe in the stowed position, with the davit arms run back so that the harbour pins took the weight.

I instructed all brakes to be removed and their condition checked. The davit arms were also in the process of being checked, and of course we found more evidence of local corrosion. After another couple of days, by swapping brakes bands, we felt confident to try number 2 boat again. This time the electric motor control box caught fire and we were back to square one.

By the Wednesday I had to instruct the engineers to check everything they could get into, even though the owner had instructed that we were not to touch anything without his permission. We already knew that the turbine had debris inside the casing, but we had not looked inside the boilers. This turned out to be an interesting exercise. The firebrick linings had been incorrectly repaired, and inside the starboard boiler you could actually look through the bottom into the bilge. If they had tried to fire it up, it would surely have set the engine room ablaze. The boiler water-feed tank was contaminated and slowly leaking, and the general condition around the outside of both the main and auxiliary boilers was one of total neglect and corrosion.

It was surely now just a matter of time. Eventually on Saturday evening I was advised by Kjell to start removing all the equipment the charterer had put on board. We began the next morning, and by 1630 hours three barges had been loaded with everything from mattresses to ropes and washing machines. A great effort by all our remaining staff.

The decision had been made by the board of the charterer to leave the dispute in the hands of the lawyers. We left the ship that evening not to return, leaving only a fire watch on board – and that was only until Monday morning, when the initial insurance paid by the charterer expired. The remaining crew were repatriated over the next few days and I flew back to England on the Wednesday evening, financially not so well off, but having gained a lot of valuable experience as to what can go wrong in these types of situations, where owners or charterers take on a ship and have little idea of what work and cost is involved to bring the vessel back into service.

Less than a month later I joined another ship in Port Said. This was *Santiago de Cuba*, to be renamed *The Empress*, which had been hastily chartered by Irene to fill the gap left by the *Empress Katerina*. Many of the original crew returned and, needless to say, they were more than happy to be on a ship that was in service, with accommodation that was at least habitable (if not the cleanest) and services that worked.

We changed it back a day or so later, and I'm not sure whether Nicholas ever saw it – but I am quite sure he must have heard about it by now.

The Empress: collision

I flew to Cairo, and journeyed onwards the next morning to Port Said along with three other senior officers to join *Santiago de Cuba*, a ship that I had previously seen in the colours of SeaEscape as *Scandinavian Song*. Built in 1966, the ship had had a chequered history, with her longest period of stable ownership being during the 1970s when, as *Saudi Moon 1*, she had operated as a pilgrim ship between Egypt and Jeddah.

And so it was that we took a hot and bumpy drive in a well-battered Peugeot down the excuse for a main road towards the entrance of the Suez Canal. The last thirty-odd miles were in almost nil visibility as we became engulfed in a sandstorm the intensity of which the locals had not seen for many years. The dusty streets of the town were reminiscent of some Wild West film and, when we arrived in Port Said, the muck had even worked its way up to the third floor of the agent's office.

Brief formalities were followed by another car ride to what can best be described as a modest Egyptian retreat – a beach hotel with none of the glamour of its Caribbean equivalent. The reception area was filled with people all clamouring for a room, the dust and dirt filling the air and covering the furniture giving one the impression of a construction site on a busy day. Somehow we managed to be given three rooms, and we passed the rest of the afternoon waiting for news. Our ship had missed that night's convoy through the canal and we had to stay till the early hours of the next day. We had a meal, tried the local beer and even some Egyptian wine – the first and, after the experience, definitely the last time.

The agent's man came for us around six the next morning,

and another bumpy drive was followed by a thirty-minute run out in an ageing workboat to meet the ship as she entered the canal – not stopping, but slowing down just enough to embark us and the rest of the inevitable Egyptian entourage that always seems to board for these canal passages. Once again I met Glan Phillips, the master I had relieved on the *Scandinavian Saga*, who was bringing the ship over with crew from the owners, International Shipping Partners. Irene Ng, the Malaysian lady who had intended to charter the *Empress Katerina*, had found the vessel when her previous efforts to start a cruise operation had flopped. She had the marketing arm of Empress Cruise Lines all set up in Kuala Lumpur and had to have a ship. *Santiago de Cuba* had just been laid up after an abortive attempt to cruise out of Cuba, so she was chartered to fill the role with the intended name *The Empress*.

We left Port Said on 23 April 1994 and sailed on towards Singapore with a call at Aden for bunkers and a slow-down off Sri Lanka to pick up a few of the new crew. The ship was old and well abused. We found many deficiencies during the delivery run, many poor repairs that competent staff would never have made – and the crew accommodation was filthy.

In Singapore we had just a few days before we were to sail again for Port Klang in Malaysia, the intended home port. There was little time to get the crew on board, let alone complete the safety drill to the surveyor's satisfaction. I had to cajole the crew by threatening hours of drills into the night if they didn't reach a proper level of competency. They responded well and we left on time, and there followed many months of trading. We gradually improved the vessel. We had our problems, small and large, but generally the ship maintained the schedule of one-day cruises out of Port Klang and Penang, with the odd call to Singapore.

I completed my contract and left in late August for a six-week break, the staff captain Martin Johnson taking over. I returned in early October for what turned out to be a voyage to remember. A collision must be a master's worst nightmare, when the speed of events makes rational decisions difficult and the outcome is truly in God's hands.

———

I had fired one of the bridge watch officers for incompetence, his lack of ability being at times rather frightening. In his place came Kyaw Sein, a tall Burmese man in his mid-thirties with the gentle manners of that class of people who have been, for too long, subservient to all they believe to be their betters.

I allowed him time to settle into his new position – he had come from a car carrier and had no passenger-ship experience – but he was in his own way keen to work, tidying out the wheelhouse and even labelling all the bridge cupboards. What he lacked became evident quickly: the qualities of leadership. I pointed out that he needed to take charge of the crew when necessary, to make them work the way he wanted – the way I wanted.

I learned from the personnel manager that he had had a bad report from his previous captain for poor cargo-work perform-ance, not a good sign when I knew that on a passenger ship I needed someone who could work and think independently should a serious problem occur during the night when I would be asleep, or in the event of some disaster such as a fire.

On the evening of 28 November we left Singapore close to

schedule on a cruise to nowhere with the intention of returning the following afternoon. The weather was fine, the visibility
was clear and we took the direct route out to sea via the western pilot boarding ground, the pilot disembarking shortly before
2300 hours.

I handed over to the 8–12 watchkeeper, Mr Lazarte, one of the
best Filipino officers I've had the pleasure to work with. He was
due to hand over to the second officer, Kyaw Sein, for the 12–4
watch. I went down below and prepared my night orders, which
were to advise the watchkeepers to stay on one engine and proceed to the northwest until such time as it would be necessary to
cross and return down the southeast traffic lane of the Malacca
Strait for our return journey. Then I returned to the bridge, made
a brief check of the traffic situation and went off to my cabin.

I must have been dreaming, when all of a sudden there was a
tremendous jolt, enough to almost shake me from my bed. For a
split second I thought I'd had a nightmare, but the ship was still
moving unnaturally. I thought, 'My God, he's hit a fishing boat!'

There have been occasions before when I have had to get on
the bridge quickly, so I have my clothes all ready to jump into.
Even so, my fingers fumbled with my trouser zip and shirt buttons. I raced out of my cabin, almost falling over the contents of
my fridge, which had thrown themselves out and were lying in
my path. I barged past the chief purser and someone else in the
corridor, reaching the bridge in something under forty-five seconds – so I was later told.

The second officer was close to hysterical, screaming at me
that there was no one on the bridge of the ship with which we
had just collided. I could see our lights reflecting dimly from the
superstructure of a vessel close on our starboard side, and went
out onto the bridge wing. My heart was already in my mouth,
but what I saw from there frightened me even more.

The port side of the tanker was against our starboard side,
the ships appearing to be sailing in tandem onwards into the
darkness. I have heard of tankers exploding after a collision,

consuming all the oxygen in the vicinity and causing all on board the two ships to be asphyxiated before a huge fireball results in the vessels being totally destroyed by fire. I knew that we had to get away from the other ship before it exploded, but I also knew that the tearing of steel could cause that little spark which would be enough to ignite any oil gases that were of the right flammable mixture.

I raced back into the wheelhouse, to find the port engine still going ahead and the rudder hard a-port. I blew the whistle in an attempt to attract the attention of the crew of the tanker, who may not even have felt the bump. The bridge of their ship was over three hundred feet behind us, the bow the same distance ahead, and below our bridge wing were the tanker's cargo manifolds. I had no idea as to the size of the ship, except that it was considerably larger than we were.

Back on the bridge wing, I looked over the side – and our bow started gently to come away as we gradually turned to port, our belting rubbed against the tanker as she appeared to move ahead, and finally the two sterns separated. My first fears were, for the moment, gone. Now I had to consider whether the collision had caused structural damage below the waterline. I closed the watertight doors, because if more than one watertight compartment was breached the ship would surely sink.

By this time all the deck officers were on the bridge. I gave instructions for the tanks to be sounded to check for ingress of water, while the Norwegian staff captain, Geir Larsen, made a public address telling everyone not to panic – a fine gesture, but the clarity of his English was not so good and I knew that a broadcast which people could not understand in this type of situation might cause further confusion, so I made another. I had to take a check on myself, to make sure my voice appeared calm, talking firmly but quietly and advising everyone that there had been a collision, that we were checking for the extent of damage and that they should remain calm at their muster stations until I made a further announcement.

I cannot remember all of the thoughts that must have gone through my brain during the next minutes and hours, but one recurring thought stands out starkly – that this event could lead to my future at sea being curtailed, particularly if I didn't do what was expected of a competent master after such an accident.

Very soon I had reports that there did not appear to be any water coming in, the ship was still upright and had not taken a permanent list, and therefore progressive flooding was not likely to be a problem – unless something gave way. I knew that the lives I had under my trust were, for the time at least, safe. A great relief.

The forward stores were checked and the lights on the foredeck were switched on, and it was then that the structural damage became patently obvious. The starboard bow bulwark was completely distorted over a length of about thirty feet, in some places having been bent down to the horizontal. Inside the bosun's store there were three large jagged holes, fortunately all well above the water line. The tanker had struck us a glancing blow in possibly the safest place, the flair of the bow. Another ten or twenty yards astern and she would have surely run over us, penetrating the ships side and into the watertight compartments – we would have sunk in minutes.

The tanker was loaded with 120,000 tonnes of crude oil, so the ship was considerably larger than our meagre 9,000 gross tonnage. One fortunate aspect was that the tanker was fully laden. A tanker in ballast is far more dangerous, as the empty fuel tanks, unless inerted, contain an oil gas that can easily become explosive when mixed with air – and a mere spark would have caused the terrible explosion I feared.

The staff captain was surveying the damage, the safety officer was walking around the ship reassuring passengers, and the chief engineer was in the engine room having stopped the main engine, after we had had to phone down to get the duty engineer to respond to the engine-room telegraph.

Within ten minutes of the collision the South Korean captain of the tanker came on the VHF radio and we briefly exchanged ships' names, etc. I was too busy to have a long discussion in his disjointed English but I asked him to stand by in case we were in need of assistance. Later the staff captain spoke at greater length with the ship to exchange further details. After our situation had become clearer I phoned my managing director and gave him the news. He took it well and assured me he would contact the authorities, the charterer and all those who needed to be made aware. My hand phone had already been ringing several times, but I had decided not to answer, as I knew it would be our charterer, who had probably been advised by her representative on board. The last thing I needed was a distraught woman asking me questions I could not, as yet, answer. As it was, a few hours later when I spoke with her, she asked me whether the ship could not just go straight back into service, the damage being repaired on route!

My accident report describes in brief detail a catalogue of errors made by the bridge and engine watchkeepers. The full sequence of events will never be known, and it was certainly not clear at the time. The following account is based on what I learned over the next few days.

From my investigations, the sequence of events started probably an hour or more before the collision. Kyaw Sein had detected the overtaking tanker, *Ocean Success*, on the radar sometime before 0130 hours. He realised the vessel was overtaking and that if it kept on the same course the closest point of approach would be five cables, or half a nautical mile – not a great deal, but acceptable in the narrow and busy waters of the Malacca Strait.

Some time after 0200 hours he detected on the radar a vessel travelling in a reciprocal direction, and ascertained that this would pass close down the port side.

From my questioning, the second officer admitted that about 0220 he realised that the tanker, which was now almost on the starboard beam, had altered course to port by some ten or twenty degrees. The computerised radar gave a new indication that the closest point of approach was zero and that it would be in just over twelve minutes. The southbound ship had a closest point of approach of less than two cables at around the same time. He therefore realised he was in what we call 'the sandwich' and his only real course of action at that time should have been to slow down – but he did not. Instead, he tried to call the tanker on the radio but received no reply, then flashed the Aldis signalling lamp at the tanker's bridge, but still no response.

By this time he must have been getting panicky. He was on his own on the bridge, as he had allowed the lookout to go and assist the fire patrolman in cleaning the swimming pool. The lookout had a walkie-talkie, but he wasn't called till after the collision. A few minutes before 0230 he realised he should slow down. By now the tanker must have been looking very large on the starboard side. He rang the engine telegraphs, but there was no response from the engine control room.

Down below, the fourth engineer left the engine room some time around 0230. He said later that he had stomach problems and needed to use a toilet, so he had gone all the way to his cabin. The junior engineer, even though told to stay in the control room, left to check around the main engine in use at the time. The oiler was also out, seeing to the boiler, and consequently there was no one to answer the second officer's telegraph command. Kyaw Sein said he also tried to phone the engine room, which would have sounded an alarm in the engine spaces, but neither the junior nor the oiler heard anything. I can only assume the second officer might have rung the wrong number in his haste – or that he lied.

For some inexplicable reason Kyaw Sein put a position on the chart at 0230 from the satellite navigator, just seven minutes before the collision. When asked why, he said that he thought the position of the collision would be important in any ensuing enquiry – in other words he had by that time accepted the fact that a collision was inevitable. Later on that morning, when checking the chart, I found that there had been some erasing of the original pencil marks, and Kyaw Sein admitted that he had done some 'correcting' as the original was not clear enough. In fact he had rubbed out the fixes not once but possibly three times, and this was evident because I had instructed the chart to be photocopied a few hours after the event, and some positions remaining on the chart did not coincide with the photocopy, some were actually missing and others did not correspond with the speed of the ship.

Regrettably Kyaw Sein forgot to call me, even though the standing instructions advised that the officer on watch should call the master if in any doubt or if concerned in any way. It may be that I could have done nothing to avert a collision, but assuming he had called me soon enough I believe I could have turned to port just before the collision and cut in behind the southbound ship.

The other 'mystery' ship appears to have passed close down the port side at about the same time as the collision, 0237 hours. Kyaw Sein believed it to have been about one cable away, but there seemed to be some doubt as to its existence, as he was the only one to have seen it. I would have thought that any ship coming in the opposite direction, seeing both visually and on radar that a collision situation was developing close to his track, would have altered course away from that point – unless of course it was yet another ship keeping a non-existent lookout.

A great many people moved very quickly after the impact, including the fourth engineer from his toilet. The casino was busy and the passengers inside were escorted to the upper deck muster station by the staff. These casino staff were one of our weak links regarding safety, and I had only the day before ensured that they knew exactly where to go in an emergency, as we had anticipated a drill in front of surveyors when we were in Singapore that day. If the collision had been a week earlier they might have been less aware of their responsibilities.

The engineers finally responded to my request to stop the engine after Lazarte telephoned them in the control room, which had become manned again after they had felt the bump. Eventually some semblance of order emerged from the chaos, and I was able to feel confident that we were not going to sink, that I could take the ship back to Singapore and that our lives were not in danger. It seemed like hours, but within twenty minutes I had made a second announcement to the passengers and crew advising them all to return to bed.

We could not immediately get under way because the second officer, in the last few seconds before the collision, had gone over to hand steering from automatic pilot, and somehow had managed to get his wrist stuck in the spokes of the small wheel when the jolt of the collision had knocked him off his feet. A pin inside the autopilot had sheared, and it took us a few hours to fashion a new one. Once that was fitted we slowly increased speed and headed back. I wanted to take it easy initially in case any of the watertight bulkheads had been weakened. By that time the tanker had also got under way and was making for Port Dickson in Malaysia to discharge her full cargo. Fortunately she had received only minor damage, and there had been no oil spilt from any of her tanks.

I retreated to my cabin to prepare my initial report to the managers. I had to retype it, as my laptop printer chose this moment to expire, no doubt having suffered from the severe jolt and instant travel across the desk at the time of impact. By the time it had been faxed off we were heading into the congested waters of the Philip Channel off Singapore. I stayed on the bridge until after arrival and then waited for the onslaught of authorities which I knew were bound to descend into my cabin. The true scale of the damage only became apparent as we looked from the dock and from one of our lifeboats, which was used to take photographs from sea level. It was impressive enough, although not the disaster it could have been. We had several local shipyards come down to climb all around and prepare quotes for the repair.

The time that the ship would be out of service was also a factor to be considered, as the cruises were booked up well in advance.

That day was to be first of many I would suffer being questioned by the Singapore authorities and the insurance surveyors. The Singapore *Straits Times* had us on the front page the next day, and fortunately I was praised by one passenger for giving 'calm announcements', although he also commented there should have been lifejackets in the cabin – not in fact required on this ship as they were all on deck at the muster stations.

Two days later we sailed round to the Sembawang Maritime Shipyard, where the repairs were to take about ten days. It was a busy time, but we managed to complete other work as well. I believe my position was vindicated, but the second officer and the two engineers were removed from the ship prior to sailing. Lessons were learned, and we closed a few loopholes in the system, the managers finally realising that a better quality of officer was required even if it meant paying a little more. Experienced men with good references would in future be employed.

For me, the morning after was a beautiful day. I looked out of my window at the bright new day and felt that it was really good to be alive. To survive such an accident with no fatalities or injuries was luck indeed – but to come out of it with my reputation intact was perhaps even a bigger miracle.

I never heard the outcome of the P&I club investigations, as I left the ship in early January and joined another vessel in March with another management company. So I have no idea whether the true story was the one the second officer gave, or whether the officer on the tanker was or was not on the bridge. One unusual aspect of the case was that the tanker was fully loaded and therefore had a deep draught, too deep to have safely navigated over the underwater banks which we had easily crossed with our relatively shallow draught of six metres. Perhaps the navigator of the tanker had realised his situation too late, and had set the new course on the autopilot taking him towards deeper water without considering that we could be in the way. Even so, it is very difficult not to see a passenger ship on a clear night when the lights are visible for ten miles or more.

Before Kyaw Sein left the ship he came to my cabin. He insisted on paying his respects to me. I was his father on the ship, he said. He went onto his knees, bowed three times and then shook my hand. I was both embarrassed and touched. He was being dismissed from a job he no doubt badly needed. He had arrived with no ships in his almost-new discharge book, and I was not allowed to add comment when he left, so he left with no ship's stamp. It would make no difference. There is a always a ship owner willing to employ sailors with a licence, provided they are cheap enough. Two weeks later he came to see me again and told me he was joining another ship the next day. Another master would have an officer who could give no evidence of his previous employment – or his reasons for leaving.

Ruminations from a master

Or how to drive an ageing twin-screw, twin-rudder passenger ship with a bow thruster but no bridge control (originally published in the Nautical Institute magazine Seaways, November 1994)

Even though I had worked on passenger ships for over ten years, the day I took over as master was probably one of the most nerve-racking in my life. I had spent three weeks with the previous captain, doing the 'driving' on some days and occasionally making a real hash of it. When the incumbent says, 'OK, I'll take over now,' and promptly proceeds to stop both engines and put them full astern it does tend to dent your confidence just a little. I would often end up kicking myself and asking why the hell the beast wasn't doing what it was supposed to do – the engines were screwing the right way, the rudders were in the right direction, the thruster was pushing the right way ... Why?

It is quite simple really. Ships do not always behave in the way you expect, in fact they rarely appear to do the things you were taught at sea school. Every docking with these ships is different in some way or another, and every ship is different. The ground rules are there – but the rules are not cast in stone. The aspiring passenger ship master has to spend much time watching his mentors, questioning what they do and why.

There will be masters who will pick up the skills quickly, there will be others who will take many hundreds of dockings before they feel confident, and there will be others who will always feel more confident if the pilot docks the ship. For all of them there will be dockings which, now and again, cause at least minor palpitations! The scary docking is a great way of finding out you are not quite as good as you believed yourself to be.

In the past four years I have been in command of five mainly ageing passenger ships, I have completed countless dockings and undockings, frightened myself a few times, been close to a breakdown watching staff captains learning not to approach the dock at over 5 knots – and always wondered how I could give to other potential drivers what I was not given myself.

So here are a few words from 'the old man'.

Rule number 1 – and probably all you need to know
Always appreciate that ships don't just go forwards and backwards. They go forwards, backwards, sideways to port, sideways to starboard. The bow can go to port and to starboard, the stern can go to port and to starboard – and when the bow goes to port it doesn't mean to say the stern is going to starboard – and vice-versa. It can crab to the left, crab to the right, and anything else in between.

In other words, just about the only direction the ship will not go is up or down (under normal circumstances). You have to feel it, wear it, sense it – just don't try to understand it.

Rule number 2
Small speeds, small dents. But sometimes this doesn't work either, because speed is manoeuvrability.

Rule number 3

Always have 'one bell' left in reserve. An old American expression for not putting the telegraphs against the stops – in normal situations.

Down to basics 1: Undocking

Taking off is always easier than landing – that's why I'm starting this way round.

I always teach the aspiring staff captain how to undock first. Sounds logical, and there is quite a lot to learn here which will make life simpler and less terrifying later. What is important is to try and treat the ship as though it was floating in air, then attempt to move it bodily in the direction you wish to go, against the forces which are acting in other directions.

When you wish to come away from the dock, the tidy way is to move bodily sideways away from the quay. This is very pretty, but not always practical, depending on the power of your thruster or the transverse moving power of your propellers and rudders acting together. To get the back end off, go astern on the inboard engine and ahead on the outboard engine, at the same time thrust off at the bow. Easy? Don't believe it.

If you do this on an engine control ship you will almost certainly discover that you cannot guarantee both engines to start simultaneously, and you'll either go marching up the dock towards the ship in front or, worse, the other way towards the ship behind. This is not so desirable, because the second mate on the stern will start to panic and give you totally erroneous distances to the impending collision. (Another rule – put little faith in the distances given to you, at least until they get below five metres.)

This method of leaving the dock is very fine for learning the balancing act with the vessel, but the best way is to thrust the bow in towards the dock first (if your ship has a bulbous bow don't be too eager), then go astern on the inboard engine and make sure you have revs before putting the outboard engine ahead. In this way, if the outboard engine does not start, then at least you won't hit anything! If, by some misfortune, the engine does not fire then stop the other. Assuming you have two rudders (it's a pain if you haven't) and you find the stern is going out too quickly, put the rudder hard over in the direction which will bring the stern towards the dock, at the same time as you are thrusting the bow away from the dock.

The master has to watch and remember where he has put the telegraph handles, watch the tachometers, watch the bow and stern, and watch a transit to the side – you have to be aware as soon as the vessel starts to move forward or astern and counteract, sometimes very quickly, for what is not going right. The more experienced master will not rush into something which he knows will need split-second thinking to counteract any problems that may arise. Therefore he will avoid trying to do a sideways manoeuvre if, for example, he only has ten metres clearance either end (normally no problem at all with controllable pitch).

Always attempt to think of your next move, what problem is likely to occur and what you need to do to correct it, and then be prepared for the unexpected. Move well away from the dock before you try to turn the vessel. Be aware of the current and the wind. Check what may be anchored in the vicinity, and what's heading your way. Turning through 180 degrees can often take a lot longer than you expect.

When the wind is blowing strongly onto the dock you may find that you can get the bow out with the thruster or the stern out with the engines, but not both at the same time. Passenger ships usually come up into the wind when going astern. Thrust the bow in as much as you can, then go half astern on both engines, and the ship will back off the quay and turn into wind at the same time. But be careful – you may have to thrust the bow off to prevent it coming into contact with the dock as you start to turn. Providing you have good stern power this should not happen, but this is a bold manoeuvre not for the faint-hearted. If you start to set down onto the dock go 'full astern'. Also beware of the ship astern, for as the bow turns towards the quay it is also turning and possibly setting down towards whatever was behind you!

Another useful manoeuvre when you need to turn through 180 degrees after leaving the berth is to turn short round right at the dock. Not quite as dramatic as it sounds. First thrust the bow in and the stern out, thirty degrees or more if possible (you can hold onto the forward spring for a while if you're worried about creeping forward). When all lines are clear, full-thrust the bow out, and usually it will come out faster than the stern comes in. Put the wheel hard over to lift the stern off the quay then go ahead on your inboard engine. I know your now thinking the stern will come in towards the dock by going ahead on the inboard engine, but in practice the twin rudders will keep the ship off. If the stern still creeps in, ease back on the bow thrust; if the stern comes off too fast then ease the rudder. Once the stern has come off far enough you can back on the outboard engine if necessary. This is a very satisfying manoeuvre which can keep the stern within six feet of the dock as you turn – any closer than that is perhaps being a little too adventurous! Probably wise to advise the pilot, as they tend to get a little nervous with this one.

If the current is coming fast from the stern and you have to turn 180 degrees then a similar move is handy, but bringing the bow close to the quay. The current is usually stronger away from the quay, hence this manoeuvre. If you do not have a bulbous bow then this makes life easier, but it is surprising how deceptively close the quay looks from the bridge, trust the distances you get from the mate (under five metres!) and make sure you can always go at least 'one more bell' astern on the inboard engine.

One way of ascertaining whether the ship is moving ahead or astern is to eyeball the thruster wash, which should be going straight out if you are turning within your own length.

If the wind is blowing off the dock (God's tug) you could try just letting all the ropes go at the same time. However, it is inevitable that one end will come off quicker than the other. I find it is best to single up then let the headlines go first, waiting then to see if the bow will blow off. Providing the stern doesn't rub up against anything nasty this can be very handy, as all that has to be done next is to let go aft, make sure all the rope tails are out of the water and power away. If the wind is very strong normal precautions should be taken to prevent the final ropes parting before being let go. The thruster can, of course, always be used to give that extra push to get the bow out into the stream.

Down to basics 2: Docking
This is where things can start getting tricky. I think the most important thing to remember is that if your approach is bad then your docking will prove to be difficult or even impossible without using a tug. Any angle between about 40 and 60 degrees to the quay is usually OK – anything less can lead to some more palpitations if the ship starts to set bodily toward the berth, and the ship you have to pass to get there.

If you have to turn through 180 degrees to stem the current (always best) leave yourself at least two or three ship lengths to sort yourself out after the turn is complete before you get to the berth. If the tide is strong you will probably drift that distance if you start the turn as you pass the berth. Do not start the turn with too much headway. With twin rudders I usually stop the engine on the inside of the turn – that way, if the ship doesn't turn fast enough you can then go astern on that engine. If you have too much speed that engine might prove difficult to put into the astern mode – the engineers may have to brake the prop by wasting air first, and air is a commodity not to waste on these type of ships.

On the majority of occasions, once I have started the turn and put the inside engine (which will be the outside engine at the berth) astern I do not have to stop it until the lines are all out and the vessel is secure. Similarly, if no turn is required, once I am committed to the approach there is no need to go 'through the gate' with either engine. The inside engine should be turning ahead and the outside engine turning astern to bring the stern onto the dock, and the speed in either direction can be adjusted with the corresponding engine and the twin rudders to control the sideways direction of the stern. The thruster is used to bring and hold the bow on.

Now, here's what we need to look out for:

1. Wind. Look at the flags. Passenger ships are affected considerably by the wind, particularly at slow speeds.

2. Current. Look at the ships at anchor, or better still, the cooling water coming from ships near the berth. You can always ask the pilot, of course, but you will be surprised how often they get it wrong.

Both wind and current must be used to your advantage, in just the same way as you use engines, rudders and bow thruster. If you try to ignore them you will come a cropper.

When you first take over command do not try to drive the ship straight onto the berth. You must work as though you are trying to park it away from the berth by about one and a half ship widths. Once you get to this point move the ship in bodily sideways (this skill you have learnt during your undockings). Don't expect to make an approach parallel to the berth initially, as it tends to be rather slow with most ships. Work the engines and rudder to bring the stern in, and manoeuvre the bow with the thruster. All ships have different characteristics, and it is just part of the learning curve to decide which end to bring in first. If in doubt, try getting the bow in so a spring can be sent ashore, then work the stern in by holding on the spring, but do not put too much ahead power on the inboard engine as the spring may break, causing much consternation on the foredeck, then even more with you as the ship starts to charge up the dock. After a while you will be able to judge relatively easily how much power to use and which way to attack this situation.

Assuming no wind or current (it happens!), then after a few dockings the aspiring ship handler will be more positive with the approach. Make sure the angle is right but be aware of how much space will be left either end once you are alongside. If you take the bow in too early the stern will come dangerously close to the ship you have to pass to get into your berth. If the sun is on the offshore side, look for the shadow your ship makes at the stern, and this will give you an indication of how far you need to come ahead to clear.

Remember, with a bow thruster, you can usually get the bow in, so leave the bow out and the stern even further out until you are quite sure the stern will clear as you come ahead into position. This leaves you with one less worry, particularly if you find the wind or current is doing something you didn't expect.

As you get close to the dock have the heaving lines sent ashore (you should not need to use a line boat) and make sure the crew only send ashore one and one first, and take in only the slack. If they put weight on, it will spoil your balance with the ship and one end or another will come into the dock. Your intention should be to hold the ship a few feet off the dock until the lines are well out of the water, then let the ship settle against the fenders and hold her there with the thruster and the engines. You will probably have to adjust the rudders to balance the push of the thruster. Do not let the men send any more lines till one and one are fast, as they will only get confused, ropes will end up in the water and may get caught up with the machinery spinning round beneath. I would be very surprised if you had enough men to handle more than two ropes each end at one time anyway.

If there is a current and you have to turn through 180 degrees remember that your ship will be moving bodily sideways, even after the turn appears to be completed, so give yourself plenty of room. I have scared myself a few times when I realised I was sliding towards the ship behind my berth. The bow thruster is not very effective when you have more than 3 knots forward speed, so don't expect it to get you out of trouble, use more astern power on the inboard engine. If in doubt stop the outboard engine and then go astern on that as well. Once your forward momentum has been taken off the bow thruster will be effective.

If the wind is onshore be wary of settling onto the dock too quickly. Again you should aim to parallel the dock about fifty to a hundred feet off and feel which way she wants to go. You may have to change the engine configuration, with the inboard engine going astern and the outboard going ahead to keep the back end off. In fact I have found that because the stern tends to 'suck up' into the wind, I often have a job to get it to settle onto the jetty in these conditions.

When current and wind are onto the jetty, the ship-handling master can have his most 'interesting' time – and much concentration and quick reactions may be required not to make a hash of the whole thing. If the wind is off the dock then much power may be required first to get the ship into the berth and second to keep it there while the men are making fast. The master will, by experience, know when the wind is getting too strong to berth without tug assistance. I have found it's usually something over 20 knots, but this of course will vary from ship to ship, and with the direction from which the wind comes.

With wind against current it's anyone's guess which one will predominate, but more often than not, depending on the strength, it will be the current.

One other point. If you come in too slow, both wind and current will affect you more. Therefore there will be occasions when a faster approach will be necessary to counteract the outside forces, and if you realise too late that you are too slow, a bump may be inevitable. If you are not sure beforehand, keep your distance or take a tug.

Finally, when you have one and one fast do not be distracted by, for example, muttering sighs of relief to the pilot. The job is not over till you've rung 'Finished With Engines'. All sorts of nasty things can happen before all the lines are secure!

Conclusion

My ruminations are just a few pointers in learning to drive this type of ship. There are many, many more situations where these guide lines won't be of assistance, but the only way the ship master can become competent at ship handling is to have constant practice, in all conditions. If you work on single-screw freighters, or on vessels where the pilot always takes over and instantly makes fast two tugs, then ditch this!

To all you experienced masters who would totally disagree with what I've written, all I can say is that this is what's happened to me. I know the type of ship I command is in the minority, but they do exist, and by becoming experienced at handling them we can save the owners or charterers money by not having to take tugs. That doesn't mean to say we will not take a tug when the need arises, it means we ascertain by experience the limits and capabilities of ourselves and the vessels that are put under our responsibility.

I 'drive' my ship in and out of port every day, and ship handling is an aspect of the job I enjoy. At first I wondered how long my heart would work under the nervous anticipation of the next docking, but now I look forward to each 'stand by', knowing I have attained a skill few of us have the opportunity to practise.

To those of you who aspire to driving your own ship, remember, every time you take over the controls it is part of your learning curve and any docking where you have no paperwork to complete afterwards may be considered as a hundred per cent success.

Command seminar 1995: a master's concerns for safety on board a casino ship trading in the Far East

The following paper was written for a seminar organised by the Nautical Institute shortly before I left the Far East 'casino trade'. It describes some of the frustrations experienced by a passenger ship master in this slightly unusual side of the cruising business, and discusses the responsibility and authority of the master when dealing with charterers and charterers' representatives.

Over the last four years I have sailed as master on four different passenger vessels, under six different charterers, in a trade that has become increasingly popular in the Far East. This trade is that of the floating casino, and the ships mainly cater for the Chinese who come from the countries in the area where gambling is against the law. Certain entrepreneurs of Chinese extraction have discovered the benefits of operating a casino at sea, and since 1990 there have been over a dozen vessels of varying sizes that have come into service. Some have gone, one has sunk after a collision, but in the main most have stayed, under one charterer or another, and more are due to come into the business soon.

The ships in general operate on one or two night cruises, with the hub ports being Singapore or Port Klang in Malaysia. So-called 'regular' holidaymakers are also carried, but none of the vessels would be able to continue in operation without the financial success of the casino and the 'junket' passengers that the casino attracts. Therefore the casino may be seen to be the prime source of revenue, and events that may hamper the performance of the casino or its operation have to be minimised.

I have been fortunate to have been employed by a reputable management company, awarded ISO 9002 status for its management procedures. They are the leading management company for passenger ships in this area and at present have four passenger vessels under management contract.

Safety

My own experience in established British companies has proved invaluable in all aspects of the business, and in dealing with all the problems normally encountered by a master on a passenger vessel – but probably nowhere more so than in the field of safety.

There is an underlying attitude among some of the charterers in the Far East that safety is a subject that must be observed providing that it will not infringe on the money-generating side of the business, although of course this would never be admitted and the attitude would be strongly denied. I have learned that in most situations there has to be compromise. I assume this is normal practice for the manager in business elsewhere, but on a ship, particularly a ship carrying passengers, it has to be the master's prime responsibility to ensure that safety is in no way compromised.

Drills

One example would be the routine of emergency drills. The industry practice is, in line with SOLAS (the international regulations for Safety Of Life At Sea), to have a drill once a week. The drill consists first of a fire exercise in which a simulated fire somewhere within the ship is dealt with by the fire teams; the scene of the fire is always different, but high-risk areas such as the engine room and galleys are repeated more often. The drill continues with an evacuation exercise in which the remaining crew members not already at their emergency stations proceed to the position where they would assist passengers to evacuate to the passenger muster stations. Finally the signal is given for 'abandon ship', i.e. for all crew to proceed to their designated boat or raft station.

▲ With *Carousel* – my first command with Sun Cruises.

◀ 'Captain Rentell's bollard' at Palma, Majorca.

▲ *Seawing* at the time of her last voyage – the tears of farewell were painted on by the crew.

▲ *Sunbird*, 'dressed overall' with passengers.

◀ Captain of *Sunbird*, 1999.

Caribbean rescue, 2000.
▼

A medical evacuation
from *Sundream* off Puerto Rico.

▲ *Sundream* in
Geirangerfjord,
Norway.

▲ A mishap with one of
Sundream's lifeboats.

▶
A Danish helicopter
visits *Sundream* in the
North Sea in another
medical emergency.
Twenty minutes later
the patient was in a
Danish hospital.

Philip Rentell

▲ Evacuation from *Saga Rose* by a South African National Defence Force helicopter off South Africa.

Philip Rentell

◀ Captain of *Saga Rose*.

▲ With Helen in Antactica, 2006.

► *Saga Ruby* and one of the thousands of gentoo penguins off Waterboat Point, Antarctica.

▲ Approaching Mombasa – at the chart table on *Saga Ruby*'s bridge.

▲ *Saga Ruby* in Dominica, Caribbean, in 2008.

▲ In the elegant library of *Saga Ruby*.

The purpose in having such regular drills is to ensure all crew remember:

1. the signals that alert them to the emergency situation

2. where they should go

3. what they should do

I work with a multinational crew, many of whom have had little previous experience of passenger vessels. The officers are mainly Filipino or Burmese except for the staff captain and chief engineer, who are usually European. I have found by experience that it is imperative for all who work on board to have their duties indelibly recorded in their subconscious to ensure that, when the smoke is so thick or the list is so great, they will instinctively understand the signals and do what is required of them. Those of us who have been in these situations will understand the concern of the master and his fear for the lives of all on board.

The casino staff, who may number well in excess of a hundred, are often reluctant to accept that their presence at drills should always be required. Their working pattern is such that it is often their sleeping time when the drills occur. However, to close the casino for a drill would be tantamount to sacrilege in the eyes of the charterer. The casino staff are not seamen and they lack the belief that they should be responsible for the wellbeing of our passengers, and yet it is the very crew who are 'front of house' that the passengers will look to first for guidance should an emergency occur, and of course it is in the casino where the majority of passengers are likely to be.

To pacify the feelings of the casino staff, the charterer and his representative will attack the master with a variety of reasons and excuses as to why his staff should be exempt from such regular drills, and where possible I have always tried to accommodate their requests, but always within the regulations laid down by SOLAS.

On some of the vessels the casino staff are not signed on the

crew list but placed on the in-transit passenger list, not specifically to avoid drills, but usually to cut down the amount of money
paid to the authorities for 'sign on' and 'sign off', as the casino
staff regularly go on leave. A passenger, on short voyages such as
ours, should only be made aware of the emergency procedures
– and therefore one could assume that the master no longer has
to ensure that the staff who are 'passengers' participate in the
regular crew drill routine. These casino staff are then taken off
the crew station bill, but are given a muster number and boat or
raft station.

Question

My opinion is that no crew or staff who work on board should be
exempted from the normal routines of crew drill, whether they
are on board as a 'passenger' or not. I feel that should an accident
occur, if any of these staff or passengers are lost or injured, the
attitude of the Court of Enquiry, on discovering that the master
had relaxed his position regarding the drills, would not be
favourable – and the master might find his future freedom somewhat prejudiced. I have, in the past, relaxed the drills to once a
month for these 'passengers' in accordance with the clarification
laid down in the SOLAS Consolidated Edition of 1992. I felt this
was insufficient to ensure the successful evacuation of the ship,
but I was under considerable pressure from the charterer and my
managers were unwilling to upset the charterers by enforcing a
rule that did not appear to exist in law.

What would be the master's position in a Court of Enquiry
should the court be aware that the master had relaxed the frequency of drills for casino staff on the passenger list?

Number of persons sailing on board

The Passenger Ship Safety Certificate has a figure indicating the
total number of persons for which life-saving appliances are provided. It also has a figure for the number of passengers for which
the vessel is certified.

The passenger ship which has a casino will, in some cases, have more crew and staff on board than the normal maximum accepted crew figure, and many of these staff will be accommodated in passenger cabins. On occasion, the charterer will attempt to overload the ship by carrying more passengers than the certificate allows, as his representative may forget or disregard the number of his staff who are on the passenger transit list and in passenger cabins.

Often on an overnight cruise the gamblers do not want a berth, or they are prepared to share the same berth. Unfortunately, safe evacuation can be compromised because the muster stations are designed for a set number of people and each cabin will only have sufficient lifejackets for the number of berths inside. On one ship the problem has been overcome by having all lifejackets on deck at the muster stations, this having been approved by the flag state before our management took over the vessel.

Another example is when the crew figure signed on the crew manifest is less than the entitlement on the safety certificate, but casino staff are on the transit passenger list, living in passenger accommodation. On a busy night the charterer again tries to overload the recognised certificate passenger figure, and I have authorised the purser to move staff from the passenger list to the crew list, where 'space' was still available. The charterers' representatives could not accept that the ship would be sailing illegally by exceeding the certificate's passenger figure, as they only considered the total souls on board figure as indicated. They were also reluctant to put any of the gamblers ashore and suffer a potential loss of revenue, not only on that voyage but also in the future if the action was promulgated between the 'junket' coordinators.

I was instructed by my managers on one vessel to take up to the total passengers as allowed by the certificate, even though they all would not have a designated berth. The result was that, on occasion, there were up to eight or ten persons allocated a double-berth cabin where only two lifejackets were available.

I instigated measures to try and advise the passengers where their muster stations and extra lifejackets were allocated, but we found that there was virtually no interest shown by these gamblers with regard to their personal safety, and the fact that an emergency could arise did not concern them.

I have never sailed with more than the number of persons for which there are life-saving appliances, nor with a greater number of passengers than the passenger certificate indicates the vessel is certified to carry, although a certain amount of 'juggling' has had to be done on one or two occasions.

Question
Should the master allow the transfer of casino staff on the passenger transit manifest to the crew manifest, and thus allow the full complement of 'normal' passengers to travel, even if they do not have an allocated berth, particularly if the lifejackets are in the cabins and not at the muster stations?

Technical safety
On one of the vessels I have had problems with the charterers regarding their performance in maintaining the machinery in line with the clauses stipulated in the charter party. In this particular instance the charterer decided to take away the technical purchasing from the managers and procure all spares and consumable stores themselves. They had already taken over the purchasing of housekeeping and food consumables, so when I observed the delivery of ship's stores in the boot of the charterer's representative's car I felt this could only be indicative of bad times ahead.

Their inexperience in the field of technical purchasing soon became apparent, as virtually no spares were delivered to the ship, and because of previous bad experiences suppliers of oils and other consumables required payment before delivery.

The managers became frustrated by the non-payment to them of bills already settled on the charterer's behalf, and in fact they were owed a considerable amount. I dealt directly with the charterer's wife, who spoke little English, and her Singaporean representative, another young Chinese lady with little previous knowledge of our business.

The lack of technical spares on board caused concern, and dealing with the two ladies only caused increased frustration when requests for urgent spares were met by assurances that they would speak to the charterer. Needless to say there soon came a time when machinery had to be stopped. One of the Pielstick main engines was the first to go, when we ran out of exhaust gas valve spindles.

I informed the managers, who asked me to fax the charterer. I advised the charterer, also pointing out the charter party obligation to ensure the vessel was operated and maintained in line with normal commercial practice. I added that if I felt that lack of such maintenance might affect the safety of the vessel or those on board, I would consider keeping the vessel alongside.

Neither the charterer nor his representatives replied, nor did they supply any spares. Within a week a turbocharger failure on another engine, connected to the same shaft, left me with two engines and one propeller. The chief engineer advised me that he suspected more exhaust gas valve spindles on the remaining engines would need replacing soon.

I informed the managers and let them be aware that I felt it was now unwise to sail. I was advised to inform the charterer.

Two hours later I had both charterer's representatives in my room, along with two technical experts from a firm of marine consultants, demanding to know why I refused to sail the vessel. After explaining the problem and showing them an A4 file with over 150 technical requisitions unfulfilled they became a little more sympathetic.

In the meantime I had asked for a representative from the vessel's classification society to attend, as well as one from the country under whose flag the ship was registered, which happened to be Singapore, the vessel's location at that time. I asked for their assistance and eventually they agreed, albeit reluctantly, to verify that the ship should not sail until the engines had become serviceable and a minimum amount of spares were placed on board. I took the ship to anchor, where we remained for four days.

Although I felt isolated against the charterer, without assistance or backup from my managers or their superintendent, my managing director advised me later that the first call he received after I stopped the ship was from the charterer's lawyer, who insisted that I be immediately removed from the vessel. The MD declined, stating that the master was simply doing the job he was paid for.

I felt that my understanding of the charter party warranted my action, but I would have been more comfortable if my managers or the ship's superintendent had backed my decision or given further advice. I felt particularly let down by both the class and flag-state surveyor, who almost had to be bullied into keeping the ship alongside.

Questions

1. Why should charterers intimidate the master or their representatives who take over the responsibility of operating a passenger ship, having had no experience before, and declining to accept the decisions or advice of the master?

2. Should the master deal directly with the charterer, or should the managers act on his behalf, particularly with apparent breaches of the charter party?

3. Was I right in refusing to take the vessel to sea?

Conclusions

These three examples are only a sample of my experiences. Fortunately my tales of woe have been spread over a number of years, and these recollections do not all come from the same ship, but I can only assume that what I have experienced has been or will be experienced by others.

Personally I feel that the United States Coast Guard has been instrumental in ensuring that passenger vessels operating into ports of the United States maintain a high standard with regard to safety. Owners and charterers are aware and committed to complying with their rules, there is no question as to whether regulations can be 'slightly' ignored, or standards of maintenance allowed to fall, as the Coast Guard insist that a full inspection plus safety drills must be carried out every three months.

Elsewhere in the world, the master must rely on Port State Control inspections, no more frequent than every six months. The inspectors, in practice, are not as thorough, nor do they appear to have the same willingness to detain a vessel, compared to those of the United States Coast Guard.

Because the charterers are not under the same pressure to satisfy the authorities we are reliant on the hapless master to ensure that his vessel stays within the regulations laid down by SOLAS. The flag state and class surveyors appear reluctant to be too firm on operators or managers, with class in particular willing only to give a 'condition' on certain defects. I cannot recall how many times I have seen 'overdue' on the Continuous Survey Cycle printout. Surveyors may give the impression of 'getting tough', but I have found that when it comes to the crunch they are usually willing to grant a period of time for the ship to 'shape up'.

Perhaps my standards for safety are too high. I am aware that there has to be flexibility in ship operation, but when it comes to standards for safety the master will not be protected from unscrupulous charterers until there is a system of inspection and detention which has as many teeth as that of the United States Coast Guard.

Addendum

A few weeks after I wrote this seminar paper the gentleman in charge of the casino concession on board approached me.

Amongst other things he discussed his firm belief in proper safety training on board and mentioned that, in the event of an emergency, his staff on hearing the alarm bells should rack the chips and hand them to the cashier, who would put them into and lock the safe. He had allocated ten minutes for his staff to achieve this task, a further ten minutes for them to collect their lifejackets and ten more minutes to abandon the ship. He had obviously worked everything out in advance. Who said a little knowledge was a dangerous thing?

Ten years of
Sun Cruises

Sunrise: the birth of a cruise line

In late 1994 Airtours, one of the larger travel companies in the UK, established a subsidiary called Sun Cruises and bought two second-hand passenger cruise vessels. The first was the ex Norwegian Cruise Line *Southward*, which under her new name of *Seawing* entered service in early April 1995. The second was the ex Royal Caribbean Cruise Line *Nordic Prince*, later to become *Carousel*.

Because of their lack of ship management experience, Airtours employed the original owner to manage *Seawing*, while *Carousel* was to be managed by a Monaco ship management company, V.Ships. This latter company had originally been part of the Vlasov group, the Italian company that had for many years owned Sitmar Line before it had eventually been bought by P&O. V.Ships was coming back into the cruise market after a five-year absence, managing and owning their own vessels.

I had returned from the Far East in early January, noticed in the shipping publications that a new British cruise company was being formed, and therefore decided to see whether I could get in on the ground floor. I first phoned Airtours head office at Helmshore near Manchester and was advised to send in my CV. A friend also told me that V.Ships were recruiting, so I gave their Southampton office a call.

After a week or so I was invited to Southampton for an

interview, which appeared to go well – but I guess it was a mistake to show them a photo of my last ship after a collision. I left and never heard a thing. But almost two weeks later I was asked by a London recruitment agency if I was available to work as master on a Mediterranean-based cruise vessel, the *Carousel*. It was clear that for some reason they were still looking for a master, so I revamped my CV, gave Captain Ridley (from the *QE2*) as a reference and faxed it off. The following Sunday I was offered the job.

Baltimore and the Atlantic

The following week the ship was to be handed over in Baltimore after a brief dry-docking. I left the UK on 7 March, and joined the ship still high and dry in a floating dock. The Crown Lounge, a bar surrounding the funnel, was in the process of being removed. RCCL had decided that this particular appendage was their trademark and therefore not to be passed on with the sale. I met the Norwegian master and other crew, moved on board and began to make myself familiar with my new surroundings.

There was a certain apprehension among the incumbents, who seemed busy trying to remove any item that might give the new owners a market advantage. All RCCL papers and official documents were boxed up and taken away. Even the computer spares system was to be removed, as Airtours considered the system outdated and not worth the asking price. This was later to cause a few a problems, as we only had one hard copy of the list that contained the thousands of spares on board.

A few of our new crew were allowed to live on board, but the majority had to wait until the official handover day, Monday 13 March. The dock was flooded down and the ship was moved to the lay-by berth without engines. The old crew departed and I was left to galvanise our new staff into action, setting an intended sailing date as the following Thursday, destination Palermo, Sicily, for refitting.

The *Carousel* was by far the largest vessel I had commanded to date, 23,149 gross tons, 194.3 metres long, 24 metres wide.

Carousel

She had been built in Finland in 1971 by Wärtsilä of Helsinki and lengthened in 1980 by adding 26 metres into her mid-section. Needless to say I was a little apprehensive when it came to manoeuvring the vessel out from the dockyard. Fortunately the weather was fine with little wind and, more to the point, she was pointing in the right direction.

We left the yard at 1100 hours on 16 March with the Chesapeake Bay pilot embarked, all four main engines having been started and on-line. Within fifteen minutes one of them stopped, and it took the engineers almost three days to get it going again. Even the three Norwegian engineers we carried had difficulty isolating the problem. The loss of one engine made only a small difference to the top speed, a reduction of only 2 or 3 knots. The pilot left us at Cape Henry shortly before 2100 hours and we set a great circle course across the Atlantic.

The voyage went without any serious mishap, the weather being reasonable for the time of year, mainly following seas that the ship coped with very well. We arrived off Gibraltar during the late morning of 25 March, and embarked six staff from the ship managers before proceeding on our way to Palermo, arriving there at 0800 hours on the 28th. The local tugs were on strike and we had to remain at anchor until the following morning, so it wasn't until 1218 hours that we rang finished with engines and completed our first voyage, a distance of well over 4,000 miles.

The vessel was due to be dry-docked again in Palermo, but the majority of the work was the refurbishment of cabins, alleyways and other passenger spaces. We were due to commence cruising on 6 May, which seemed to give plenty of time for the task in hand. The chief engineer, John Mealing, had set himself a considerable work list, knowing that this period would be the last for some considerable time when much of the machinery plant could be closed down.

Palermo and the refit

In the event we found that the local shipyard was extremely slow in achieving results, although much was promised. The UK subcontractors for the hotel refurbishing work started well, but towards the end were overstretched and failed to complete the work to our satisfaction. Many plumbing problems had to be sorted out over the ensuing weeks, after cruising commenced, to correct poor workmanship. The last few days were extremely hectic, the ship still being in the dry dock – which was not flooded up until the night before sailing. Stores were taken on, a mammoth operation in itself and only just completed in time.

The rest of the ship's complement arrived during this period, and there was much safety and occupational training to be carried out. Peter Greenhow was the safety officer, and he worked with great diligence to ensure the programme ran as smoothly as could be expected. The affable and competent Alfredo Romeo, an Italian from Costa Line, came on board as my staff captain and quickly took over the role I had been monitoring. My own workload had increased dramatically as the weeks progressed, so I was very pleased when Alfredo arrived, on a night, as it so happened, when Peter and I were ashore for a few hours taking a meal. One of the laundry water tanks, in the process of being slowly filled, overflowed into the forward pump room through a pipe which should have not existed, and Alfredo found himself immediately getting involved with making decisions in our absence. He no doubt wondered what he'd let himself in for.

I remember that it was very touch and go that we should leave on time. Airtours wanted us to be in Palma on Thursday 4 May, ready for some show rounds, a christening of the new name on Friday and sailing on Saturday with a full load of passengers. Before that, however, we had to berth in Barcelona to take stores. I have never seen anyone look so tired as John Mealing before we sailed from Palermo – he must have had no more than ten hours' sleep in the previous four or five days. An older man I am sure would have cracked under the mental and physical stress, not only because of the sheer number of repairs and maintenance jobs, but also because of the quality of his staff. Several had poor English, one Polish officer was fired because he had none and managed to pollute the dock with fuel oil, others had insufficient experience for a complicated plant, and the Italian staff engineer was riding his officers so hard that they threatened to walk off.

There was no time to go first to a lay-by berth, and I piloted the ship out of the dry dock, under our own power, to sea. The departure and subsequent arrival in Barcelona were all part of my own learning curve in how to handle the ship. In fact I found things a lot easier than on *The Empress*, my previous ship. *Carousel* had bridge control and was relatively responsive to adjustments of the pitch controls on the bridge, except that, because of her size, things took that much longer to happen – and this I had to learn quickly.

Barcelona was one mad scramble. But, much to the surprise of the local agent, all stores were placed on board in reasonable time, so we sailed the same evening for Palma. Down below in the stores area it was just a mess: far too much had been ordered, enough in fact to keep the ship going for at least two weeks. A new programme of storing weekly had to be worked out for the future.

Palma and the commencement of cruising
In Palma the final work should have been completed ready for the passengers, but the subcontractors left us in the lurch and

there were many problems all over the vessel. On Friday I took the ship over to the ferry pier ready for the naming ceremony. Now, more than ever before, I had to wear the hat of the social captain. I met many of the senior people from Airtours including David Crossland the chairman and Hugh Collinson the managing director, whose wife was to launch the large champagne bottle. The bosun had very ingeniously prepared this so that it would swing down onto the name and break when the ribbon was cut.

A crowd of over two hundred was present for the ceremony, including local dignitaries and a brass band. The day was beautiful, and everything went off without a hitch, the bottle breaking spectacularly over the name on the bow as planned. A reception was later held on board.

The next day was probably even more frenetic. The passengers started arriving by ten in the morning, and a certain amount of confusion seemed to be the order of the day. Unfortunately the company had booked us with a full ship, thus not allowing any leeway for unfinished cabins, floods and so on, which are the norm after a major refit. Four coaches arrived after our scheduled departure time, and the correlating of passport numbers took several more hours. We eventually sailed just after 0100 hours on Sunday morning.

The first week was of course new to all the crew and staff, with over 1,100 passengers to feed, entertain and look after. Many problems came to light, some of which were expected, many of which were not. There was a water leak forward, causing wet carpets in crew accommodation. The new officers' mess had not been completed, and consequently the officers had to eat their meals at the deck buffet. There was a problem in pumping ballast caused by valves passing, which in turn created problems for the staff captain in keeping the ship upright. The lack of cleanliness in the galley also gave me cause for concern.

Our itinerary for the first week was Malta, Catania in Sicily, Naples, Alghero in Sardinia, and Mahon in Minorca. We were late arriving at Malta because of the late departure, but we stayed until after 2300 hours, when a large fireworks display was staged to celebrate VE Day. Alghero was the only anchor port, and it proved to be a non-starter when we arrived due to swell conditions. Unfortunately it had been planned as an afternoon call and, having had much experience on *QE2*, I realised that in order to get over 1,100 passengers off and back on board again safely in the time available, the conditions had to be just right. I took the ship away and closed the cliffs of Capo Caccia, which are spectacular seen from the sea. The water is very deep, and I could get within a third of a mile from the surf breaking on the rocks.

The following week was the alternate itinerary, Ajaccio in Corsica, Civitavecchia, the port for Rome, Elba island, Villefranche and Barcelona. We had to anchor at Elba, while at Villefranche the pilot advised me to use mooring lines forward to a buoy in the bay. This turned out to be a poor move, as the wind and swell increased during the morning causing the pontoon that had been provided by the port to move up and down dangerously. There was no lee provided, and consequently I decided to call the pilot back and manoeuvre the ship to a safer position. Needless to say, in the unpleasant weather conditions, this operation took a few hours as I had to slip the buoy, place the ship in a broadside direction to the swell, drop the anchor and then back down to the inner buoy and pass a line though the buoy shackle and back to the ship. There were a few pulse-increasing moments, but we succeeded eventually and continued the launch operation. Because of the delays some passengers didn't manage to get ashore and were then put off by the torrential rain – not a good day!

Problems

There had been quite a number of diarrhoea and vomiting cases during the trip, and I started pushing hard for the food department to get their areas cleaned up. Neither the executive chef nor the food manager appeared to realise the gravity of the situation, one which was about to erupt quite spectacularly, justifying my original concerns.

The chairman, Mr Crossland, came aboard on the next Saturday evening. He saw me later and asked what needed to be done to improve the food, having just had a meal in the restaurant. The food was certainly the worst I had tasted on a 'proper' cruise ship.

During the third week we found out that a passenger was reporting back directly to Mr Crossland with some alarming and damning facts about the operation, going so far as to say that a major outbreak of food poisoning could erupt at any moment due to our unsanitary conditions. In the meantime Alghero was changed for Olbia, a ferry port on the northeast coast of Sardinia. At least we went alongside, but the passengers were not over-impressed with this one-street town.

Mr Crossland came aboard for the overnight journey between Minorca and Palma, and I had a chance to talk with the man who had initiated this cruise-ship operation on the lines of the traditional package tour. He gave me the impression of being not only very intelligent, but also committed to giving good service and a good product to those who might have been unable to cruise before because of the high cost, which he believed was not justified. With his own fleet of nineteen planes and over 650 retail outlets in the UK alone he knew that, given the right professional people, his cruise operation should be a great success, and at a fair price that would be particularly attractive to first-time cruisers.

He was critical the next morning of the poor results observed in the questionnaires which passengers were asked to complete. Unfortunately the D&V figures for the week were still climbing – sixty-four in seven days – and the situation was not helped by the fact that our doctors were locums from the Spanish clinic in Palma who stayed only for one week and intended the cruise to be a holiday, not a job. The last one couldn't really converse in English.

The next cruise, number 004, could be described as our disaster cruise. By the end of the week 177 passengers had come down with diarrhoea and vomiting, with a further eighty-two having one symptom or the other. The medical staff were so inundated that two nurses and another doctor from the Palma clinic were put on board in Villefranche to assist. Two microbiologists from London also came aboard to conduct tests. To cap it all, the weather had been poor, and seasickness was an additional problem over the last two days. Regrettably I also had to dismiss one of the nurses in Barcelona; she had been causing problems for a number of weeks. The local agent did not assist us with her repatriation, which, because of visa problems, meant she had to stay on board till Malta the following Monday.

Tom Waslander from Airtours came aboard to organise 'damage limitation' in an effort to reduce adverse publicity. He was quite successful, as no major newspaper reported the sickness problem.

Out of the trough
That was our low spot, and from then on things began to improve dramatically. Ratings climbed to over 90% for the food, the summer came at last, and passengers in general had a good time, stating the cruise was great value for money. There were further problems, of course. The sixth doctor decided he didn't like his situation after he boarded and was about to walk off on the Saturday evening, which would have left us unable to sail, at least legally. Fortunately he was talked round and stayed, albeit grudgingly. Then the seventh doctor spoke no English, and the eighth was so emaciated he looked like a refugee and some passengers couldn't believe he was a doctor.

V.Ships became very sensitive regarding all operational matters, to the extent that the managing director appeared nervous and concerned about the possibility of losing the contract. A new hotel director, David Sinton, came aboard – an old friend from my days in Singapore. He galvanized his team and set many new

255

standards, though regrettably his manner was at times abrasive and some of the management were offended. I tried to support him but I was criticised for informing too many people of my professional respect for him. After I went on leave he was fired.

Beverly Paul, the cruise director from the *Seawing*, replaced ours, who was 'let go', and the entertainment scores started to improve. But the standard of the shows could not be compared to that of the established companies. The entertainment concession had not worked on ships before, and it showed.

The two-week alternating itinerary continued with no major operational problems, hygiene and food standards rose dramatically, but we often sailed late from Palma because of delayed flights. Alghero was put back in after also trying Porto Torres in northern Sardinia, but always there was a problem of trying to get too many people away in a short time after lunch using only two of our launches and one shore tender to cover the fairly long run in to the pier.

Captain Jean Marie Guillou came aboard in Civitavecchia on 11 July; he was a Frenchman of great charm and was to be my relief during my first vacation. The following Saturday he took over and I left 'my' ship for seven weeks. Yet again my contract had been one of interest, a new challenge that had eventually been concluded successfully with much hard work and heartache having been put in by many of the officers, crew and staff.

Returning just seven weeks later, I remained on board until the end of the year. The first summer season continued and settled into a comfortable routine, with our quality of service improving all the time. The winter season saw the ship based in Santa Cruz, the main port of Tenerife, from where we were to complete seven weeks of three- and four-day cruises to the other Canary Islands. Scheduling was hectic, and made even worse for the pursers and housekeeping staff as every Tuesday and Friday over a thousand passengers would arrive and leave. Some had a cruise and stay holiday, others just flew out for the short cruise segment before flying back home. The travel operator forgetting the distance between Santa Cruz and the airport in the south did not help berthing times. On Tuesdays, in order for some passengers to be at the airport in time to check in, we had to arrive alongside before 0300 hours. Friday wasn't much better, with an 0530 arrival.

I managed another six-week break before returning for a series of one-month cruises to the Caribbean from Tenerife. The westbound voyage out across the Atlantic is one of my favourites, long days of comfortable seas, reaching the trade winds and the equatorial current, which bring the temperatures up as the days at sea increase. Seven days after departure we would arrive at the islands, Antigua or Barbados, and then a port call most days until it was time to return. The company had little idea of what a passenger would expect or enjoy, so I found myself adjusting the schedule to stay later on some evenings and getting the cruise director to employ the services of a local steel band to play on deck under the tropical stars.

I believe the cruises were a success and particularly good value for money, but after two or three weeks on a ship some passengers tend to get restless, and one or two find fault or reason to complain, particularly when the weather starts to cool on the return journey and they are unable to top up their tans. Two seven-day periods at sea are only for the true cruiser, the person who can relax with a good book and let the world just sail by.

Winter moved swiftly into spring, and more short cruises were followed by a return to Palma for the weekly summer season of 1996. Both *Carousel* and *Seawing* were making money for the tour operator; the word went around that the company might be expanding. Lurking on the horizon, however, was the increasing threat of competition. Thomson's already had an active cruise operation with chartered ships, and the package tour operator First Choice were making preparations to enter the market. We had to ensure that we maintained our market lead.

Carousel, 1996–97

The summer season of 1996 went without any major problems. There was a certain amount of uncertainty regarding which management company would take over the management of both *Seawing* and *Carousel*. By the middle of the summer it was a foregone conclusion that V.Ships would be the one, and also for the new ship which was to join the fleet in the spring of 1997. The next vessel, about which there was much speculation, was to be the *Song of Norway*, to be renamed *Sundream*. Airtours paid $40 million, substantially less than for *Carousel* even though the two vessels were sister ships.

Following the decision on who would be the ship manager there was then concern on the part of Airtours to ensure that they should keep as many of the existing staff on the *Seawing* to ensure continuity during the change-over. We on the *Carousel* watched with interest as V.Ships and Airtours made their moves, offering the crew on the *Seawing* exactly the same conditions and salaries as they were getting under their employment with Norwegian Cruise Line, which in most cases was considered to be substantially higher than that normally offered by V.Ships.

The majority of the NCL people accepted the offer, knowing perhaps that if they remained with NCL they would be downgraded due to the loss of one ship from their fleet. Jim Evans at Airtours expressed his desire that the two ships should be 'a team' and that liaison between the two should be encouraged.

In the meantime a rift was developing, unknown to me, between one of the new Airtours-appointed security officers on our ship and Peter Greenhow, who was staff captain at the time. He became frustrated with the capabilities of the security officer and it became apparent a month or so later that this particular officer had gone back to Jim Evans and suggested that Peter was working against the morale of the crew on board. If anything, it was the opposite, and I attempted to support Peter's reputation when I spoke with both the technical superintendent and Jim.

On board we eventually had two Nepalese gangway security petty officers and, following the guidelines from the V.Ships manual, I set in place a higher status of security at the gangway, which is what I believed were the wishes of Jim Evans. An event occurred shortly before my leave in early November that took us a little by surprise.

The cruise director from *Seawing* came over in Palma with a young lady in tow, and on the gangway he happened to meet Peter, who had yet again been instructing the new petty officers, one of whom was a little slow in understanding his responsibilities. Peter asked the cruise director to wait while someone was called to meet him, explaining that this was a new rule on board – which in fact it was not regarding senior staff, and Peter was probably a little pedantic in trying to enforce it. Unfortunately the cruise director became upset and eventually, after some brief acrimonious discussion, walked off back to his ship. Regrettably he wrote a fax to the director of Airtours saying that he was refused permission to board our vessel, and the whole thing blew up out of proportion.

I attempted to pour oil onto the troubled waters by explaining what had happened in the past when we allowed crew from other vessels free access, but it did not have the desired effect and I was later accused of making decisions on board based on my emotions rather than company policies, and informed that Jim Evans and John Drysdale were concerned at my less-than-willing participation in their policy of integrating the *Seawing* and *Carousel* teams to build an Airtours team for the future. I was very surprised, as I felt that I had always worked with the management ashore to make the ships as professional and successful as possible.

During a visit to the Southampton office while I was on leave, Jim Evans brought up the matter of integration. He had made up his mind that Peter Greenhow should no longer work on any Airtours ship, and it was obvious from the conversation that I could say nothing to change his mind. I am convinced that persons unknown had generated some gossip and, unfortunately, our bosses had preferred to listen to tittle-tattle rather than the professionals they employed on board.

The saga left me with an uncomfortable feeling, and when I returned from vacation I found that Peter had left that day and was not to return. All his V.Ships appraisal reports had been very good and the ship managers were at a loss as to his demise. We were left with the loss of a good man, experienced with the ship, and whose presence would have been of great use when the *Sundream* came on-line.

I also found that four of the engineers had left just before my return, including the staff engineer who had been destined for promotion to chief early the following year. He was a character who gave the appearance of being incredibly efficient and always 'on the job' down below, but his failing was that he felt he should be 'one of the lads', and it was not unusual for him to be drinking late at night long after a sensible head of department would have retired to bed. The staff captain often complained to me that the staff chief had promised assistance and cooperation, but it rarely seemed to materialise – or at least not with any great urgency. We were left with a technical team who had a certain lack of experience of the ship and its plant. This was a situation we had been in before, and it caused me some concern.

The morale of the engineers had never been good, given the long hours and the continual need to repair ageing machinery. To get ahead with the planned maintenance seemed to be impossible, and the lack of spares, due to budget constraints and slow delivery, resulted in engineers working hard and partying hard – sometimes too hard.

Some time earlier, one night in late September, one junior engineer officer had already crossed the limits. He phoned the bridge as we were preparing to sail from Palma. I happened to take the call, and he advised me that there was no tea or coffee available in the lido cafe machines. I explained that we were at stations and that it was the concern of the food and beverage manager. He continued to talk, and was obviously intoxicated, so I had to put the phone down.

I went back onto the bridge wing, and just as we were letting go the ropes the engineer came with a crash through the bridge-wing gate. He proceeded to abuse me verbally, saying that 'no c—' was going to talk to him like that. There were passengers above so I moved into the wheelhouse, and he followed. Peter Greenhow managed to get him to leave, but he reappeared, without jacket, just as Peter was manoeuvring the ship off the dock. He again used foul language and indicated he wanted to thump Peter, but fortunately the security officer was close by and led him away. Needless to say I was not amused, particularly as Peter was under training and distracting him could have resulted in the ship hitting the dock.

Obviously the officer could not stay. I interviewed him the next day, when he was still as belligerent, and he flew home on the Monday from Malta. He had a chip on his shoulder and obviously was not happy with the discipline required on a passenger ship. We were well rid of him, as I found out later that he had been a bad influence just about everywhere on board.

But we were also losing experienced and reliable engineers, and, for whatever reason, the company's aim of keeping its staff had backfired. It might have been due to the lack of qualified men available, or to the uncompetitive wages, but for me it meant that further problems 'down below' – mishaps or worse – could be expected.

***

We sailed from Tenerife on 3 December, with around a thousand British passengers bound for Antigua, Martinique, Saint Lucia, Sint Maarten, Tortola, Tobago, Grenada, Barbados and finally Aruba. Half the passengers disembarked in Barbados, and on the whole they had had a great time, while the remainder stayed on to Aruba – and some were a little disappointed as they indicated we were more interested in preparing for the new winter season with Canadian passengers than we were in looking after them. Not really true, of course, but there were a number of changes that had to be completed.

They finally left on 12 December, and we started our first major embarkation at a new port and with a different type of passenger. It was a disaster.

The embarkation of the new passengers was a debacle. In my voyage report I recorded that it was reminiscent of our first time in the Med in May 1995 – in fact it was worse. Some passengers said they had to stand in three different lines for over three hours; this was true, as the flights arrived very close to each other, no proper computer list had been forwarded to the vessel, and there were no table reservations. The Canadian tour company had not considered the problem of embarkation correctly and they had no ground staff to complete the check-in. The other US operator was similarly ill-prepared – their representative had only worked for them for one week and had never been on a ship before. Ship staff assisted by our own UK management gradually sorted the embarkation process out, but not before we had lost tremendous good will from the passengers.

We were very late leaving and could not catch up the time to enable us to arrive on schedule in Barbados, so the passengers effectively lost half a day at the island. The American passengers in particular commented adversely about the cruise. Many had been on bigger, newer ships, and they were not at all impressed with our vessel or the fact that the holiday had been sold as a 'dream' cruise. I recorded the following in my voyage report:

> Regrettably the voyage started off on the wrong foot even before we had sailed. The debacle in the arrivals hall can only be an indication of the tour operator carrying out insufficient research. The general mood of some of the passengers after embarkation carried on throughout the cruise with further rumblings of discontent. By departing late we were unable to recover lost time. Due to a control problem number 2 main engine refused to stay clutched in when going up to 410 RPM, thus the passage to Barbados continued at 350 RPM and we probably lost an hour or more.

The entertainment programme was adjusted to take into account the mood of the passengers, as the first two nights' shows were not received favourably. The casino was in demand, but had insufficient staff to open all the tables; the fact that many of the machines were out of order was also an obvious disadvantage.

From the questionnaires it is immediately obvious that the 'Dream Cruise' was not so for many passengers, particularly those who had cruised before on more modern vessels. The comments reflected severe dissatisfaction with the embarkation procedure, while the entertainment and food also came in for some direct and unpleasant criticism. Margarita Island is not appreciated by the majority of passengers, particularly those who did not take the tour, as there were few taxis and the berth is many miles from anywhere.

One passenger's comments, although rather caustic, could perhaps sum up the feeling of some on board –

'There was never any hot water, bathroom smelled like sewage, very disorganised at airport, some of the employees are rude, events are never on schedule, always waiting in line.'

There is no doubt some truth to this person's reaction, and there must be a radical rethink on how to cater for our North American 'cousins'.

The second cruise was not much better, and we were to receive quite a few complaint letters over the next few weeks. However, menus were improved, entertainment was altered and gradually things did get better. Within a few weeks, cruising became more routine and the scores from the questionnaires, although not great, were getting close to those we had received in the Mediterranean.

I had to take a week off the ship to attend an operational meeting in Southampton where several captains and chief engineers were to get together and thrash out operational procedures for the fleet. I managed to get eighteen hours at home on a Saturday night after flying from Curaçao, but my return was straight out to the ship in Aruba with an overnight stop in Miami.

The remainder of my contract went off with only the usual hiccups, though the actions of the chief engineer were slowly frustrating me. In late February it was discovered that the non-exclusive surveyor he had called in at Barbados to survey engine items was in fact not accredited to the classification society, and they refused to accept his work. This left the ship with much egg on face and meant that these items were out of class, plus all the work that had been done since November might have to be opened up and resubmitted. In the end I wrote the following memo to the technical superintendent when he came to visit:

Dear Sir,

You are aware, I believe, of some of the difficulties that have ensued as a result of the actions and attitude of Mr Rivers, the Chief Engineer on board *Carousel.* Both the Hotel Director and the Staff Captain have approached me at intervals with their frustrations regarding Christopher's somewhat cavalier remarks and response to the needs of their department and the ship in general.

I have been made aware of a certain amount of unpleasant and unprofessional hearsay, which one should of course ignore, but there have been occasions when I have listened to statements made by Christopher first hand and felt uncomfortable with his attitude.

Regrettably there have also been times when I have felt that I have had insufficient explanation or feedback from the Chief Engineer with regard to technical matters. There have been other occasions when I have learnt of problems from other sources and had to go to Christopher and ask for information. Some of these occasions I have recorded as an addendum to my voyage reports, and these are attached.

I have felt that there have been times when problems have been 'glossed over' by Christopher's explanation, and I have tried to ensure that he has kept you fully informed at all times. Perhaps this has been the case, but it has not always been made clear to me that you have been given the whole picture. In turn I have in the past copied him with all technical matters I have sent to your office.

I have attempted on several occasions to advise Christopher that he must maintain this important aspect of communication that is required between the Master and the Chief Engineer. However this week I have again been disappointed by his actions.

After your two faxes to the Chief Engineer regarding DNV survey work completed in Barbados and overspend on budget I tried several times to discuss the situation with Christopher, but it was only on the third occasion that he eventually came to my office. His explanation of the problem with the non-exclusive surveyor was not very satisfactory, and you will no doubt attempt to understand the reason for not ensuring Mr Massiah's credentials were acceptable to DNV. The budget over-spends were put down to 'Operation bilge clean' and he assured me that he would be able to provide costs involved with that exercise which would in turn enable you to discuss the situation with the owners.

He had apparently allowed the Staff Chief Engineer to take over his responsibilities, which included stand-by duty in the engine control room, without at least making me aware that this was going to happen. He also proceeded to dress out of uniform in public spaces, which might be considered a small matter, but he had been introduced to the passengers as the Chief Engineer and I explained to him that I felt it improper not to continue to dress in the uniform provided by the company.

I realise that there have been a great many technical problems over the past three months, but in fact it has ever been thus for the past two years. I am not qualified to judge Christopher's technical ability; however, with regard to his management ability, I feel that Christopher is at times either being deliberately perverse or that he does not have the common sense to understand that he is being foolish. This perhaps I can accept. However, when it comes to the safety of the vessel the Master must have complete trust in explanations given by and discussions held with the Chief Engineer.

I regret to inform you that I do not have that trust with Mr Rivers.

Philip Rentell, Master, *Carousel*

A new chief came some weeks before Christopher paid off. Mark Cameron had recently left a ship which had been my first command, the old *Scandinavian Saga*, so he was well used to mechanical nightmares, and he was also keen to maintain the normal communication expected between master and chief engineer.

John Brocklehurst joined as staff captain, and we immediately developed a good working relationship. In fact we had met once before, some time in late 1982 when we had both been invited to the Royal Naval College at Greenwich for a mess dinner organised by the Royal Navy for a few of the Merchant Navy participants in the Falklands campaign. John had far more right to be there than I as his ship, the *Atlantic Conveyor*, had been hit by an Exocet missile and set on fire. The crew had to abandon ship and several, including the master, were killed. John had been the chief officer, and with others had had to climb into a raft out of the cold waters of the South Atlantic.

Of note during my last weeks of Caribbean cruising were continual problems with generators, main engines or other auxiliary machinery – not unusual or unexpected, but a source of continued frustration, particularly for the engineers, as often their supply of spare gear was limited.

We had an outbreak of gastroenteritis, or diarrhoea and vomiting. This resulted in two health consultants flying out from the UK to advise and monitor our sanitising procedures. By the time I left the problem was still around; even one of the consultants went down with it and both of them had to be isolated for a couple of days.

Alfredo Romeo took over the ship and I flew home from Barbados in the middle of March, glad to leave the Caribbean after over three months of routine, which had become at times a little humdrum, but one where tensions had been high on occasion.

I rejoined the ship in Palma in time to start the new season of weekly cruises, very much the same as previous years, with two different itineraries, except that Corsica had been replaced by Portofino and Sardinia by Tunis.

Alfredo went off for a couple of weeks' vacation before taking over the *Sundream* from John Reeves, who had brought the ship through refit and the first few cruises. Alfredo was of course to have his own problems and we communicated often to ensure routines and operation were as similar as we could make them on the two sister ships. Chris Rivers, the chief engineer, did not return from vacation. He had been asked to comment about my letter and chose not to, effectively terminating himself from Airtours employment.

The weather was to be very mixed for the first part of the season and that was to be the cause of one or two problems. Portofino, a beautiful little village some twenty miles to the east of Genoa, caused all the masters headaches from time to time. The anchorage is very exposed, and to run a safe launch service the sea conditions had to be calm.

On my first call in May there was too much chop. I tried to secure the shore pontoon but the gangway was jumping and in the end I decided to cancel and move on to Genoa, where we arrived around eleven o'clock. The passengers were a little disappointed as Genoa is very much a working port and the surrounding area is rather scruffy. It was even pointed out to me that one street seemed to be full of 'pimps, whores and homosexuals' – not quite the ticket for our old ladies.

A few weeks later on leaving Palma there was a strong onshore wind. I allowed the bow to come out by using the thruster, bringing the stern out only slightly. Once I thought the angle was right and the wind would not set the ship back onto the dock as we moved forward, I allowed the ship to move ahead, easing back the rudder at the same time. The wind caught the stern and pushed it back towards the quay. I corrected, but the delay allowed the ship to drop sufficiently for the painting cradle secured to the outside of the promenade deck to touch the crane on the dock, becoming rather squashed in the process. This caused great amusement, and the damaged cradle subsequently became known as 'Phil's Folly' – so called by our humorous Glaswegian chief engineer Ronnie Keir.

The weather continued to be unpredictable. We made Portofino on the second call, but heavy rain and squalls marred the call in Villefranche, with one of the squalls causing the stern line attached to a mooring buoy to part. Fortunately the ship remained fairly central in the anchorage with the starboard chain out to seven shackles. That turned out to be fortuitous, for when the chains were brought home we found one of the joining shackles was cracked. This was the port side chain and it could have easily have parted under stress. A new joining shackle had to be purchased at around £2,000, shipped out and then fitted on board.

The following time in Villefranche the rains came again, this time as a result of a passing frontal weather system. I anchored the ship with the starboard anchor, but even before we had secured the stern line to the buoy the wind changed and conditions started to deteriorate. The buoy line parted within an hour and the ship swung to the anchor, this time too close for comfort towards the rocky eastern shore.

After an interval of waiting to see how things panned out I decided to have the engines started and everything ready to make a move – just in time, because the wind strengthened and as I heaved away the anchor the ship drifted even closer to the shore. I had to back out on full power, thrusting at the same time to ensure I could make a new approach to a safer position. There was an amusing moment when the technical superintendent, Ron Ellison, who was waiting for a boat to bring him out to the ship, called me up on the security officer's radio from the quayside. He asked me if I was having problems. My answer was fairly short and went something like 'Hi Ron, yes things are getting interesting out here, at the moment I'm staring into some chap's bedroom window.'

After yet another seamanlike performance I anchored again, got soaked though to the skin and changed ready for our management staff to come on board.

———

Other incidents were interesting in different ways. One morning I fired three members of the band because they refused to get into a lifeboat during our safety drill. When I asked why they refused, they said that it was far too dangerous and that there had been many accidents in the past. It was a particularly bad day to get my back up, as I had just spent an hour in discussion with shore management regarding the revision of working schedule and salary, the conclusion of which had not been particularly satisfactory.

There certainly had been no accidents in my time on the *Carousel*, and I explained to them that if they refused during a drill to get into a boat, they might refuse in an emergency and therefore I had no alternative but to dismiss them. They seemed quite happy with the outcome, and in fact they had been causing problems for the cruise director for the month they had already been on board so their leaving would be no great loss. Unfortunately the assistant cruise director had taken over for a few days and she was already having difficulty coping, and when she heard the news that there was no band for the remainder of the week she just held her head in her hands and said 'Why me?'

The entertainment concession were very apologetic, understood the situation, and sent another band the following Saturday. What they never discussed was why the bandleader had been re-employed when he had been fired from the *Seawing* in 1995.

A few weeks later we had a report that there had been a male passenger photographing young girls. This was initially hard to substantiate, but within a few days there was another complaint from a passenger, and after a few hours the man was identified and followed to check his cabin number. The next morning the hotel director, Adam Scott, entered the room when it was vacant and found three rolls of exposed film and a notebook apparently recording the subjects of the photographs, including such notes as 'girl in blue shorts and white ankle socks', 'girl in black bikini', etc, etc.

I had the notes copied and the film removed so that it could be developed on board. Within a few hours we had the results, and sure enough he had been taking photographs of one or two girls in their early teens sunbathing on deck or sightseeing. There was a propensity for taking shots of girls' bottoms in tight shorts, and although they could hardly be described as lewd I decided that the man should be interviewed.

Adam and I invited him to the hotel director's office just before lunchtime when the ship was in Malta. I explained that I had received complaints from other passengers and he immediately admitted that he assumed that it was because of the photographs. I hadn't informed him of our evidence but asked him to explain his actions. He was rather pathetic and gave the impression of being a naughty schoolboy who has been found out by the headmaster. A man over fifty, who looked perfectly normal, but who had a social problem that he could not repress.

We taped the conversation and he asked me if I was going to throw him off, or could he just stay, but not carry his camera around. I suggested that it would be in the best interests of all if he were to leave the ship as soon as possible, and he had the gall to ask if he would be recompensed for the lost days of his cruise. I agreed to arrange his flight through the agent, for which he would have to pay. He asked if he could write an apology to the parents, but I told him keep a low profile until he was called to leave the vessel.

In fact I was very surprised that he went without a fuss. I had checked with the company to ensure they would cover his flight costs if necessary, and also with the local agent to ensure that police would be available if he refused to leave the vessel. In the end of course that was not necessary, but I did advise the company of his flight details, and I believe that the authorities were advised of his peculiar habits, and that he was interviewed when he landed in London.

John Brocklehurst, my relief, was already on board as staff captain and was handling the ship often to gain experience. It had already been decided that I would move to *Seawing* while John and Kjell Stokerite would work three months on, three months off in command of *Carousel*. Jim Evans came out to Barcelona on the day I was due to leave, with the prime task of thanking me for my efforts over the previous two and a half years on board. In turn I expressed my thanks, commenting that this period had been the most professionally satisfying of my career.

As I walked down the gangway on 15 August, the whistle was blown three times – quite touching, really.

The captain's table

For many masters of cruise ships, the table becomes a chore which is suffered on just the formal nights. I imagine the problem is that they get rather cheesed off answering the same old questions. 'How long have you been at sea, Captain?' 'What does your wife think about you being at sea, Captain?' 'Don't you get terribly bored doing this, Captain?' And perhaps the most repeated question of all, 'If you're down here, who's driving the ship?'

Well, of course, it goes with the territory. I've always said that if you don't like talking to passengers then you should go back and work with cargo ships. There's plenty of silence there! Over my years spent watching other captains I picked up what I thought was the right approach to take – and one technique that was definitely not the right approach.

Basically, the captain must be able to communicate if he is going to enjoy the social side of his job. Unlike some other professions these days, where the general public are more likely to question the pearls of wisdom that are given by various professionals, at sea the captain is still awarded an automatic respect no matter what kind of person he is. Perhaps it's because the average passenger imagines that this man has learnt all the experience of hundreds of years of seamanship, or just because he may be in charge of their destiny should the unfortunate occur. Perhaps it is the uniform, his seeming unavailability – or maybe it's their own lack of knowledge of the sea, or what keeps them afloat, or how he gets them from A to B.

Whatever it is, if the captain really needs to master the social side of passenger-ship life, he must come down off this invisible pedestal the passengers have placed him on. There is only one way to achieve that – he must communicate.

On board I have always managed to get around and be seen, stopping briefly to say 'hello' and perhaps have a brief chat. I speak on the public address fairly frequently, initially to read out the passenger safety drill speech while passengers gather at their designated muster station at the beginning of the voyage. After arrival in port and before departure, I usually come on to talk briefly about what they may expect in the hours ahead, and I always try to add a little humour, because it catches their attention. This type of communication lets passengers hear your voice. They become familiar with it and, usually unknowingly, develop a respect for the captain, so that they are more likely to listen and respond to the 'voice' should there be some kind of emergency.

The captain's table is a natural extension of this need to communicate, and if it is to be enjoyed by all, including the captain, it has to be managed correctly – but of course without the passengers being aware that they are, to a certain extent, being manipulated.

It was rare for us to get anyone famous on the Sun Cruise ships, but on my table there have been some very interesting people from all walks of life. Prison guards, policemen, firemen, nurses, undertakers, bankers, doctors, a walking-stick maker, plumbers, builders, refuse collectors, they have all been there. Most people are not too worried whether they come or not but, inevitably, when that invitation gets posted under the door, a few start to get all excited. Not to sit with the captain particularly, but to be able to say, after the event and perhaps quite frequently, that 'we had dinner with the captain!'

Originally I used to keep the same table of passengers for the whole week, which was the way the system worked in Cunard, the idea being that the captain would buy wine for the table on the first night and suggest it wasn't compulsory for him to buy the wine every night, thus gaining revenue for the company. Sun Cruises decided, after reading a few adverse comments in the customer questionnaires, that it was unfair and other passengers should have the chance of sharing the captain's table. With the best will in the world I can only sit with approximately fifty passengers in one week so I thought it rather pointless, but it did make the decision easier for other less sociable masters to avoid the dining room whenever possible. It also meant that I bought the wine every night and therefore it cost the company a fair amount of money!

Constantly meeting new passengers meant that every night I had to introduce myself, put them at ease, and of course talk about myself. I developed a technique of meeting the passengers at one of the bars for half an hour before dinner – it broke the ice, and they also started to talk to each other. Alcohol has the great effect of loosening the tongues of even the shyest. "Where do you come from?" "What do you do?" "Do you have any children?" are the normal questions to get people going, and it's true that most people are happier talking about themselves. By the end of the week many people have heard me so often over the public address system that they think they know me and are therefore much more relaxed, with the result that conversation can skip a few jumps and become quite interesting. Most people do have a story to tell, it's just a matter of asking the right questions.

Picking the table is also something of an art. My instructions to the maître d' are to look for people who probably like a drink and are often seen to be chatting with the rest of their normal table. Often, as I meet passengers at the 'handshake' part of the Captain's Cocktail Party, I will observe how they greet me, ask a quick question or two and see how they respond, gaining an impression quite quickly as to whether they may be suitable 'victims' for a future evening on my table. I may take their cabin number and give it to the maître d', and he will try and place them one night.

My guests are escorted to the table and make themselves comfortable while I chat to a few other tables on the way. By the time I sit down, my guests are often talking amongst themselves, which is exactly how I like it. I pity the poor master who arrives to his table socially 'cold' – the passengers are often afraid of what to say or even whether they should speak before being spoken to. It takes ages for the 'ice' to thaw.

A good table is one that doesn't want to leave at the end of the meal, when all the other guests have left the dining room and the waiters are clearing up all around, or preparing for the midnight buffet. I have had many and I have enjoyed most of the tables I've attended. There have however, been a few notable incidents.

It is unfortunate that, on occasion, some folks have just one too many and go over the precipice between having a good time, laughing, talking normally, and making an absolute fool of themselves. I can remember two occasions when a passenger definitely had one or two 'over the odds' and ended up going over the back of the chair, taking everyone but the head waiter (who was on hand to catch them) and myself by surprise. One poor lady was so inebriated by the time we sat down that she only just managed to push the soup around the plate with her spoon, her conversation was slurred and her head wobbled in time with the words she was trying to say. Her husband, realising the fact, eventually decided she needed him to help her out to the toilet; as she tried to stand up and push her chair back she just went with it. All of us at the table thought that would be it and were very surprised to see them both return about ten minutes later. Her efforts to eat the main course were obviously hampered by her inability to remember how a knife and fork worked. In the end, her husband realised they had to go, and two waiters were on stand-by to catch her as she yet again fell back from her chair.

Conversation is usually absolutely fine and, depending on how I see the table, sometimes the jokes are more 'adult'. There have been occasions, though, when one of the guests has been rather overwhelming, full of anecdotes about themselves or their own knowledge about absolutely everything – they've done it, seen it and probably eaten it. This type makes it rather difficult for everyone else and, in a quiet way, I try to turn the conversation for the benefit of the others. Unfortunately, I have been known to be slightly acidic in my comments to loud guests when I have felt it necessary to regain the table.

Perhaps my favourites have been one or two of our older guests, who are usually genuinely grateful for being invited. The most interesting have been those of great age who still had all their mental faculties. One particular gentleman was ninety-two, very tall and still with a straight back, I asked him what he could remember from his early days at work. He proceeded to say, in a quiet and slow voice, 'In 1922, when I was asked to open the office of Marconi in London ...' and he continued for about ten or fifteen minutes with the whole table in rapt attention, listening to these tales so well remembered. Another old lady could remember the ships on which she had travelled as a little girl, and she was quite surprised when I told her I knew of them and had original postcards in my collection.

Lord Justice Kelly and his wife sailed with us in 1997; he was well over seventy and had recently retired from the bench in Northern Island. I fell in to conversation about his work. He had tried and imprisoned many IRA activists and still had a police guard at the bottom of his garden. When I had first met them at the cocktail party I did not realise his status and asked, as I normally do, if they were settling in OK. He was very polite and said 'Yes', but his wife, who I later found out was born in India during the days of the Raj, said she thought the food was 'very poor'. I decided I should keep an eye on them. A few days later I asked her how the food was and she said, in a very posh voice, 'Oh, it's improved dramatically.' Of course it hadn't, she had just become used to it. That cruise was a whole month across to the Caribbean and back, and I always used to stop when I passed by, just to say hello and see how they were. Far from snobs, they turned out to be two very charming people, and communication broke down any social barriers that may have existed when they first boarded. By the end of the cruise, he was asking my opinion of California as a place to retire to.

Two of the most memorable experiences at the table were in my early days with Sun Cruises.

During the summer of 1996 I left *Carousel* for what was meant to be my long vacation of the year, nine weeks. I had in fact planned to have my vasectomy during this period, and it was perhaps a little unfortunate that three days after the operation Captain Guillou, my relief on board *Carousel*, had to be hospitalised with high blood pressure (apparently as a direct result of the Greek doctor's medication – but that's another story).

The head of personnel from the vessel's manager, V.Ships, phoned me on the Saturday to ask 'Was I busy?' After I was advised of the situation I volunteered my services, but explained my predicament. The decision to fly me back to the ship was not made until the Sunday; Alfredo Romeo took the ship out of Palma, his first chance in command. The company wanted me to fly to Ajaccio for Monday, but that would have meant an all-night taxi ride to Gatwick, a flight to Paris, a change of airports and a flight down to Corsica. I really didn't fancy the idea, because the swelling from the operation was causing life to be just a little uncomfortable, and I was walking around like John Wayne after a week on horseback.

Eventually I left home on Tuesday morning, took a flight to London, another to Rome, and joined the ship the same day in Civitavecchia – far more comfortable. Alfredo was doing a great job, so I explained I was going to baby-sit for a while and that he could do all the driving until I decided it was time for me to leave him and fly back.

Life was gradually becoming more comfortable as the days continued. Even so, I found myself at the dinner table moving from one buttock to the other. I never mentioned my situation until Thursday. I was sitting next to a lady who was obviously slightly inebriated, and she started to quiz me about my family.

I explained that we had one child, and she asked if we were going to have any more. I said no. She asked 'Why?' I replied that because of our ages, our long separations, etc, etc ... She again said 'Why?' so I eventually mentioned that in fact I had just had a vasectomy – and she said 'Why?' By this time the rest of the table were getting slightly embarrassed, but she continued to ask direct questions and said that she believed it was unfair for men to be sterilised because they might go and marry again and the wife would naturally want children. She believed it was OK for the wife to be sterilised after she had 'done her bit'.

I can deal with most little annoyances, but this lady was becoming a nuisance and I could see little way out except by leaving the restaurant, which I was loath to do. Fortunately, at that moment the lights went out, the room went dark and the Baked Alaska parade commenced to much 'oohing' and 'ahhing' from the other passengers. My relief was immense, particularly as that was followed by the introductions of dining room staff. By the time it was all over, the poor woman had forgotten what she was talking about and left me in peace for the remainder of the meal.

I was reminded of the event about a year later when some passengers asked me if I remembered them. 'You know,' they said, 'We were on that table with that awful woman who criticised you for having a vasectomy!'

And finally, here's how not to do it –

My Sunday evenings were usually taken up for a period of about three hours by the Captain's Welcome Aboard Party, where it was my duty to greet the passengers at the door to the lounge, usher them through and, of course, have a picture taken. The captain's photo is a great revenue earner for any company, and I quickly developed a stance to ensure the best results.

I greet the passengers by the hand and place the couples, one either side, with my arm behind their backs to ensure that they are positioned correctly for the photographer to grab his shot. If it is at all rough my arm is ready for some support, particularly if the lady is wearing high heels. It was on one of these occasions that the lady, just as the camera clicked, moved backwards as the ship took a slight roll in the moderate sea conditions we were experiencing.

She apologised and said that she had 'just felt a little swell'. I immediately, and perhaps rather naughtily, replied 'It's been a long time since I've had a lady say that to me!'

Needless to say she was just a little embarrassed, but went off into the crowd and I forgot all about it – that is, until the conversation at the dinner table came round to embarrassing situations. I then mentioned that, funnily enough, one had occurred tonight, and I proceeded to tell the story. The table were most amused, all that is except the lady on my left, who said 'That was me!'

I apologised, of course, but I was rather tickled and in fact it turned out to be a great ice breaker. The whole table turned out to be good fun for the remainder of the week.

There are, of course, other stories. I could mention a birthday of mine, and the belly dancer who emerged from the cake ... But I think that must wait for another time.

Haps and mishaps

Bollards

In my early years of service with Sun Cruises I had some unusual experiences of one sort or another. One of my favourites occurred on *Carousel* while she was lying alongside the quay in Palma. She had been berthed since early morning one Saturday, and passengers were both disembarking from the previous cruise and embarking for the cruise ahead. This was quite normal when we would have well over forty different flights from all over the UK and Scandinavia carrying a proportion of our passengers amongst their complement. Alongside the dock there would be a hive of activity, with stores and water being taken, containers being unloaded and garbage being carried off and put into skips. The first of two passenger gangways placed to try and ensure a smooth flow of passengers was the accommodation ladder, which could be described as a set of steps secured by hinges to a platform, itself secured outside the shell door one deck above the quayside. The shipside lower shell door had the second, shorter gangway, a brow placed so that its weight was supported by the quayside ashore and by the shell door frame inside the ship.

During the afternoon the wind increased considerably, pushing the ship bodily away from the quayside. The polypropylene ropes are designed to stretch a little in order to prevent breaking during mooring operations or when the ship is affected by increased swell conditions in unprotected harbours. The ship's side, however, acted like a great sail, resulting in a gap opening up between ship and shore. I was called to the bridge and immediately had the brow taken aboard, as it was very close to dropping into the harbour. The port authority was called and two tugs ordered to assist in pushing the ship back into position while we secured more ropes, but I anticipated, correctly as it happened, that it would take some time for them to get alongside. It was siesta time.

Down below, the engineers were ordered to prepare the engines and start the bow thruster. If everything broke I didn't want to end up as the largest boat in the yacht harbour, which was immediately behind us. Fore and aft mooring stations were manned and I decided to try and manoeuvre the vessel myself and attempt to ease the strain on the ropes at each end, but this is never easy and, as it turned out, I was being a little overoptimistic with regard to my ability to overcome the effects of the weather.

I used the thruster to push the bow closer to the quay, but we gained little on the headlines. I thrusted the bow off the quay and used the engines and rudder to assist the stern. All of a sudden, two headlines, secured to a bollard at the corner of the quayside, literally shot back towards the ship. The bollard foundation had given way, no doubt as a result of the extra weight placed on it. The ropes pulled the bollard away from the quay so that it fell into the dock, taking about five metres of wall with it.

I eased back on the thruster immediately in order to prevent the other head lines from breaking, but the officer on the fo'c'sle had obviously experienced nothing like this before. For about the next twenty seconds he gave a tirade of Polish English over the walkie-talkie. I didn't understand a word of what he said but I had no doubt as to what he meant! When he finally released the 'press to talk' button I instructed him in no uncertain manner to send two more lines to the shore.

The two tugs eventually arrived and a certain degree of normality returned. The ship was held alongside, and more lines were put ashore and tightened to hold the ship in position. I took a walk onto the quay to inspect the damage my ship had inflicted. It was quite spectacular. The corner of the dock was completely missing, the bollard was nowhere to be seen and there was a jet of water reaching about four metres into the sky as a result of the freshwater service main being torn apart when the quay wall had disappeared. What was interesting, however, was that there had been an access tunnel built into the quay only a few centimetres under the surface. The bollard had been sitting in only thirty centimetres of concrete, hardly sufficient to support the weight of a ship in bad weather conditions.

Needless to say the harbour authorities were not over-impressed, and wanted to charge the ship for damaging their pier. I in turn told them I expected the port to pay for the two tugs I had had to order because their quay was badly designed and of insufficient strength to hold the ship.

Over the next few weeks the corner was shuttered up and tons of concrete was poured into the hole to repair the quay. The final job was to place a new bollard into the final pour of concrete; it was much taller than the previous one and looked very substantial. It had not been painted, so the deck crew went ashore to paint on the finishing touches – a black base, a round white top and, stencilled in white paint, 'Captain Rentell's Bollard, replaced July 1997.'

I never did see a bill for the repair, but we did pay for the tugs. The artwork remained on the bollard for the whole season.

Anchors

Anchors are inevitably another piece of hardware to give the master a headache from time to time. One morning during a sea passage between Civitavecchia and Palma, I had been up to the bridge around about seven a.m. to see that all was well. The wind was coming from the northwest and fairly strong, but no great concern even though we were endeavouring to make full speed. We were approaching the Strait of Bonifacio, a relatively narrow stretch of water separating Corsica from Sardinia. It is not uncommon for the winds to increase considerably between the islands, and over the next hour we started to register over 40 knots on the anemometer.

The sea state started to increase, but the ship ploughed on quite happily with spray being shipped over the foredeck when we hit larger waves. I was at my desk below when I heard a deep rumbling and felt a certain amount of vibration through my chair. For a few seconds I was trying to imagine what this could be when I realised it had to be only one thing, the anchor and chain running out!

The sea, with its constant buffeting, had caused a relatively small movement of the anchor, but in turn this had resulted in the securing arrangements on the deck above failing. A metal claw became detached, allowing anchor and chain to plummet towards the seabed at a great rate of knots. Under normal circumstances the weight alone of anchor and chain would have ripped its securing pin from the anchor locker. The officer on duty, however, was very quick to respond by pulling back on both propeller pitch levers in order to stop the vessel's forward motion. The anchor hit the seabed some sixty to a hundred metres below and, quite remarkably, the chain stopped its downward rush into watery oblivion. Rushing to the bridge to take over, I also gave instructions for a couple of guys to go forward and recover the errant anchor while I held the ship in position. Everything was soon secured, but we had been near to stationary for about fifteen minutes.

I was aware that passengers would be curious as to why the scenery had stopped moving past them, so I came onto the public address system and made a brief statement: 'Good morning, ladies and gentlemen, you may be aware that for the past fifteen minutes we have been stopped. This was to recover an anchor which had gone ashore without permission.'

On another occasion we were in the process of departing from the beautiful bay of Villefranche, which is situated between Nice and Monte Carlo. The ship had happily sat at anchor all day with two lines secured to a buoy at the stern; these were cast off and recovered. I was manoeuvring the ship so that it remained above the anchor while it was being heaved up by the windlass. The officer on the fo'c'sle gave the 'anchors aweigh', which meant that the anchor itself was off the bottom but had not been sighted. Under these circumstances it is normal for the prudent master to wait until the officer has reported 'sighted and clear', thus informing him there is nothing snagging the anchor, such as a wire that may have caught over the flukes, that part of the anchor that digs into the seabed to hold it in place.

The report came as I was thrusting the bow to starboard; I increased the propeller pitch levers in order to depart the bay. The weather was simply beautiful, and as I stood on the port bridge wing I could hear the last of the chain coming across the gypsy before it dropped down into its locker. All was well with the world. There was a metallic thud, the anchor coming home into the box, the recess in the shell plating designed to protect the anchor from the worst of any heavy seas. But then there was a more pronounced bang – not normal, I thought. I waited just seconds for the report from the now very surprised officer, who stated quite loudly over his radio, 'The f—ing anchor's just disappeared!' Much to the amusement of those passengers on the deck immediately above me, who had been watching the operation with idle curiosity.

There was not a lot I could do about it so we continued to Barcelona where, next day, the chain remaining was examined. It appeared that the D shackle which connects the anchor to a swivel had failed, sending the whole anchor back down into the relatively shallow waters of the bay. On the foredeck was a spare anchor, so a local shipyard with crane was employed to remove it and hopefully connect it to the swivel. Nothing at sea is guaranteed to go smoothly, particularly on old ships, and this minor operation was going to be one of those. The steel holding-down straps were burned off and the anchor was lifted onto the dockside by crane. The chain was lowered and the end was also brought onto the dockside, but the swivel proved to be seized and had to be removed by burning through its adjacent shackle. The anchor flukes were also seized, no doubt due to the years of long exposure to the elements, so it was decided to remove the whole lot to the shipyard workshop, where heat and pressure could be applied to free up the seized parts.

The day progressed, and I went over to the yard to inspect the progress. They couldn't do it, at least not in the time available. The ship had to sail in order to maintain schedule and make the next day's arrival in Palma, where passengers were disembarking to make their flights home. From having three anchors on arrival in Villefranche, I had ended up with just one by arrival in Palma two days later. Not particularly good news, and I advised the office that if I should lose the last one, the ship would not legally be allowed to sail.

The Barcelona anchor was repaired and sent back to us in Palma for the following week, but even then there were problems with the joining shackle. This is a special link designed to come apart in order to join adjacent stretches of cable, or in this case, to connect the cable to the swivel. A local yacht repair yard helped us out and we sailed that evening with an anchor on either side of the bow – very reassuring for the master, as we have a saying at sea, 'Don't run aground with both anchors in the pipe!' In other words, you take every measure to ensure anchors are dropped in good time to prevent an unintentional grounding.

The Villefranche anchor had a slightly longer journey. It was recovered by a diving team within the week, along with the remains of the broken D shackle. The failure was attributed to metal fatigue, possibly due to bad casting. The anchor itself was carried by flatbed truck to Livorno in Italy, a new D shackle was fabricated, and the assembly eventually placed back on board some three months later.

That is not the final anchor story, however. A year or so later, when my good friend John Brocklehurst was in command of *Carousel*, I was on *Sunbird* and given the task of carrying another errant anchor across from Barcelona to Palma in order for it to be placed on board his ship. Apparently the anchor had become damaged and was landed for repair in a shipyard. When the job was done it was inadvertently placed on the wrong ship, or at least on a ship which would not be going to a berth suitable for eventual transfer back on board *Carousel*.

By the time it reached us I believe it had been on several ships and had also been on a container journey, so it was becoming a most expensive repair. John heard a rumour that because of its now enhanced value it had been painted with a gold primer by another ship's waggish staff captain. He asked me to ensure he would not suffer the embarrassment of receiving a gold-painted anchor by repainting it with a more suitable colour, i.e. black.

'No problem,' I said, and duly had the anchor painted in a mix of colours that came out a shocking pink. When we reached Palma the anchor was lowered down onto a flatbed truck and driven across the quay. I phoned John to tell him it was on the way and, if he was interested, he could look out of his cabin window to watch it arrive. He said, 'Fine, thanks very much Phil,' and then he saw it. Fortunately he saw the funny side of it, and to this day, when we speak on the telephone, he often opens up with 'Hi Phil, Pinky Brocklehurst here!'

Stabilisers

I should imagine that most people understand what stabilisers are meant to do. They prevent the ship rocking around too much in bad weather. What people often do not understand is what they look like and how they work. When explaining their function to passengers I try to make it as simple as possible by telling them that the stabilisers are like the ailerons on an aircraft wing. They are approximately four metres long and protrude from either side of the hull when the vessel is at sea. Before coming into port they are retracted into a housing set inside the hull. When the ship rolls, for example to starboard, the port fin rotates on its axis to dig in to the sea in an attempt to bring that side down. The fin on the starboard side turns in the opposite direction to assist in bringing the ship upright. A simplified explanation that is usually sufficient to satisfy all but the most technically curious of minds.

I usually do not need to add that it is imperative that the stabilising fins are retracted before coming alongside upon arrival at the next port. On the bridge it had been common practice for a large board stating 'fins in' or 'fins out' to be placed in the region of the propeller pitch control levers. When the master arrived on the bridge he would ask the officer of the watch to confirm the status of the fins before taking over control of the vessel.

I had come back from a short break during the summer of 1995. *Carousel* had been in operation for less than six months and we were still on a steep learning curve, both as a company and also as a team on board. In my absence problems had been experienced with the stabilisers, and I was told they were not available for use until a new electronic card had been fitted to the starboard side fin.

We approached Naples after travelling from Palma. The weather had been calm, and the need to extend fins, even if they were available, had not arisen. I took over from the officer of the watch prior to the harbour pilot joining outside the port, conned the ship into the harbour and, with the pilot's acknowledgement, continued towards the berth. The allocated berth was one I had not been to before and I questioned the pilot as to the shallow water indicated on the chart. The pilot replied, in the fairly casual manner of so many Italian pilots, 'Nothing to worry *Commandante*, the berth, she has been dredged.'

The berth was only just long enough for our vessel, and I had to reverse the ship into the basin in order to go starboard-side alongside. We approached carefully, with the ship almost in the correct position but some five metres off the berth. My intention was to 'work' the ship sideways with thruster forward and propellers aft, but the stern started to come in for no apparent reason. I adjusted the controls, and the stern came out but the bow came in. There could be no logical explanation other than that the ship was pivoting on the end of the extended stabiliser, which must now be resting against the dock wall – but I had been assured that it was housed inboard.

I quickly ran into the wheelhouse and phoned the chief engineer down below, explaining that I thought the unimaginable had occurred and for him to go and check. I could almost see his white face as he called back to tell me that the fin was out!

Nothing for it but to carefully lift the ship back off the dock while the engineers attempted to rehouse the fin. This was soon accomplished, and I was able to dock the ship normally. We reviewed the situation after mooring operations were completed; no one could shed any light on how the fin could have become extended.

I filed a report and forwarded it to the company. To say they went ballistic would be an understatement. Technical superintendents came out to the ship. The owners sent disparaging letters to the ship managers, accusing them of putting incompetent staff on board and to dismiss the person or persons responsible. The reason for such high drama was that if the ship had been brought close to the jetty with any speed, not only would the fin have been severely damaged, but a hole could have been ripped out of the hull as steel was torn apart. The engine room could have been flooded, and if watertight doors had not been closed quickly enough the ship might have sunk alongside the berth. A sobering thought for me as a fairly young master who had been with the company only six months.

We never found the culprit. However, one of the electricians had been seen replacing the computer card on the starboard fin the day before while the vessel was at sea. It is quite possible that he had extended the fin to test the card and had not housed it correctly, or had not set the securing pins and it had come back out on its own. A combination of mistakes had compounded the error: the indicator panel on the bridge showing fins in or out was not switched on, and the engineer on watch had not physically gone down to check the securing pins at the stabiliser housing.

The furore eventually died down, we compiled new checklists for both engine room and bridge, and now I ensure that the indication panel is on permanently. Even with all these measures, as I walk onto the bridge wing to bring the ship alongside, I make a point of glancing at the indicator panel. I still partly blame myself, but I learnt from that incident that you can never rely completely on the word of someone else. If it's important enough, check it yourself.

Lifeboats
Lifeboat drill is probably one of the most potentially dangerous events that we have on a regular basis, and it is for this reason that I have always been very particular in ensuring the officers in charge are well trained. When there are large heavy boats being run up and down, wires going round sheaves, ropes round blocks plus tricing pennants to let go and bowsing tackles to make fast, there are plenty of opportunities for disaster.

I have always taken boat drill seriously, I always watch from the bridge wing the boats go down and then come back up. I have always ensured that the officers learn to have eyes in the backs of their heads, to always follow a set procedure and never to let the crew perform any action unless all those involved, both in the boat and on the boat deck, are ready to deal with the unexpected. Here is a report I had to make from *Sundream* in late 2003 after a drill where the unlikely became reality.

Incident to number 4 lifeboat

10 November 2003. Port of Corunna.

Please be advised that during a routine emergency drill this morning, a failure of the aft block swivel to number 4 lifeboat allowed the aft end of the boat to drop approximately 2 metres before its weight was held by the after bowsing tackle.

The forward block and hook remained attached and the boat lay stern down at an approximate angle of 30 degrees. Of the seven crew members in the boat at the time, two received very minor injuries and one fell from the boat to the water below. He was recovered by another boat and apparently has relatively minor bruising to the chest. The doctor will compile and forward the medical reports.

The boat could neither be lowered nor recovered on board and it was necessary to employ the services of a shore crane contractor to lower the boat to the shore. The ship was turned on the berth between 1500 and 1530 hours to allow this operation to be completed.

The security officer is compiling reports from all persons present. The safety officer will compile an incident report.

I was monitoring the launching of the lifeboats from my position on the bridge wing. All the remaining five boats on the port side had been lowered safely and the tender, number 4 boat, was about to be lowered, with the safety officer Magne Johansen on the deck and two second officers in the boat. It would appear that the pin at the base of the swivel failed as the aft tricing pennant was being released and the transverse weight of the boat came onto the after bowsing tackle. From my vantage point it appeared that all normal precautions had been taken and that this incident was caused by a structural failure of some sort.

Investigations as to the failure will continue on board and ashore by the technical superintendent who is proceeding to Corunna. *Sundream* sailed from the port at 1954 hours without number 4 boat on board, having received a dispensation to complete the voyage from the classification society, DNV.

In my fourteen years in command it was the first time there had been a serious incident, and I watched the whole scene in what seemed like slow motion from the bridge wing. I saw the boat fall and then come to a sudden stop, and as I waited for something else to break I saw the crew member make a graceful descent into the harbour some ten metres or more below. I waited for him to surface, and watched to see whether his lifejacket, which should turn him so his head is above water, would exhibit a lifeless face, neck broken by the impact.

Everyone was shocked, but I was surprised at quickly how they all recovered and started doing the right thing. The guy in the water surfaced and started spluttering, so he was OK; I sent another boat to fish him out. The guys still in the now partially suspended boat gingerly made their way up and out onto the boat deck, and the officers on deck, after assisting them, tried to fathom out how they could prevent the boat falling even further.

The fact that the only injury was a broken finger was a miracle. On other ships where an accident of this type has happened there have almost always been fatalities. If the manila rope and three sheave blocks, known as the bowsing tackle, designed to hold the lifeboat alongside the ship whilst being loaded, had parted, the aft end of the boat would have dropped to the vertical position. The forward fall block or the securing foundation in the boat might have given way, and the boat would have dropped onto the crew in the water. Anyone still in the boat as it fell would have suffered serious, if not fatal, injuries, and then could have been trapped as it filled with water. It's the stuff of nightmares, and as I watched all the officers and crew performing exactly as they should I realised that my demands for regular and proper training in the past had finally been justified.

The problems this incident caused the company were many. We were about to cross the Atlantic for our winter season in the Caribbean. To sail with one boat short would mean that the passenger complement would be reduced, not just by the capacity of this tender, but also by the capacity of the tender on the other side. This is as a result of the way the life-saving appliance rules are written. Unlike a cargo ship, where there should be enough lifeboats on each side to hold the ship's complement, a passenger ship must have sufficient boats between the two both sides, plus an extra 33 per cent available space, which can be in life rafts, to take the total souls on board. This is a slightly complicated formula which does not allow for the master's inability to launch boats and rafts on the weather side should the sea conditions be too rough. My paper for the Command Seminar in 2000 (see pages 357–365) was an appeal for the authorities to look again at the rules, particularly in light of the huge cruise ships that started to be launched in the 1990s.

We also needed both the tenders in the Caribbean, as there would be several ports where we were to anchor and send passengers ashore by boat. Our own tender, after being landed ashore, was going to take a week or more to repair. The solution was a sensible one: we would take the number two tender from *Carousel* when we met in Las Palmas a few days later, and they would take our boat after it had been repaired. They were based in the Canary Islands for the winter and had no anchor ports. An easy plan to devise, but not quite so straightforward to carry out. Dispensations had to be obtained from the country the ship was registered with in order to complete the cruise, and the same for the *Carousel*, as they would have to sail without a boat. The flag state, the Bahamas, would insist that the total complement on board was reduced to reflect the life-saving capacity on board, so passengers would have to be cancelled or crew landed.

In the end, the logistical nightmare was somehow sorted by our incredibly hardworking, ever-present and knowledgeable marine operations manager, Myra. We had a test run in Las Palmas, offering *Carousel*'s boat up to our falls; it fitted perfectly but we had to return it to them in order that they might finish their cruise in Tenerife. We were meant to sail that evening for Antigua, but I told the passengers we were making a slight diversion. They sailed early; we followed shortly after and arrived in Tenerife about five hours later. They had already docked and were making preparations to bring the boat over. Within an hour we had their boat secured in our falls and were on our way across the Atlantic on the repositioning voyage. Lost time was picked up and we arrived on schedule some six days later. *Carousel* eventually took our boat a few weeks later, after it had been shipped down to Las Palmas for repair. To my knowledge they were never changed back. An eagle-eyed ship spotter might have noticed that the ships had tenders that were slightly different in appearance. The side fendering was constructed differently, and for *Sundream* it was orange while the fendering on the *Carousel* was black.

Bumps and holes

I'm not so sure that anyone can be lucky enough to drive their car all through their life without having one or two little bumps or scrapes, and it's much the same with ships. Apart from the excursion of my somewhat inexperienced Burmese second officer on board *The Empress* in 1994, I have been, to date, relatively fortunate. It is quite true what they say – 'Any docking without paperwork at the end is always classed as a 100% success!'

There are some ports and some days, however, that catch you by surprise, and a notable one for me was the island of La Palma in the Canary Islands. *Carousel* was in the middle of a winter season cruising Morocco, Madeira and the Canaries, not a bad itinerary for a little winter warmth, but the sea conditions are not always that perfect. In fact quite large swells coming from North Atlantic depressions can travel thousands of miles to give a particularly uncomfortable ride.

It was on a day when an Atlantic depression had come much further south than normal. We arrived early in the morning and docked bow-in towards the port without any problem, even though outside the winds had started to increase from the west. The port and small town of Santa Cruz is on the eastern side of the island, well protected from any weather except that which may come from the east, which was fairly rare. The local agent informed me, however, after we came alongside, that a westerly gale could cause problems. The island is of volcanic origin and very high, and the tall mountains are horseshoe-shaped, with the open neck towards the west.

Strong westerly winds rise up through the mountains, cooling as they do so; they then tumble over the top of the Caldera and spill down the eastern side, towards Santa Cruz directly below. This phenomenon is supposed to occur very rarely, perhaps only every fifty years or so, but I was to discover that, unfortunately, this was to be the day. The morning passed quite normally, with no extreme weather forecast, but by lunchtime things had started to change. While I was taking a bite to eat I felt the ship heave on its mooring lines and bump back onto the fenders. Concerned, I went up to the bridge where the officer on duty told me the wind speed had just shot up to over 30 knots for a few moments. Not for long, but long enough to have an effect on our relatively high-sided ship.

I stayed on the bridge and it wasn't too long before another gust came down from the top of Roque De Los Muchachos, 2,423 metres above. The port is situated so that these winds dropping down from the mountain are funnelled into the harbour, speeding up considerably before reaching sea level. I ended up staying on the bridge for about the next eight hours, watching severe gusts passing across the water, making mini-waterspouts as they swirled around and regularly reaching 60 knots. One gust went over 80 knots on the anemometer, roofing on the cargo sheds ashore was peeled off and scattered onto the road, and the ship surged on the ropes as the weight increased. Extra lines were put out and secured as best we could, the gangway was lifted clear of the quay and passengers advised to stay inside the ship. As the ship moved around it would come back heavily onto the fenders and the steel hull plating was not only marked with black rubber, but was actually dented.

Departure at the scheduled time of 1800 hours was a definite 'no-no'. The local airport was closed shortly after we saw a German holiday jet drop probably a hundred feet or more as it made its approach. We had our worries, but I was very glad not to be in that plane. Eventually, by about 2000 hours, the wind started to drop. I had the engines started ready to leave when there was a lull long enough for us to get off the berth. I had been worried because the wind had been veering during the afternoon; if it had come round to the starboard bow it would have been pushing the ship off the jetty as opposed to on, and a sudden squall could have broken the lines and cast us adrift onto rocks just a few hundred metres off our port side.

The agent had advised me that, even in this unusual situation, there was a chance that the wind would drop as the sun went down. It did, but there were still gusts of 15 knots or so. I wanted to go immediately, but was held up by the freight ferry leaving first. The engineers started the larger bow thruster, some one thousand horsepower available to push the bow off the quay as we came astern, but then there was a problem. The thruster motor stopped and the engineers couldn't rectify the fault straightaway. I asked for the smaller thruster, about five hundred horsepower, still strong enough under normal conditions to hold the bow off the quay as I screwed the stern off with the propellers and backed out.

It didn't work out like that. I got the stern out to a reasonable angle, kept the thruster on, and started to increase the sternway. As we moved astern off the jetty a squall came across the harbour, probably greater than 20 knots, and the ship started to move bodily sideways back towards the quay. Thrusters lose their ability to move the bow one way or the other as speed is increased. We were only doing 3 or 4 knots, but the thruster could not keep the bow off. I adjusted the pitch on the main propellers in an attempt to bring the stern back parallel with the quay. But it's not a motorcar, and these things take time – perhaps only ten seconds or so, but I didn't have that time.

The ship landed heavily against the fenders, pushing them in so much that the shell plating just behind and below the bridge wings actually hit the concrete surface. Not much I could do about it, but the fender acted like a big spring assisting the thruster and pushing the ship away from the wall. The squall had also passed, and within seconds I found myself back in control of my vessel. We continued out of the harbour with our wind-blown agent and pilot, who hadn't come aboard anyway, looking down at the quayside and at the hull. He gave me the thumbs up sign, so I guessed there was not too much damage apart from the inevitable black skid mark down the side of the ship.

The next day in Tenerife we went down to inspect the ship's side. Not so bad, except there appeared to be an indentation in the hull about two metres long, formed, no doubt, as the ship came into contact with the concrete. The indentations caused by the ship surging onto the fenders during the afternoon were deeper – deep enough to need repairing at the next dry-docking.

The classification society surveyor, who acts on behalf of the country who registers the ship, has the duty to inspect, amongst other things, everything of a technical and safety nature. Indentations in the ship's hull plating of less than a couple of inches are normally accepted and do not have to be cut out and repaired, unless the framing inside is distorted or cracked. My crease was not particularly deep, so the ship would, in all probability, remain with 'Rentell's mark' for the rest of its life.

There were a few other heavy landings when I was in Sun Cruises, but nothing of any significance except one. I had flown over to the States to take over the *Song of America*, which was to become our flagship, the *Sunbird*. At around 38,000 gross registered tons it was the largest ship I had commanded, and a slightly daunting prospect with its sophisticated bridge and control system. I had been with the ship since Los Angeles, spending two weeks on board as it completed its final cruise for the original owners, Royal Caribbean Cruise Line, around to Florida. I had time, therefore, to watch the master handle the ship.

It is not until you handle the ship yourself that you get to understand its little quirks, what it can and cannot do, and how well it will manoeuvre in varying conditions of wind. I took over and, fortunately, it was a straight drive off the quay, no turning and no weather to speak of. After a seven-day passage across the Atlantic we arrived off the Mersey, bound for the dry docks of Cammell Laird at Birkenhead. The harbour pilot boarded and gave all the indications of having an intimate knowledge of the river and its currents. He may have done, but it turned out that he was not inclined to share his knowledge until I asked him, by which time it was way too late.

We had to pass into the dry dock at an exact state of the tide, when the sill of the dock would be sufficiently deep to let us slide over the top. He made the approach, we were right angles to wind and tide and the wind were strong. Initially the manoeuvre went well. I held the ship in position a few hundred metres off the open dock entrance, and the minutes ticked away as the dock master was constantly advising the pilot of the changing depth of water over the sill.

When we were given the go-ahead, I increased the forward speed, making allowance for the current to ease off at the bow as we reached quieter water close by the dock entrance. But then the bow started to go the other way. I couldn't hold it with the thrusters, and the tug was now incorrectly placed to assist. I asked the pilot whether there was a counter-current at the entrance and it was only then that he said yes, there was!

Time was running out. We continued, and as I brought the forward speed down to a minimum I realised that I must allow the bow to rest gently on the corner of the dock entrance and then slide the ship gradually into the dock. Unfortunately, from the conning position it was impossible to see the corner once the ship was closer than ten metres, and it disappeared below the flare of the bow. The bow came down fairly slowly to rest on the corner, but still too fast to avoid putting a one-metre crease into the shell plating. With all the weight of thruster and tugs it was still impossible to keep the ship up against the wind, so we gradually slid along the wall and into the dock until all effects of the river current had disappeared.

Damage was minimal, except for a good scraping of the paint, but of course there were a good many 'managers' down from the head office in Manchester eyeballing the whole operation. I don't think they were over-impressed with the master's driving of their new pride and joy. Of course, there wasn't a single one of them on the dock who had the slightest understanding of how a ship is manoeuvred, so I wasn't particularly concerned.

Even though it was judged by the surveyor that the shell plate indentation could remain, the director of Airtours taking responsibility for the ship decided to have a section of plate about one metre square replaced. The dent would have been fairly close to the new name above, and therefore would have been in any photographs taken during the renaming ceremony.

The relief master, a hairy Norwegian, was not going to let me forget that one, even though he'd had a few classic dents in his time with the company. I didn't worry – there was no great love lost between us.

The story of the hole may seem unlikely to the land person, but unfortunately on old ships one must expect the unexpected. After enough of these experiences one starts to develop a rather calm manner in dealing with them, often to the surprise of others who, shall we say, are more emotionally inclined, and who may see shouting and waving of hands as part of the sorting-out process.

During the first winter season, the *Carousel* made three long cruises to the Caribbean, first from Palma and then from Tenerife. I was on board for the first and third, and it was during the last that we had yet another unusual experience.

We had left Guadeloupe on 4 March 1997, bound east for a seven-day Atlantic crossing back to Tenerife. The cruise had gone particularly well, with good weather and a relaxed passenger complement of over one thousand, all of whom seemed to be enjoying themselves.

On the evening of the 5th, at 2235 hours, the duty fire patrolman reported water coming in from the ship's side down in the laundry. We investigated the situation and it appeared that water was coming in from under some stainless steel cladding, under which was rock-wool insulation. The cladding was removed, and underneath could be seen an area of corroded steel between frames 137 and 138, out of which was issuing a steady flow of sea water, estimated to be about three tonnes an hour.

The bilge pump could, of course, cope with such a small amount, but we had no way of knowing whether the hole would increase in size. We certainly were not going to hammer away with a chipping hammer! I informed David Carter, the Airtours technical superintendent who was travelling on board, and he decided on the steps to be taken to strengthen the area.

I could do little to help, and if I stayed awake all night just to watch the repairs I would be of no use should a bigger emergency arise. I retired to bed and spent a few moments thinking about what potentially could go wrong. Regrettably, the watertight bulkhead behind the main laundry was severely corroded at the bottom where it joined the tank top; if the laundry became flooded then the next compartment aft would also flood. *Carousel* was a two-compartment ship, meaning that, theoretically, with two watertight compartments flooded, she would remain afloat; however, if there were water ingress anywhere else, she would surely sink.

During the night a steel plate was welded between the two frames and cement was then poured in to try and harden around the corroded area. The pressure of water made this very difficult, and in the end a smaller drain hose with a valve attached was led off to relieve the pressure. This was successful, and when the cement had hardened the valve was closed. Another larger cement box covering the valve was constructed the next day – what you might call a 'belt and braces' temporary repair.

On the other side of the laundry there was similar cladding, and this was removed to show also what appeared to be sea water seeping through the hull. The rock wool had effectively trapped water and held it against the steel, causing it to corrode between the frames over an area of about half a metre square. A strengthening repair was also made to this side.

With both David Carter and Peter Whitehead, a technical superintendent from V.Ships, on board, I left them to do the reporting back to the managers and owners. We realised that the classification society would have to be informed and also that, because of the corrosion on the watertight bulkhead at the aft end of the laundry, there would be little chance that a surveyor would let us sail with passengers after we had reached Tenerife. A decision had to be made to cancel the next two or three cruises, and also to find a dry dock which would be able to take us.

I also had to consider the fact that, should the leak become worse, I would have to turn the ship back to the nearest safe port. I was sure the word would come out and the passengers would be made aware of the problem, thus causing anxiety and potentially damaging media coverage.

Dry docks were considered in Gibraltar, Cadiz and Lisbon, but none was available for over a week. The next two cruises were cancelled on the Friday, and the director of Airtours cruises, John Drysdale, wanted me to inform the passengers on board before someone from the shore phoned in and let the cat out of the bag. I held off until Saturday lunchtime, some four days after the incident and only three days before our scheduled return. I spoke over the public address system as I always did after noon with the information about the day's run, speed, weather, etc. I then said that I was sure they would like to know what was happening over the next year with the ship, that there had been a problem early in the week and that the ship would be going into dry dock for a precautionary inspection. I followed the statement with information about future cruises, hoping to lose some of the importance of the problem in a smokescreen of detail. The ploy worked quite well, as there was never any real concern, although a few passengers tried to hazard a guess as to the problem. I don't think anyone really found out the truth. I certainly did not tell them, and they all left happily upon arrival the following Tuesday.

Our arrival in Tenerife was on schedule, even though the weather had been far from pleasant considering the latitude of our crossing – a force 8 northerly gale the previous day had made a few passengers ill. By 0730 we had docked, and during the morning Arne Stavelin from Det Norske Veritas, our classification society, came aboard to survey the problem areas. In the meantime an underwater welding and repair company from Belgium, Hydrex, sent their representative – and it was decided that an in-water repair could be made rather than send the ship to some distant dry dock. These repairs could, therefore, be finished in good time to resume cruising a week later.

A local diving company inspected the area, and using a chipping hammer on the wasted steel they made a hole about fifteen centimetres by ten, thus proving our suspicions. If we had chipped away at sea it would have been doubtful if the pumps could have coped with two to three hundred tonnes of water per hour.

Initially there were a few problems because the local diving company believed they should be doing the repairs and would not offer any assistance to the Belgian company. Eventually it was accepted that Hydrex were the experts, and a compromise was reached, with the local company being given all the other work, which included an in-water hull survey for the annual safety certificate. Three British divers employed by Hydrex were flown in the next day, and on the Thursday they commenced work.

The work entailed a steel doubler plate approximately one metre square being welded over the corroded area on the outside of the hull, about three metres under water. By Saturday evening the work was complete and the hull watertight again. Even so, a company from Las Palmas was employed to weld reinforcing plates and frame to the area inboard. All of this work would eventually have to be cropped out during the next scheduled dry-dock and a permanent repair inserted.

The Las Palmas company, Nico International, also worked on the corroded bulkhead of the laundry, adding an L-shaped doubler to ensure the watertight integrity. The forward bulkhead was also badly corroded, and this had doublers welded in from the reverse side, which happened to be inside freshwater tanks 22 port and starboard.

Airtours felt that all these problems were due to a lack of maintenance by the previous owner, RCCL, plus a lack of proper survey by the classification society, and therefore they intended to pursue a claim against them. An independent surveyor from London arrived to review the damage. A loss adjuster from Special Risks Limited came aboard to ascertain the degree of 'loss' with regard to his client's expense for the 'loss of revenue insurance'. He, in turn, was being monitored and advised by a claims manager from Silver Line, a V.Ships London office subsidiary. All rather complicated, but an example of how the financial side of shipping works.

On Monday 18 March I donned the ship's diving gear and took a look under the hull, at the new doubler plates, the rudders and propellers, the stabilisers, the grids for sea suctions and the bow thrusters. Everything looked reasonable – a few dents, barnacle growth on the grids, scratched paint around the bulbous bow where the chain moves around when the vessel is at anchor, some light weed here and there. I found it reassuring to be able to inspect these things myself, even though the class surveyor had been satisfied with the underwater video inspection.

On Tuesday morning, between eight and nine o'clock, we shifted the ship back to our normal berth and within a few hours were embarking passengers for our next cruise. Another problem in the running of a large cruise vessel had been rectified with the minimum of fuss, the losers unfortunately being those passengers who had to miss their holiday on board, plus, of course, the insurers who would have to reimburse the company for at least some of their expense and lost revenue.

Meridian passage:
Sun Cruises at its zenith

I joined the *Seawing* in the south of France on 2 October 1997, and was to be attached to that vessel until December of the following year. It was a time when Airtours and Sun Cruises were really starting to make their mark in the UK cruising market. We all felt rather pleased that after less than two years a third ship had joined our fleet and we were carrying up to three thousand passengers a week, year round. *Sundream*, the ex *Song of Norway*, was now well settled in, with John Reeves and Alfredo Romeo as the designated masters.

In fact *Sundream* was the oldest ship, having been built in 1969, but as she was a sister to *Carousel* and the price was right, it made good sense to buy her. I felt it a little strange, though, that the management should put a new man to the company as the first master, as he would not understand all the little intricacies of company policy that I had had to learn, particularly as the ship was to be managed by V.Ships, the same management company that *Carousel* was with. In fact there had been some degree of friction between the two parties, as the ship managers were concerned that marine director Jim Evans of Sun Cruises was cutting the operating budget too close to the knuckle, while at the same time demanding greater and greater efficiencies.

The move turned out to be a very pleasant change for me, as the *Seawing* was to transfer to Cyprus, where her operating base would be Limassol. During the summer months we operated weekly cruises to the Greek islands, carrying up to eight hundred and fifty passengers. In the winter we started what is often referred to as Holy Land cruising, making three- and four-day cruises from Cyprus to Egypt and Israel. Unfortunately, there was an attack on tourists at the Egyptian resort of Luxor early in the season and the bottom just fell out of the market to Egypt. Airtours cancelled our calls at Alexandria and Port Said, the entrance to the Suez Canal. We attempted various alternatives to bring back passengers, including stops at Antalya and Alanya in Turkey, Rhodes, overnight in Haifa, but unfortunately the travel operator could not sell the ship at the right price. Later in that first winter season *Seawing* repositioned to Tenerife to operate weekly cruises around the Canaries.

In November 1997 I was taken off the ship to attend a conference back in Southampton. All six captains were instructed to go along so those at sea handed over command to their respective staff captains for up to a week. We had two days of talks with the tour operator, and the mood was very upbeat, but one thing they did tell us was that they found it very difficult to sell the ships at the right price during the winter season. The company was attempting to be vertically integrated with its different divisions; the cruises, for example, would be sold by their Going Places shops on the high street, the Airtours airline would carry the passengers to the ports where the ships were based and we in Sun Cruises would take them on the cruise. Sun Cruises was a wholly owned subsidiary of Airtours, and Airtours, the tour operator, would charter all the berths on the ships at the beginning of every season at a fixed price. As a cruise operator, Sun Cruises would have to operate to a working budget set at the beginning of each financial year. To my knowledge we never made a loss on budget, and by 2003 I was told we had made a profit of eight million pounds over budget. In fact, pro rata, I was

Seawing

told that Sun Cruises were making more money than any other division within Airtours.

The cruise conference, as it was referred to, was, we believed, very beneficial, and some of us were quite forward when it came to suggesting ways we could further integrate and assist each other in selling the ships to what was now a booming cruise market out of the UK. There was an underlying feeling, however, that the tour operator was having a problem in selling a cruise rather than a package holiday; in fact our customers were just a small fraction of their overall turnover, which was huge. I had the distinct impression that we were a nuisance factor that had to be tolerated. Perhaps I was wrong, but finally I believe I was proved right.

In the meantime the *Seawing* carried on regardless. She was the smallest ship of the fleet at a mere 16,710 gross tons and a length of 163 metres. Compared to *Carousel* she felt much smaller, but first-time cruisers loved her. She had an intimacy that the modern ships will never achieve. If you met someone one night you would see them the next, whereas the new leviathans are so big you are sometimes lucky if you find the same lounge the next evening. The Piano Bar was just aft of the main lounge, and the resident pianist, Paul Madden, had the passengers at his fingertips with his superb playing, excellent singing and casual banter. Upstairs in the Crows Nest the disco kept very late hours, and the atmosphere with the waiters in the restaurant was electric at times.

The Greek island cruising was a very pleasant change from the Palma itineraries. We had calls at Heraklion in Crete, Rhodes, Piraeus for Athens and Santorini, the latter being a firm favourite. Santorini, or Thira as it is sometimes referred to, is the remnants of a terrific volcanic eruption that took place approximately 1500 years before the birth of Christ. We normally anchored in about twenty-five metres of water, on the plug of an extinct volcanic side cone and the only available place where it was shallow enough. To find the spot we had to use both radar and echo sounder. If I made a mistake, or passed over the anchorage too quickly, the anchor and chain could have gone hurtling down to the depths, the securing pin in the chain locker being torn from the securing point by weight and momentum. To make matters worse, all this had to be done in the hours of darkness to ensure we were the first vessel to arrive and grab the spot – 'first come, first served.'

The small village lies at the top of the cliffs and can be accessed by a cable car or via the zigzag track by donkey. The chief engineer, Ian Dimblebee, and I would walk up. We considered it our exercise for the week and were justly rewarded at the top by a couple of bottles of Mythos, the rather pleasant Greek beer. On average the walk took us just under nineteen minutes, though we were often be hampered by donkeys, and their 'residue', passing either up or down. But to sit at that bar, with a cold beer, and take in the view was superb. I have not yet met a passenger who has been unimpressed by Santorini.

Our first calls to Israel and Egypt were not without amusing incident. On entering Haifa, I think on our second or third call, an elderly pilot boarded. As was the custom, I asked him if it was OK for me to continue to 'drive' and take the ship alongside the allocated berth. He said quite categorically that he would drive. Fine, I said, and watched with interest. When berthing a ship, the approach is everything; get that wrong and you'll probably make a mess of the docking. Similarly, with a bridge control ship, it's not so easy to give the right orders with someone else on the controls as there is no such thing as 'half ahead', 'dead slow astern', etc. It can be like teaching someone else to drive a car and them pressing the pedals, you never know if they'll press the right one or to the right degree of pressure.

In the end the pilot completely messed up the approach, and eventually I asked him to confirm which berth he was taking us to, no doubt with a certain amount of cynicism in my voice. He gruffly replied that I had the con, and stepped away.

On another occasion, when we were leaving Alexandria, a pilot had boarded to take the ship the one mile from just off the berth to the breakwater. For some technical reason of which I was not immediately aware, we lost all power to the propellers. This had happened once or twice before and I wasn't too perturbed, as the chaps down below usually managed to restore power fairly quickly. So I didn't tell the pilot, but let him continue with the con, knowing that if I did he would want to anchor the ship and order a couple of tugs. For three or four minutes he noticed nothing, even though the ship had slowed down from 12 knots to less than 4. He only cottoned on when he realised there was an unusual amount of bridge-to-control-room communication taking place and the scenery on either side had almost stopped passing by. When he did, I explained there was no need to panic, and fortunately the power came back just before he grabbed the VHF and shouted in gruff Arabic to the port control office.

A little more serious was an incident that occurred while the ship was berthed in Istanbul, one of our irregular port calls. The chief and I had gone ashore on an all-day tour to visit some of the wonderful sights of that historic city. I received a call from the staff captain about 1000 hours, advising me that the port authorities were now in discussion with our appointed shore agents over an oil spill that they said had come from our vessel. Should I return? 'Not necessary at the moment,' he said. So we continued with the tour and later received a message saying all had been sorted – well, to a fashion!

In fact, two roving officials had noticed some lubricating oil slowly rising to the surface near the gangway. Apparently an engine room rating had topped up the stabiliser header tank and, unknown to him, a seal had deteriorated sufficiently to allow very small amounts to escape. Our estimation was that it could have been no more than a couple of litres, but the Turkish authorities are extremely intolerant with regard to any oil entering their harbour. The fine depends not on the amount of oil but on the size of ship. Our agent explained that the fine could have been in the region of US$42,000, and because it was a bank holiday the ship might be detained. However, he had negotiated with the two officials and, in the way business is often done in some parts of the world, a decision was made that in exchange for a much smaller sum passed directly to the men next day, further action would not be necessary.

Meanwhile, back in the UK, the initial Sun Cruises team, which had consisted of just three people working from an office above a Going Places shop near Portsmouth, had moved to new larger offices which had been built at Hedge End near Southampton. The number of staff had increased dramatically, and within six months the offices were already too small. It was obvious to us all that the company was working towards managing their own vessels, and the services of V.Ships were shortly to be dispensed with. Rumour had been rife that Sun Cruises were about to purchase another ship, probably the *Song of America*, and eventually this was confirmed.

For many months there was speculation between the ships as to who the first appointed master would be to the new ship. I was the master with the longest service with the company, but it was made perfectly clear by Jim Evans that the position would be granted on merit, and then not until much closer to the time of handover. Mark Cameron, one of our chief engineers, went over during the summer of 1998 and spent many months observing the operation and becoming totally familiar with the technical plant.

Eventually, Jim advised me that I would be the first master

and that Kjell Stokerite, a Norwegian who had originally come from Norwegian Cruise Line with *Seawing*, would be my opposite number. I was to leave the *Seawing* in early December, take some leave and then fly out to join *Song of America* in Los Angeles for her last voyage with Royal Caribbean Cruise Line passengers around to Miami, then up to Norfolk, Virginia, for dry dock. I was then to take over command and bring the ship back across the Atlantic to the UK for a refit in Birkenhead at the Cammell Laird yard.

Before all this, though, there were changes afoot within the management of Sun Cruises. The first managing director, John Drysdale, had left and been replaced by David Burns. He took a long look at the economics of having an operating base for the fleet in Southampton while the main body of Airtours was based up at Helmshore north of Manchester. The decision was made to relocate, and our shore staff were forced to move or leave the company. Jim Evans decided he wasn't prepared to move and consequently left before the launch of *Sunbird*, our newest vessel. In many respects I felt this was a great shame, as both John and Jim had been the driving force behind the cruise operation and they were both outspoken enough to ensure their message got across. Perhaps things may have turned out differently if they had stayed.

Sunbird was a truly superb ship. I was told by the RCCL staff that it was by far the best ship the company had, and by that time they had a handful of ships over 70,000 gross tons.

Built in 1982 by Wärtsilä in Helsinki, *Song of America* was 37,584 gross tons, 214 metres long with a draught of 7 metres. Four Wärtsilä Sulzers provided the main propulsion, giving a total brake horsepower of 22,000 and a service speed in excess of 18 knots. For an experienced ship master she was a delight to handle, with no funny quirks and plenty of power in the two bow thrusters, enabling the ship to be turned around in her own length, even in fairly windy conditions when berthing. She was the second generation of cruise ship built for RCCL, and

Sunbird

everything which the naval architects had not got quite right on their first trio of ships they had sorted with this, their fourth.

Having spent a couple of weeks watching the Norwegian master handle the ship, I was eager to take the controls after it was handed over to Sun Cruises in Norfolk on Sunday 21 March 1999.

I had planned what is known as a composite great circle route across the Atlantic, up the US eastern seaboard, passing south of Cape Race in Newfoundland then north of Ireland and down to the Mersey. Of course it all depended on the weather. March is not always a favourable time of year in the North Atlantic – and the Norwegian master was quick enough to shake his head and remind me of this fact.

In fact, the worst weather was experienced during the first two days, and then the last as we picked up our landfall. High pressure fairly well south meant that we would experience following wind and sea if I went to the north, and this is exactly what we got, plus the added bonus that the northwesterly wind cleared any fog which might have been lurking off the Grand Banks. Ten years of experience plying the route from New York to Southampton paid off, and saved the company at least a precious day of time which would undoubtedly be needed in the refit.

Arriving off Liverpool we picked up the Mersey pilot and we discussed the arrangements for docking, the critical factor being the depth of water over the sill at the entrance to the dry dock. The events that followed have already been described in the chapter on *Bumps and holes,* so I need only say that the docking did not go as smoothly as one would hope. We ended up with a nice little paint scar and small dent on the starboard bow, but the damage was not serious enough, according to the surveyor, to consider cropping out and repairing.

Kjell Stokerite was already on board, having done the transatlantic, and he was to take over for the refit and the initial run down to Palma some three weeks later. I shot off home for a spot of leave and returned to Liverpool to complete a radio course a few weeks later. The refit went as well as could be expected, and a quick trip over to Dublin and back was made with Airtours staff before heading down for the Mediterranean, where she was officially renamed at a ceremony in Palma.

The initial cruise was perfect, unlike just about all start-up operations I have been involved with. There were no serious glitches, and if there could be a criticism, it would be that, because of the ship's size, it wasn't quite as intimate as our other vessels. I worked hard to rectify that, making my usual announcements, getting around the ship, and basically just doing what I believe a captain should do, communicate.

For the next twelve months Kjell and I worked three months on, three months off between us. Then I heard that he was being sent to the *Sundream* with immediate effect, but I was to stay another twelve months. The reason given was that a couple of our other masters had been on one ship for over three years and the company had decided on a policy of senior officers changing vessels after two or three years. Understandable I suppose, but I found it difficult to disguise my disappointment for a while.

The company ashore was still changing, David Burns left and Frank Pullman became the new Sun Cruises MD. By now the older ships were getting tired, there had been a couple of disastrous refits and an occasion when the *Carousel* turned around mid-Atlantic. Her master, John Brocklehurst, took the courageous decision to tell the company that, in his opinion, the ship would encounter even more serious problems if he attempted to continue the voyage to the Caribbean.

Later in the season, after *Carousel* finally reached her winter cruising ground, she was unlucky again. With a relatively inexperienced Italian master on board, she ran aground when leaving the difficult Mexican port of Calica. Unfortunately, the investigations became acrimonious and the master left our employ.

There was a growing need to try and replace our older tonnage. Old ships can become very expensive to run and, as they depreciate financially, so does their standing in the eyes of the experienced cruising public. So many new larger ships were coming onto the market that our competitors were able to reduce prices but still maintain profits. The cost of operation is looked at on a passenger berth per day basis, so if all available berths are sold at brochure price it actually costs less to run a larger ship. We were advised that, because *Sunbird* could carry almost twice as many passengers as *Seawing*, she was actually about 15% cheaper to operate on a passenger berth basis. All the tour operator had to do was fill the ship year round.

Frank Pullman, after protracted negotiation, had managed somehow to do a deal with a Greek cruise company, Royal Olympic. The *Seawing* would be transferred to the Greek company on some sort of lease-back arrangement. Royal Olympic would operate the ship for Airtours, still under the Sun Cruises banner, for the next four summer seasons. Airtours would pay them a fixed amount for the cabins and Royal Olympic would pay a fixed amount in return at the end of each year for the lease of the ship. At the end of the period the ship would effectively belong to Royal Olympic and we would have one less old ship. The theory behind all this was that the company would then have the financial capability to negotiate for further tonnage, another more modern and larger second-hand vessel, or perhaps even a new ship.

I signed on the *Carousel* in May 2001 and stayed for two

voyages, and it was like stepping back in time. Six years on from when I first joined the ship in Baltimore it seemed small, shabby and basically rather run-down. A new positive-pressure sewage treatment system had been fitted, but it used existing ventilation pipework, with the result that unpleasant odours seemed to filter up through corroded pipework to various parts of the ship – which had, amongst some of the crew, become known as the *Carousmell.*

One of our masters resigned, and I was asked if I would prefer to stay or transfer to *Sundream.* I needed the move, and furthermore the ship was operating out of the UK during the summer on Baltic and Norwegian itineraries, new territory for me.

Looking back, it was probably at this time that the star that was Sun Cruises had reached its zenith. The office had moved yet again to a new building at Parkway, just outside Manchester, part of the Airtours head-office complex, and the number of staff there seemed to grow every month. All that is required to run a cruise operation professionally was in place both on board and ashore, and the ships now had a continuity of good experienced staff. Even though the vessels were fairly old and possibly reaching their 'sell by date', the guys knew how to fix things when they broke, which happened not infrequently with some of the old equipment and plumbing. Unfortunately, although there were rumours of further tonnage, and even a visit by management to a shipyard in France, it all came to nothing.

Sunset

On 1 March 2002, having missed my connection in Bogotá the night before, I joined the *Sundream* in Cartagena, Colombia. Fortunately there was no problem: I was given a hotel room overnight and caught the first flight to the coast the following morning. Once again I was to work in partnership with Kjell Stokerite, and I spent two days with him going up towards Montego Bay in Jamaica. He left, I took over. The ship was much the same as the *Carousel*, with just a few differences in layout. For example, some changes had been made in the main lounge during the initial conversion of *Carousel*, but it had not really worked well and therefore retained its original form in *Sundream*.

I was to stay until the end of 2003 and, all in all, it was a very happy ship. The teams from engine room, bridge and hotel worked well together, particularly in my last year on board. We had some real characters – Mark Cameron as chief engineer, partnered latterly by Simon Graves, Andrew Clark as hotel director, Svein Mentzen and Kostas Gritzelis as the alternating staff captains. We all knew the ship was old, tired in places, prone to problems of one sort or another, but we just got on with it. They say that the old ships are often the happiest, and I think this was the case with *Sundream*. There was a good camaraderie, I always felt that the guys were keeping me informed, and thus I had little need to wield the 'big stick'. At times we laughed so much we were fit to burst.

In the meantime Airtours was changing in a big way. Chairman David Crossland was taking a back seat as a fresh team came in to manage the day-to-day operation. The company had grown considerably, taken over many foreign travel operators, and had a workforce of well over 20,000 worldwide. Four ships, over sixty planes and more than seventy retail outlets on the high street had created the second largest travel operator in the UK and possibly the largest air inclusive package tour operator in the world. A change of name and corporate logo had been decided upon. There was a board decision that the Airtours company name no longer represented the entire scope of holidays and packages that it sold. The new corporate name would be My Travel, and the logo was entirely different, basically blue and orange with an emphasis on the word 'my'. On board we were told we had to change the funnel logos of all four ships.

The company had budgeted a considerable sum to achieve this, but in the end our sailors dismantled the old raised logo and painted on the new one for virtually the cost of the paint. For the aircraft it was a different matter, and over two years later they still had a variety of markings. This was a management decision which we saw as a ridiculous waste of money – and perhaps we should have seen the writing on the wall, as it was just one of many such decisions they must have made, bringing the company almost to its knees.

On the *Sundream* we completed the winter season in the Caribbean, repositioned to Southampton and commenced the initial few cruises to the Mediterranean before repositioning again to Harwich. I had again the great pleasure of working opposite John Brocklehurst, and he handed over the ship to me for the second of two cruises up to northern Norway. Although I had been up there many years before on the *QE2*, and on a variety of cargo ships, I had never been through the inside route all the way to North Cape, a fantastic journey of over a thousand miles. The scenery was superb – mountains, fjords, and even a couple small glaciers. Of course, it meant many long hours on the bridge, but sometimes the views in the Arctic daylight of the night were just spectacular. In the two weeks the sun never set for over seven nights, North Cape was clear and we passed under the cliffs at midnight with the sun up to the north at least fifteen degrees above the horizon.

Returning to Harwich, I had the pleasure of my family, Helen and Richard, joining me for a full six weeks, three two-week cruises to the Baltic. Oslo, Stockholm, Helsinki, St Petersburg, Tallinn, Copenhagen and Amsterdam – it was fantastic. It rained for one day on our first call in Oslo, but then the sun just shone, and remained shining until our northern season of cruising was over. During the days the temperature rarely dropped below seventy-five degrees Fahrenheit, St Petersburg was stifling, Amsterdam was unbearable – it just went on and on.

I had decided to undertake a challenge, with Helen, to raise five thousand pounds for the charity Mission to Seafarers in order for us to join a small team journeying to Peru in October.

We were to spend two weeks travelling the country by road and rail. Lake Titicaca, the highest navigable lake in the world, and the Inca Trail to Machu Picchu would be on our itinerary.

In order to raise the money I had permission to 'pester' the passengers. We raised over three thousand pounds from the sale of my first book, and the rest from various means, such as raffling places at the captain's table and receiving a one-pound donation for a certificate I made up for 'surviving' very bad weather we had one night later in the season. It was printed over a photograph taken with the ship ploughing through mountainous seas (albeit a year before!) and we sold five hundred of them. The company were equally generous, donating a thousand pounds.

I took leave in early October 2002 and flew off with Helen to Lima. We made the trip, hiked the trail and returned safely to Cusco, the old Inca capital. One of our travelling companions returned from checking his email at an internet café. 'Did you realise your company is having financial problems?' he said. Apparently the share price had dropped to below twenty pence. I have to say I was surprised to say the least, particularly as many of us had signed up to a sharesave scheme and were banking on a return of well in excess of two pounds per share. This was probably the first time that I became aware that things were not exactly rosy in the My Travel camp.

We continued as normal. The winter season cruising out of Barbados went well and the ship always seemed to be full, even though we heard that there had been some very good late deals to be had. Many of our retired regular passengers admitted to me that they scanned teletext frequently and had a suitcase packed ready to go. Three or four hundred pounds for a week in the Caribbean, including flights, was not unheard of.

We received several emails from our Sun Cruises MD, who passed on to us policy statements from further up the management tree. We did, however, get the distinct impression that cost savings had to be made. They came gradually at first, with indications that operating budgets must be cut, dry-dock periods would become wet docks and reduced in length, only safety items were not held back or reduced in number when ordering spares. Entertainment costs were slimmed down by reducing the number of specialist acts, the band was taken off all ships except *Sunbird*, investment in new stage shows was cut back. By sourcing cheaper products food costs were reduced, as was the daily feeding rate per head, and only two midnight buffets were prepared instead of five. Then there was a pay freeze for all.

The options for two new ships that had been discussed with the French shipyard were dropped, which was particularly bad news as it had involved the shipyard taking our two oldest vessels as a part payment. It would have meant that again we would have been the market leader in our style of cruising.

Morale started to deteriorate on board, and there was much uncertainty. Ships are just about the last place you want to have rumours of impending bad news. There is always a minority of seafarers who will not accept that they must be patient and wait before speculation is confirmed. We call it 'galley radio' – the second lettuce chef knows more than the captain and the voices of doom and gloom start to wear everyone down. Sun Cruises then confirmed that *Sundream* would be taken out of service at the end of the 2004 summer season. *Seawing* was to also end about the same time and My Travel believed that, with just two ships, they would rationalise their cruise operation and would not have to discount passenger ticket sales in the winter periods. This was definitely not good news if you were appointed to the *Sundream*.

We all had almost a year's notice to get used to the situation, and by the end of 2003 the company were starting to transfer some of the officers they knew they would keep to the other ships. Kjell had resigned and I was advised unofficially that I didn't need to worry, which was fine for me, but didn't stop Helen being very concerned. Furthermore, there was continuous speculation that our flagship, *Sunbird*, was about to be sold for the Thomson operation.

The share price continued to drop, and a disastrous set of

annual accounts was announced by the new managing director of My Travel in April 2004. They had made an operating loss of almost one billion pounds. In his statement the MD referred to the cruise operation briefly, stating only that it was being reviewed.

It certainly was. Within a few days we heard that Louis Cruise Lines of Cyprus were bidding to operate the ships. Phone calls I received at home from friends on board indicated that half our office management team, along with a Louis management team, were already in the Caribbean waiting for the official announcement to be made. They were to walk onto the ships, at whichever island they were docked, and inform them of their fate. *Sunbird* and *Carousel* were being sold to Louis, while *Sundream* would be managed by Louis until the end of the summer season, when it would be put up for sale. All our people were to be made redundant within the month.

At home I waited for the inevitable, but then Myra phoned me up and explained another problem she had to rectify. The *Seawing*, which for the past three years had been managed and manned by the Greek company Royal Olympic, was laid up in Piraeus near Athens after the Greek company had gone bankrupt. It had been handed back by the Greek courts to Sun Cruises in order that they might complete a scheduled summer season. Would I be the captain? She could guarantee me perhaps six months' work. Of course I said yes, and I waited at home for further news.

This return to Sun Cruises' own management had been on the cards for several months, Royal Olympic having apparently failed to fulfil their obligations under the contract by not ensuring that the hull and machinery insurance were in date. A small team had gone over earlier in the year with the intention of taking possession, but had been turned away. The matter had gone before the Greek courts as the ship had been arrested by many of the creditors waiting to get money owed to them. Our own Sun Cruises captain, George Delagrammatikas, was on leave in Athens and finally accepted re-delivery towards the end of April, but there was less than two weeks to get the ship ready and cross over to Malta in order to start another summer season of cruising in the eastern Mediterranean.

It was an impossible task. The ship was a shambles and, apart from Sun Cruises having to pay off numerous creditors, there was just too much technical work to ensure all trading certificates would be in place in time. George managed to bring the ship to Malta, in foul weather, and put her in the dry dock, where both propellers had to be pulled as the oil lubrication system for the variable-pitch props was ninety per cent seawater. Ian Dimblebee was on board as chief engineer, and he let me know some of the things that were not working, which included both stabilisers, the sewage treatment plant, the oily water separators, both the evaporating and reverse-osmosis fresh water manufacturing plants. In addition the watertight doors took over four minutes to close when they should take no more than one, one boiler had collapsed, and the berthing controls on the bridge wings were inoperative. Fuel oil remaining in the bunker tanks was of such poor quality that it had to be removed by a firm of specialists. In the end, just two weeks of cruising were cancelled – but it was only through the hard work and professionalism of our own people that the ship managed to get away for the third cruise of the six-month season.

In the end I didn't join until June, by which time George had nicely settled the ship into its routines. He'd had a hard time and was very grateful for a seven-week vacation. By the time I arrived, Sun Cruises officers on the other three ships had already been made redundant and Greek officers from Louis Cruise Lines had manned their ships. A small minority had accepted the terms offered by the new owner, but in general their salaries and conditions were very poor in comparison, and no senior officer stayed on. They felt they had been sold down the line.

The 2004 summer season

Although the ship still looked fairly shabby, it was obvious the team spirit had taken over and all were working hard to ensure passenger satisfaction would be as high as we could expect to achieve. The ship was pretty old and looking 'tired' in many of the public areas. While she had been under Greek management little had been spent, not only on the technical side, but also cosmetically within the passenger areas. Even crew cabins were dirty and untidy. I set about getting things into some degree of order. Some of the crew were our own, while others were employed because they had worked on the ship within the previous few years – and it was these who had to be shown the standards we required. It didn't take long.

The ship had already started to settle into the two-week itinerary: Malta on a Sunday, then one week Dubrovnik, Venice, Corfu and Messina, the other week Heraklion, Rhodes, Santorini and Piraeus. It was the saving grace for the season, and both itineraries were popular with passengers and crew alike. For the first few weeks of my contract various bits of equipment failed from time to time, but we got by. Backing out of Rhodes in early June became interesting when the port propeller pitch became stuck halfway as I was building up the astern thrust, but it was temporarily sorted out by the chief officer giving the control lever in the wheelhouse a hefty wallop.

For a few days we were down to one not entirely satisfactory radar. An experienced technician from Malta dry docks came and sorted all three out in one go, using spares cannibalised from old sets over the years. Leaving Venice for the first time on 16 June, the gyrocompass jammed. The pilot could see what had happened but said nothing, and continued to con the ship using helm orders only. In theory he should have called up the harbour office and taken the ship to anchor until the problem was rectified. Perhaps he just wanted to get home, as it was early in the morning. As we pulled away from the pilot grounds in heavy rain, the gyro was given a 'gentle' shove which forced it past the point where it was sticking. At the first opportunity our electricians gave the equipment a good clean, and all was fine from that point on, yet another example of lack of maintenance. We continued through the month of June. Technical problems cropped up from time to time, but basically there were none that could be considered a 'ship stopper'. Routines became established and the crew gelled into a happy team who, although they knew the writing was on the wall with regard to their employment, were prepared to make the best of six months' work. I took the ship through the islands off the Croatian coast north of Dubrovnik, past the beautiful walled town of Korčula, and then found out that the authorities were banning the liners from using these relatively narrow waterways during the summer months. Apparently local windsurfers used to career across the paths of big ships, either for fun or to get from the mainland to the islands, causing so much of a nuisance that the authorities felt the need to act – and not in our favour. A great shame, as future passengers missed the lovely scenery of the Dalmatian coast – except, that is, on our last voyage, when I just went up there anyway.

I remember on one occasion there was a tremendous downpour just as I was docking in Corfu. I was so wet I had to change every item of clothing, and those white uniforms take on a different opacity when wet! Elsewhere we had our usual problems from time to time with pilots and harbour radio stations. The pilot in Rhodes tried to insist we should take a tug or two in the strong winds during our initial calls, but eventually gave up when he could see the ship was manoeuvrable enough and I was a capable of driving it without incurring damage or resulting paperwork. I joked with him and said I thought he had shares in the tug company. Valletta Harbour Radio seemed at times a little incapable of understanding developing situations when more than one ship approached the port at the same time, and on occasions we had close encounters which could have been avoided if they had given correct instruction in good time. On the other hand, I once had my ear 'bitten off' by Piraeus Traffic for approaching the harbour entrance without permission – but their shouting into the radio did nothing to improve clear or precise conversation.

On 9 July the ship was arrested, but then released, apparently over yet more bills the previous operator had not paid. In Venice a few days later an Italian Port State Control inspector gave us a hard time, but eventually gave us a 'clean' report. Later in the month I reported a Greek ferry to the harbourmaster in Rhodes when he made a very irresponsible manoeuvre in front of us as we approached the port – fat lot of good it did! One stabiliser was eventually repaired, but then other odd bits of machinery broke, or at least stopped working till our long-suffering team of engineers managed to get them up and running again. Seventeen cabins were flooded when a saltwater sanitary system valve blew off on a B deck cabin loo early one morning. Not really very nice, getting out of bed into six inches of water.

On one occasion the rain top on the starboard funnel blew off and landed on the deck below, smashing a deckchair completely. Fortunately the deck was empty of passengers. Sewage smells, bridge-wing controls failing at critical moments, engine overspeeds followed by unrequested stopping at critical moments – all these things came and went without even much of a raised eyebrow. We simply expected the unexpected, and when it happened we just got on with the job as best we could, no tears, no drama, just wry smiles and often some very hearty laughs. On one occasion we had so much rain that the plastic matting on the sun deck started to float around, while the pooling water seemed to find unknown holes, and proceeded to enter the public spaces from above.

Various people came to take a look at the ship with a view to purchase, including a consultant working on behalf of an Israeli casino concern. One old lady was landed with pneumonia, while another two were almost put ashore for excessive drinking and being a general nuisance. Two crew were dismissed for fighting.

The saddest incident was when a couple had to disembark just after we sailed from Malta after they heard their son had hung himself.

By late September the season was drawing to a close, and rumours started to fly – first that the company was going to cancel the last four cruises and Louis Cruise Lines was going to take over the ship. Royal Olympic, who were once more operating with just two ships, were again close to being stopped from sailing: in fact their ships were arrested and then released while in Turkey. Myra gave me a call in the middle of October and said we might have to cancel the last call to Piraeus, as Royal Olympic were somehow going to have the ship arrested.

On 25 October she called me again. It was the last cruise and we had left Valletta the evening before, the whole itinerary taking us only to Greek ports. She said the My Travel board were now very twitchy and I might get a call ordering me not to enter any Greek port in case we might be arrested. If that happened we would have to send all our passengers home and the ship would become the centre of some prolonged legal battle. It all was getting just too bizarre for me, and making a decent itinerary at this late stage out of only Turkish ports was a non-starter. That evening I instructed the electro-technical officer to shut down the satellite, so even if the company had wanted to stop me from making our first Greek call they would not be able to do so. I felt a little like Nelson looking through the telescope with his blind eye.

The satellite went back on the next day, but only after we were safely alongside in Heraklion. There was a message waiting, but it was instructing me to continue the itinerary as planned, except Piraeus would be dropped for Kusadasi in Turkey. In fact there were no problems in any of the Greek ports, and the week went brilliantly with good weather and all the passengers in a buoyant mood. The staff were in good form, knowing that the time for going home to their families would soon be upon them, and then I had sad crying eyes painted onto the port anchor. Myra came out, along with most of the remaining office managers, and when I showed her the artwork, out came a short four-letter expletive, quite unintentionally. My amusement was heightened by the look from a passenger from another cruise ship walking past nearby. She did take it in good spirit, but I had the offending paintwork removed once we arrived in Malta the following Sunday.

The passengers did not actually find out they were going to Kusadasi until they woke up, and even though they were expecting Piraeus not many seemed too concerned when I explained the reason why. After we sailed that evening we found out that the Royal Olympic owner had been searching for the ship, and when he realised it was not in Piraeus he had even tried to get the Turkish authorities to arrest us, but without success – for probably obvious reasons!

Then I found out that the ship might still be arrested once we arrived in Valletta. The managing director of My Travel was fortunately talked out of sending us directly to Sicily where, for some strange political reason, the Greek courts could not touch us. We arrived alongside at 0700 hours on Sunday 31 October, all passengers were disembarked by midday, and we slid away soon after. It was all rather nostalgic as, after a turbulent beginning, the ship had a superb summer season, receiving many favourable comments. Everyone on board had contributed their all, and it must have been one of the happiest ships that sailed the Mediterranean that year.

We sailed from Malta on Sunday lunchtime, and by 0830 hours on Tuesday 1 November we were safely alongside a lay-by berth in Palermo. I had plans already made, and left the ship two mornings later for a flight back to the UK. Within two more days I was in Monaco having an interview for a possible command with a fledgling cruise line, Easy Cruise.

Royal Olympic never did get the *Seawing*. The ship was sold to Louis Cruise Lines and renamed *Perla*, joining *Carousel* and *Sunbird*. The former became *Aquamarine*, while the latter was renamed *Thomson Destiny* and was in the end chartered to our main rivals. Only the *Sundream* went elsewhere, and the last we saw of her was lying alongside in Piraeus, where she had been renamed *Dream Princess* and was waiting to be converted into a casino ship destined for operating out of Israel. It was truly the end of an era.

Sun Cruises miscellany

Medivacs

Our business is one of giving a great many people the pleasure of seeing the world, experiencing countries and cultures different from their own, and hopefully making sure their holiday is an experience they may wish to repeat with us some time in the future. Of course, when you carry many thousands of passengers every year, some will have experiences that are beyond both their own and our control. People get sick.

All ships that carry more than one hundred people on board must, by international maritime law, also carry a doctor, but the rules don't actually say how many doctors or medical staff, so in fact with a total complement of fifteen hundred passengers and crew we would only carry one doctor and one nurse. Both of the medical team were usually trained in emergency medicine and had experience of the accident and emergency ward at a major hospital.

If a passenger developed a serious or life-threatening illness we would try and get them ashore as soon as possible. On a regular itinerary this was not normally a problem. The passenger would be disembarked as soon as we arrived, and it was not uncommon to see an ambulance, complete with blue flashing lights, on the quayside as we docked. It is quite surprising how many serious heart attacks have survived the night and have been landed 'intact'. This is, in the main, because the medical team are there within minutes when the emergency call is put out, applying first aid with the specialist equipment needed to resuscitate the patient and stabilise his or her condition.

There are occasions, however, when a medical disembarkation must be undertaken when the vessel is at sea. Fortunately I have only had a few, but it's not always an easy call to make, as I must also consider the other passengers and the effect it may have on their holiday. I have at times put a certain amount of pressure on doctors in order for them to assure me that the life of the patient is in danger if we cannot arrange to get them ashore one way or another. It becomes a little easier when the patient is obviously in a bad way, for example with a fading heartbeat or irregular breathing. Similarly if we had a passenger in labour – there would not be much doubt as to what I should do in that situation.

Then there is always plenty of paperwork to complete after the event. Here is an email I sent to the company shortly after I disembarked a passenger from one of the San Blas Islands, situated just off the Caribbean coast of Panama.

Mr Peter Sumner, a 39 year British passenger travelling on his own, had an apparent seizure during breakfast this morning. By the time the medical team arrived he had stopped breathing and his heart had stopped. His heart was revived within approx ten minutes. After being moved to the hospital his blood pressure and pulse came back but he was unable to breathe without assistance.

I contacted Adrian Homes at C B Fenton in Cristobal; he immediately started the process to see whether a helicopter or fixed-wing aircraft was available. The only helicopter did not have the ability to carry a stretcher so a medical team of three was organised, with an Islander aircraft, to fly out to the small airstrip on the island of Porvenir some five miles away.

The local Carti Island Chief, Tony Adames Harrington, was instrumental in setting up transport for the medical team to the vessel after they had landed. He did require $100 cash, which he said was needed to buy the fuel for his boat. This amount will need to be reimbursed to the company from the passenger's insurance company. The Chief Purser has already forwarded the Passenger Disembarkation Form, SMS 150.

The plane landed just before 1400 hours and the medical team were on board 45 minutes later. In the meantime the tender service ferrying passengers back and forward to the island of Carti was complete by 1500 hours. We therefore weighed anchor and proceeded towards Porvenir.

Because the passenger was a very large man, a team of sailors and security staff assisted the medical team in taking him from our hospital to the ship's pontoon and into a local boat. He was disembarked at 1555 hours. The whole team were also required to go with the boat and assist lifting the passenger into the plane, which was not specifically designed for medical emergencies. I understand the passenger is to be taken to the Clinica Einstein, Panama 5.

We cleared the area at 1654 hours, by which time the plane had not taken off. I anticipate our arrival in Cartagena on schedule tomorrow.

With best regards,

Philip
Philip Rentell
Master, *Sundream*
sdrcaptain@suncruises.co.uk

This one was unusual because we were actually at a scheduled stop when the emergency took place, though unfortunately it was one of those out-of-the-way places where there are absolutely no medical facilities except those for basic first aid. The San Blas islands are inhabited by South American natives who live in mud huts with straw roofs, choosing to live a life without all the trappings of modern civilisation and making a living by fishing and producing a few handicrafts to sell to the tourists who come ashore from the odd cruise ship and gawp at their unusual habitat.

The email contains little feeling of the excitement and effort that the emergency created. There was obviously much work done by our medical team, but there was the planning with my officers on the bridge as well. We had to pay the local head man in cash beforehand to ensure his services. I had to decide whether

I should move the ship close to the next island so the boat ride for the patient would be relatively smooth, and not aggravate further his condition by being bounced about in the choppy sea conditions.

Here is another report made a month or so earlier during a relatively routine three-month contract for me on board.

Herewith a more comprehensive report regarding the medical debark yesterday with a couple of photos for your files. I was called around 0430 hours, Friday 28 November, and advised by our doctor that Mr Arthur Southwell, an 80 year old male British passenger, was suffering congestive heart failure, having respiratory difficulties and heart irregularity. Doctor Payne considered he should be evacuated to a shoreside facility at the soonest opportunity.

We were still five hours from our next port, Catalina Island, and although we had passed the island of Puerto Rico I considered the facilities the US have at their disposal would prove to be the quickest solution. US Coast Guard were contacted around 0445 and after the expected preliminaries they asked that we reverse our course and approach the northwest coast of Puerto Rico. Our helicopter check list was commenced and the after sports deck area prepared.

Over the next hour their medics were in contact by telephone directly with Doctor Payne and an air evacuation of the passenger was confirmed. The helicopter, 'Rescue 6575', first made contact with the bridge at 0621 hours and was on scene some 18 minutes later. By this time the passenger had been brought by stretcher to the sports deck.

The pilot briefed me of his intentions and, after dumping some fuel, the helicopter approached and lowered by wire their diver onto the deck to evaluate the patient and request the correct lifting arrangement from the rescue crew. We continued to hold our course and maintained our speed at 17 knots. A 'litter' was subsequently lowered, the passenger secured inside and then lifted to the helicopter along with a portable oxygen unit supplied by the ship. He was followed by the diver.

The aircraft left the scene at 0710 hours and had an estimated 45 minute journey to San Juan, where the patient was to be transferred to the Centro Medico at Rio Piedras. The position of evacuation was 18 degrees 18 minutes north, 67 degrees 30 minutes west, some 15 miles west of the Puerto Rico coast in the sea area known as the Mona Passage.

We resumed our voyage to Catalina Island, having had to divert a total of 56 miles from our intended track. The anchor went down at 1255 hours and we had commenced tender operations by 1330, with all passengers ashore by 1430 hours. I delayed our departure by one hour and to my knowledge all passengers were quite happy with the call.

With the assistance of the local agent, Mrs Southwell left the vessel in the early afternoon to be escorted to the airport. A flight was arranged to San Juan where she was to be met by our appointed agent in that port and transferred to the hospital to be with her husband.

I am happy to be able to inform you that the company procedures for helicopter operations worked faultlessly and all staff involved carried out their duties in a most professional manner.

With best regards,

Philip
Philip Rentell
Master, *Sundream*
sdrcaptain@suncruises.co.uk

This medical evacuation required me to proceed in the opposite direction to our intended course for several hours. By the time we reverted to our original course there was insufficient time left to ensure a scheduled arrival, and so I had to advise the passengers as to why their time ashore would be less than they had anticipated. Many of the passengers did not even realise we had been involved in a little drama, and had been unaware of a helicopter hovering very close over the ship around breakfast time. Those that did were surprised, to say the least, but I believe they thought it was something we did every other day, and hardly an eyebrow was raised.

Another helicopter evacuation took place off the coast of Denmark during August of 2002 when an older gentleman was found to be suffering from fluid build-up in the lungs. Time was critical and I requested assistance from the local coastguard, who in turn were able to scramble a Danish Navy chopper within half an hour. The diver was lowered to the deck and went to the hospital to confirm the doctor's diagnosis. Meanwhile, the gentleman's wife asked whether she could go with her husband. This wasn't normal but we asked the pilot anyway and much to our surprise he said he was happy to take her. The lady went up on the wire, secured in a harness and held by the diver. When she reached the sill of the door she turned and waved with a large beaming smile to the ship's safety party below. No doubt if it had been in less uncertain circumstances it would have been the adventure of her life. Perhaps it still was.

In the last few years I have had to call in help on more than one occasion, and I have seen a variety of helicopters hovering over my command. Most incidents, like the one off the Puerto Rico coast, have not resulted in a port or itinerary having to be cancelled. The birth of twins, however, was a different matter.

In the summer of 1997 the *Carousel* was operating out of Palma. We had two different weekly itineraries, and the second took us to Tunisia and La Goulette, the port for Tunis. We left one afternoon for a fast run up to Minorca, where the vessel was not due to arrive until lunchtime the next day. That evening Helen and I had dinner with passengers and, as was my normal practice, I went up to the bridge afterwards in order to check progress and leave my night orders. As I returned I ended up in conversation with our very competent Canadian nurse Maureen, who informed me that there was a lady in the hospital complaining of stomach pains. She was Danish and six months pregnant with twins.

I went down to talk with our Greek doctor, Spiros. He was worried and explained to me that the mother would not accept that she might be in the initial stages of labour – in fact she thought it was seasickness or something she'd eaten. Both doctor and nurse were very concerned because the ship was not equipped with what would be required for the delivery of twins, nor was there any blood or plasma on board should the mother suffer further complications. I explained that if they had real concerns then I was prepared to divert the ship to the nearest port.

Returning to the bridge, I took out the charts and checked

what options I had. If the lady did give birth then time would be of the essence. There was only one option, Cagliari in southern Sardinia, a port for which we had no harbour charts, and where I had no experience of docking. A phone call from Maureen a short time later advised me that the mother was definitely in labour, her waters had broken. I started to make a few phone calls, and our Italian general agent told me they had a sub-agent in Cagliari and he would get things moving with the local hospital.

I went back down to the hospital. The parents, who had been adamant they wanted to stay on board until Minorca, were now very apprehensive, but I told them the decision was out of their hands, I had altered course and within three hours we would be in port. Spiros was understandably agitated – he was not an obstetrician – and Maureen could not remember the last time she had delivered a baby. Could I find out whether there were any specialists or midwives on board?

By now it was gone midnight. Most passengers would be well tucked up in bed, so I decided to make a broadcast from the bridge through the passenger areas, including the cabins. This was probably one of my more memorable announcements.

> Good evening ladies and gentlemen, this is the captain and I'm sorry to disturb you, but we have a lady in our hospital who is shortly going to give berth to twins. If you are a midwife or doctor experienced in these matters would you be so kind as to pick up your cabin phone and dial zero.

Within minutes five doctors and a midwife had phoned the purser's desk and were on their way down to the hospital.

On the bridge I was studying the small-scale chart that included Cagliari, which unfortunately also covered just about the whole of the western Mediterranean, so Sardinia was about three centimetres by two, and Cagliari was a dot. Even so, I could not see any serious navigational hazards, shoal areas, oil-rigs, etc. So I continued at full speed, as we consulted the pilot books for any available information that would be of use to us and checked the harbour pilot's radio frequency. I stayed there until the bright lights of this busy ferry port started to give a glow ahead in the dark night. A pilot on duty was expecting us and came out a mile or so from the port. By now the area of the chart we had was unusable to record positions, but the blue lights of ambulances on the quayside were an indication that we were heading in the right direction.

In fact the arrival proceeded very smoothly. The pilot boarded, gave us a big 'Welcome to Sardinia' and he guided us the last half mile or so – and I berthed the ship on a convenient jetty where three ambulances were waiting with their rear doors open. Down in the hospital both babies had been born apparently without any particular problem, but one of them was having breathing difficulties. We had neither incubators nor any technical means to assist them. We had arrived just in time.

Within minutes parents and babies were taken ashore and rushed to the local hospital, and our doctor and nurse looked relieved to say the least. Our guest medicos had included a retired Danish doctor, a midwife, a lecturer from a leading London teaching hospital and a husband and wife team who were both very experienced doctors, though in different disciplines. The mother probably could not have been in better hands, bearing in mind the circumstances.

I needed to get the ship under way, but I had to wait over an hour for the formalities required by the local officials to be completed. By the time we left, the dawn was starting to enter the sky to the east. We heard that one of the babies had died but the other was doing well considering the premature birth. After clearing the port I went to bed and managed just a few hours' sleep before I had to get and up and prepare my report for the company. Regrettably the diversion had cost us precious time and, although we could have made Minorca, the time in port would be less than an hour. I decided to cancel the call and proceed direct to Palma, so as to arrive on schedule the following day.

I informed the passengers over the public address system later that morning and everyone was most understanding. Or almost everyone. There was one complaint in the pursers diary, from a couple for whom Minorca had been the only reason for booking the cruise, and they suggested that the company should offer some financial remuneration in order to reduce their disappointment! Other passengers remarked that they were at first alarmed by my coming on the PA system, but as soon as they heard what was said and realised they couldn't help, they went straight back to sleep.

The team of passengers who had helped out were invited to my cabin for a drink and my thanks later that day, and somewhere at home I have a letter from the retired Danish doctor, who thanked us for our efforts. We never received any further acknowledgement from the parents, or even any information as to how the surviving child was progressing.

I still use the Waterman biro that Spiros later gave me as a token of his appreciation for getting help down to the hospital and the ship into a port so quickly. It is not every captain who gets the chance to complete the 'births' section of the 'return of births and deaths' in the official logbook.

Caribbean rescues

Here is the news, courtesy of the *Scottish Daily Express* one January morning in the year 2000. All I can add is that it must have been a slow news day, as the story was accompanied by three photographs including the old photograph of me I used on the cover of my first book.

> The British captain of a Christmas cruise was hailed a hero last night after saving the lives of a boy and a young man who had been drifting helplessly in the Caribbean for 10 days. Passengers on the cruise liner *Sunbird* spotted the 15-year-old and his fellow fisherman, 27, drifting in a 12ft wooden boat as the liner sailed from Aruba to Barbados.

The ship's captain Philip Rentell, 49, ordered the liner to turn around as soon as the alarm was raised and plucked the young men from rough sea 200 miles from their island Grenada.

Last night Captain Rentell – who lives in Cornwall with his wife Helen and their nine-year-old son – said the boat had only been spotted by chance as he had changed course 45 degrees to avoid a storm hours before.

'It was a miracle we saw them, as the boat was too small to be picked up by radar,' he said. 'They'd have died if they'd been in the water much longer.'

Around 1,500 passengers from all over the UK were on the nine-day trip organised by Sun Cruises, an arm of Airtours. Captain Rentell had left the bridge to prepare for lunch when his first officer spotted a small blue craft in the sea on the ship's starboard side. He paged the captain as passengers ran to the bridge to raise the alarm.

Speaking from Barbados last night, Captain Rentell said: 'I ordered the boat to turn around and as we got nearer, I could see they were waving a red flag. They were in an obvious state of distress and as we got closer I saw one of them make the sign of the cross.'

Captain Rentell ordered a crew to prepare a fast launch for the rescue – but the sea was too rough.

He said: 'We opened the pilot door and arranged a scrambling net as I manoeuvred the ship to within 10 feet of them. We sent a heaving net out and one of them caught it and jumped into the sea. The other lad was too weak and one of the sailors clambered down and brought them on board.'

Terence McGuire, who was on holiday with his wife Joan, said passengers gathered on deck to watch the dramatic rescue. Mr McGuire, from Fife, said: 'A huge cheer went up when the crew reached the dinghy and saved the pair.

'The captain later made an announcement that the young men had been in the sea for nearly two weeks after setting out from Grenada and we were the first boat to pass them. It was a tiny boat and they only had oars. No one knows how they managed to drift out so far.'

The fishermen, Kellon Ashton, 15, and his friend Davies John, told the crew they had set sail at the beginning of the month in their boat *Kenda* but the outboard motor failed. They drifted out to sea, despite desperate attempts to row back.

Captain Rentell said: 'We took them to our hospital and the doctor and two nurses on board put them on drips because they were so dehydrated. They were covered in blisters, not just from the sun and salt from the sea, but because they had tried desperately to row back. Once I got the ship back on course, I went to see them and they were extremely happy. When the doctor introduced me, they just gazed up and took my hand.' The fishermen were looked after by the ship's crew until they were dropped off in Barbados on Monday night.

The holidaymakers were so moved by the plight of the pair that they started a collection for them and the young men will be presented with hundreds of dollars when the ship returns to Grenada.

Myra Shacklady, of Sun Cruises, said: 'All ships have clear procedures for rescues at sea and there will have been no inconvenience for passengers. The *Sunbird* docked on time the next morning.'

Of course there was a little more to the story. The two young men had left their village in Grenada for a morning's fishing and had found themselves being taken by the prevailing wind and current when their engine had failed. They were well off the normal shipping lanes and would probably have drifted for another ten days or so until coming up against the Caribbean coast of one of the Central American countries, by which time they would certainly have been dead. The United States Coast Guard had been looking for them, but I can only assume that the estimated drift had not been calculated correctly, as we neither saw nor heard any kind of search activity. Some would say it was a miracle we saw them, considering we were probably four or five miles to the right of our intended track due to our change of course in order to avoid the heavy rain showers.

They were so exhausted they could never have rowed to us, and the trade winds were causing a fair degree of swell and sea that would have caused problems in launching and recovering our sea boat. I opted to bring the ship to them, and fortunately it worked well. I just made the manoeuvre in the same way I would in coming to a berth. The only problem was to avoid forcing their boat away with the wash generated by the starboard propeller going astern as I held the ship up against the wind. I made a lee for the boat that left them in relatively calm water (see colour plates), and they were recovered fairly easily.

The first line thrown was caught by one of them, and our guys pulled on the line and literally pulled him out of his boat and into the sea. Fortunately he held on and they fished him out and took him up the pilot ladder. Another line was sent and the other chap must have tied it off to the boat as the whole lot came alongside. He was brought aboard and I gave instructions to sink the boat. We had no means of recovering it on board, and leaving it adrift would have been a hazard to navigation, at least to any yachtsman who might have come across it in the middle of the night.

There was an amusing conclusion to the story. The passengers donated over one thousand dollars, and some ten days later I asked the local agent in Grenada to come down with these two characters so I could pass the money on. They trooped on board looking a little sheepish, and understandably so, as the agent informed me that the boat hadn't been theirs, they had borrowed it.

'Who from?' I asked.

'The local policeman,' was the reply.

Needless to say, I gave them the money, but suggested they should pass it straight on to the local constabulary and hope for the best.

———

Three years later, when I was on *Sundream*, I came across another boat adrift in the Caribbean, but the circumstances now were slightly different – as the following two emails show.

From: Sundream Captain
Sent: 25 March 2003 09:59
To: Shacklady Myra SCR
Subject: Rescue. 'Wander' 25.3.03

Hello there Myra,

Further to my telephone conversations of this morning regarding the above 'rescue', I can advise you of the following timetable of action regarding the incident.

0614 hours local (Z–4). OOW noticed drifting fishing boat with 3 persons on board. Master informed and vessel's course altered to effect closer observation.

0625 hours. Situation confirmed and Master brought vessel alongside the boat which was approx 5 metres long, open, with failed outboard engine, name 'Wander'. Occupants said they were from St Lucia and had been drifting since yesterday p.m.

Position 14 degrees 39' north, 061 degrees 22.8' west, some 13 miles from the coast of Martinique.

0655 hours. MRCC Fort de France, Martinique informed. They advised the vessel had been reported overdue and was suspected of being involved in smuggling narcotics. After some discussion the Master was asked to wait until a French patrol craft could come to our position.

0922 hours. French police cutter G8002 arrived on scene and took in tow the boat with the occupants. Sundream was released from further action regarding the incident. Now proceeding towards San Juan at maximum speed, anticipated ETA 0630 hours Wednesday 26th.

The three occupants, who appeared to be in good health, had not been allowed on board, but were given food and water whilst alongside the Sundream.

Should you wish further information please advise. Photos to follow.

With best regards,

Philip
Philip Rentell
Master, Sundream

From:	Pullman Frank SCR
Sent:	25 March 2003 14:24
To:	Sundream Captain; Shacklady Myra SCR
Subject:	RE: Rescue. 'Wander' 25.3.03

Hello Philip,

Are these the same chaps you rescued a couple of years ago?

I reckon you must employ them to sail their boat to your ship so you can rescue them as a new form of passenger entertainment!

Seriously, well done and full marks to OOW for spotting them. The name of the boat appears to be singularly appropriate!

Many thanks,

Frank

This story also had a bit of a twist in the tail. The three guys in the boat hadn't realised they were finally going to be taken ashore by a boat of the French police, as the 'gendarmerie' lettering painted on the roof of the launch was only visible from our vantage point above. We had passed down a cooked breakfast, and passengers had thrown them a few tokens, and as they were being towed away one of the scallywags was shouting up, 'Thank you *Sundream*, thank you!' Little did they know that they would probably spend the next few months incarcerated in some sweaty non-air-conditioned Caribbean prison cell.

Unsavoury incidents

I suppose it is inevitable that, on occasion, a passenger ship with many young male crew will have incidents of a social or sexual nature that can at best be described as unsavoury. The ship will always have specific rules forbidding any social interaction between crew and passengers, with any breach of the rules punished swiftly by what may be considered draconian measures.

Passengers are often surprised when they get a negative response to their request to invite their bedroom steward or their table waiter for a drink in one of the lounges. They are no doubt unaware of why we, acting on behalf of the company, have to draw a line. I consider the crew to be our greatest asset when it comes to passenger satisfaction, and we must be fair to them, particularly when it comes to dispensing discipline – which fortunately does not happen often. But from time to time some of the young men, particularly those with relatively little experience at sea, try to push the boundaries of the ship's code of disciplinary conduct. They rarely succeed, but if they do, and if they are caught with a serious breach, dismissal and a flight home at their own expense is more often than not the result.

Perhaps it seems harsh, but the following two incidents will help to explain why the rules are necessary. Over the years I have come across just a few relatively minor instances of crew members being found holding hands or even kissing young passengers on deck. But these two incidents were much more serious. They happened on the same ship within a month of each other, and I felt no sympathy whatever for the crew members involved.

The first involved a young man who had been employed as a disc jockey on board. He came from an entertainment agency and had been with us just five days. Apparently during the first few days of the cruise he had befriended a young family that included two sisters and two brothers, all university students except the younger boy, who was sixteen years old. When the nightclub closed, usually around two or three in the morning, the DJ would come over to chat. On the fifth morning, last orders had been called and the three young men were still in the bar. The DJ had been buying drinks for the boys, and when they were finally finished he walked the brothers back to their cabin, then apparently asked the younger brother if he would like to come and see his cabin down on the crew deck.

The younger brother agreed, the cabin mate of the DJ was not there, and they both sat on the DJ's bed. When interviewed with his parents later, the boy said he could remember little about it, possibly because he was intoxicated. However, it was apparent that the DJ took advantage of the boy.

The boy must have been traumatised, and later that morning he told his sisters, who in turn informed the parents. They must have taken a few hours to take in what had happened, as it wasn't until the early evening that they came to the purser's desk to ask to speak with the security officer. The ship was alongside in St Petersburg in Russia and my wife and I were ashore with a tour to the folkloric show. When I returned around 2230 hours the staff captain was waiting to give me the news.

My instructions were to have statements prepared in order that I could read them first thing in the morning. I phoned our marine operations manager, Myra Shacklady, and passed on the information. She in turn contacted the company lawyers. We could both see that apart from the distress caused to the family, the company might also suffer significantly, both financially and from a public relations point of view.

The following morning I read the statements and interviewed the disc jockey, who admitted to the incident but stated that he thought the boy was a willing participant and 'experienced', whatever that might mean. I was disgusted, but in my position as master I had to ensure that my personal feelings did not cloud my judgement or my duty to follow correct company procedure. He could have been dismissed instantly for any one of a number of violations of the company's code of conduct, but I had to tread carefully and take advice from our office ashore. Apart from civil proceedings, the family might wish to pursue criminal proceedings against the crew member.

Myra had ensured that the P&I (protection and indemnity) club, which covered the ship for civil liabilities, was informed. They were quick to send down their local representative who, along with our two port agents, met in my office. Discussing incidents of this kind with three complete strangers seemed a little unusual, but their English was fine and we could understand each other completely. We had first to confirm where the incident took place and therefore which country had jurisdiction. By checking the charts it appeared that it was in Russian waters, and that if the parents wished they could ask the Russian authorities to come down and pursue a criminal investigation. I asked what this would entail for the family and for the disc jockey, and was informed that all of them would have to leave the ship, and any investigation would take several days. As the DJ had already confirmed that the act had taken place, and given that the legal age for homosexual sex in Russia was eighteen, it would mean that the he would almost certainly be locked away in prison, and for a very long time.

So what to do? The family were on a tour, so I asked the staff captain and the security officer to meet with them when they returned. The 'Russian' option had to be offered, which probably would have meant delaying the departure of the ship. We were also investigating the possibility that the family could take the case to the British police when they returned to the UK, and thus avoid having to spend an unknown amount of time in a country with which they were unfamiliar.

They chose the latter, and the company worked hard with British officials to ensure that the family could report the affair when the cruise ended back in England in a week's time. I interviewed the parents and listened to their concerns. They were not so much angry as distressed, particularly for the boy's long-term emotional and possible physical health.

The DJ was then brought before me on a disciplinary charge. The breaches of company conduct were paragraphs 27.9.16, 'behaviour which seriously detracts from the social wellbeing of any person on board', and 27.9.17, 'taking passengers into crew accommodation'. For either of these offences the company manual states that 'if proved to the reasonable satisfaction of the master to have been committed,' they 'are those for which dismissal from the ship either immediately or at the end of the voyage will, according to the circumstances of the case, be considered appropriate apart from any legal action which may be called for.' I dismissed him at the next port, Tallinn. Unfortunately, as the DJ was waiting to leave the ship, the family came back on board from a trip ashore. They were shocked to see him, as we had promised that the man would be kept below decks while they were still with us. It did not help matters that distress had already given way to anger, and if it had not been for the prompt action of one our security staff I think the DJ would have been throttled there and then.

The incident did not just go away. The parents did see the police in Harwich, but apparently they were still looking for some kind of redress six months later when the *Daily Mail* published banner headlines with 'Cruise ship scandal' and 'Tour giant rocked by gay "rape" of boy aged 16.' Apparently the British police could do nothing until the Russian police decided what to do, as the offence occurred in their waters. The company was accused of being 'appallingly insensitive'.

That particular article came just three weeks after another lurid headline in the same paper. The incident to which it referred had occurred four weeks later on the same ship. It was just as unpleasant, but far from so clear-cut with regard to responsibility.

A female passenger of just fourteen was travelling with her younger sister and mother. Apparently the father had died a few months before and the mother had decided to take the children to see the 'Baltic Capitals' as a form of therapy. In fact they made two cruises, with exactly the same itinerary, and with just a two-week break between. We were not quite sure of the real reason for the family's return because, during the first cruise, the younger daughter had been bullied by some of the other young female passengers, who found her, apparently, very precocious.

The incident in question occurred late one evening halfway through the second cruise. One of the Indian waiters from the restaurant had befriended the fourteen-year old over the previous few days, and on this night he was said to have invited her to his cabin. Later, in the early hours, the girl approached the purser's front desk with friends and asked to see the nurse. When the nurse arrived the girl requested a 'morning-after pill'. Of course our security officer was immediately called, and after a brief explanation he phoned the mother to advise what had been requested. By the time I was given a report in the morning, there was much to deliberate over.

The girl had willingly followed the young waiter to his cabin, possibly to get some beers for her friends. At the time there were others inside watching a video, but they all left apart from the two men who shared the three-berth cabin. The girl apparently sat down on the waiter's bed and a certain amount of fondling

341

and kissing took place, followed by intercourse. When questioned, the waiter admitted having sex with the girl, but stated that she was a willing participant and he believed she was sixteen. Prolonged investigation with the other two crew members only revealed that one remained on his top berth writing a letter while the other remained on his own lower bunk watching the video. No matter how we asked the questions we always received the same story, bizarre as it may seem.

The girl was not in distress when she saw the nurse, but needless to say when her mother arrived all hell let loose. That day was spent by the security officer and staff captain taking statements from all concerned. I informed Myra Shacklady, and interviewed all three crew members myself. I had decided not to speak with the mother until I had seen all the statements and informed the company of my findings. I needed to know what legal advice they were being given so that I would not compromise the position of the company in any conversations I might have with the mother. It was a complex case, made more difficult by the fact that it possibly took place while we were sailing through Russian waters and we were now in the waters of Estonia. Because the three suspects were not of British nationality and the incident took place outside UK waters I was told the British police might refuse to deal with the case. In the evening while I hosted a cocktail party I was accosted by the mother, who was now past shock and very angry. I agreed to meet her the following morning. Here is a transcript of an email I sent to the company after the meeting:

Good morning again all,
    Having just sat and spoken with the mother, she has asked for the following, to which I replied I would consult with the company:

1. She wants the three crew members tested for sexual disease, and to be told the results.

2. She now wishes to pursue a criminal case. (She did not yesterday morning in Tallinn.)

3. She wishes to pursue a civil case and wants to know exactly whom she should sue.

4. She wants provision of a direct line from the ship to the press now so that she can ensure their presence upon arrival Harwich.

5. She wants counselling for her daughter today.

The conversation was not exactly without acrimony on her side, and she believes I am acting only for the ship, company and crew members. I would say she is now irrational and requires help herself, which I offered via the Chief Purser or the Doctor and to which she replied 'I'm on enough already.'

My opinion is that she should at the earliest convenience receive counselling herself. She has already been down to the crew accommodation twice and has stated she has a pair of scissors in her bag with which she will 'cut their knackers off'.

Her daughter, in public, appears to have suffered no apparent long-term mental trauma as she still cavorts around the deck with her fellow young passengers. I consider she is more likely to come to some harm from her mother, who now believes her daughter to be 'filthy and disgusting'.

The family, which also includes a slightly younger daughter, were on board for the first Baltic cruise and have returned after a two-week interval after having 'such a good time', even though we have a medical report from the Doctor indicating the daughter was attacked on three occasions by other young passengers, the last of which was on the day before they disembarked and resulted in many bruises and contusions.

I have to say the company supported me throughout. It was not an easy or pleasant situation to find myself involved in, but it is another example of the variety of problems that can come across the desk of a passenger-ship master.

The following day, in Copenhagen, two UK lawyers appointed by the P&I club came aboard and we discussed the situation at length. By this time the girl, no doubt influenced by her mother, had made a statement that all three men had raped her against her will. We invited the Danish police to attend the vessel on the behest of the mother. They first spoke to me and then had an interview with the mother. I could tell they were reluctant to take action as the incident was not within their jurisdiction, but they listened patiently and waited for the outcome of a call the mother had with the UK police in Harwich, our terminal port. When the mother was satisfied that the UK police would attend, the Danish officers left, no doubt somewhat relieved.

Numerous reports had to be prepared from anyone who may have been witness to the incident, before and after. The clothes of the accused were bagged up in order for them to have forensic tests carried out in the UK. In the meantime we went through the routine of disciplinary procedure with the three young men. There was, of course, no doubt that all three would be dismissed, because they had admitted to having a passenger in their cabin. It was just a matter of when I should pass the sentence and when they should leave the ship.

On arrival in Harwich a detective inspector came on board, and before he interviewed the mother he listened to my tale of the events that had transpired so far. I advised him of my conclusions and showed him the various emails that had been sent between ship and company. He returned after interviewing the mother with a sort of 'yes, I can see what problems you may have experienced' look. A senior officer of the immigration service also came to see me. They had been informed of the situation and were aware that the mother had threatened to contact the tabloid press if she didn't see the three crew members being taken away by the police.

The problem was who should be responsible for pursuing a criminal charge against the men. British victim, Indian accused, incident occurred in Russian waters, Bahamian-registered ship. In fact the UK police said they could only act on behalf of the Bahamian authorities if officially requested. It was the task of Sun Cruises to try and convince the Bahamians to pursue an investigation, which eventually they did.

I dismissed the crew members for breaching the company

code of conduct, and on disembarkation they were met by officers of the immigration service, who took them to a secure holding unit to await the issue of a warrant and an extradition order from the Bahamas authorities. The mother was advised of what was happening and eventually drove off, with her two girls, in her large Mercedes.

For us on board, that was effectively the end of the incident. A few more reports were required to tidy up the case, but now it was in the hands of the lawyers. The men were to wait for extradition hearings to take place. Apart from the young man who foolishly invited the girl down to his cabin in the first place and then proceeded to take advantage of her, I felt that justice for the other two should be based around the fact that they let the incident take place. I wasn't at all sure that they had been involved in a physical way. In my own mind I questioned why the mother should bring the two girls back on a cruise when it must have been obvious that the younger girl had received a rough time from the other young passengers she had met on board during the first cruise.

It would appear that once the case landed with the lawyers, the whole process was going to take some considerable time, and at the UK taxpayer's expense. It was not until six months later that the first extradition hearings were heard in London, and these were reported in the tabloid press. To my knowledge these proceedings had not been completed two years later, with the men still in the UK, unable to return to their families, and reporting to a police station every day. The press, as might be expected, chose to print only what they deemed 'newsworthy' – and the coverage was, as far as I was concerned, rather one-sided.

I have always tried to be firm but fair with the crew on board, and these cases indicate why there is a need to have rules that may seem to others to be very strict. The system of rules and regulations does work most of the time, and on the few occasions when it is abused the crew are fully aware of the punishment they might expect.

Cruising North 2003

Norway

I rejoined *Sundream* on Friday 20 June in Southampton. The previous master was not on board, as he had been requested to leave in Lisbon three days previously, and the staff captain had taken over his position temporarily.

Within an hour of boarding I was talking with an intelligence officer from the UK customs. Apparently they had reason to suspect that a quantity of drugs was secreted on board. Two passengers had inexplicably disappeared in Cadiz a week before; they had gone ashore and not returned, leaving items of clothing behind. Our company were on excellent terms with the British authorities, and suspicious behaviour was always passed on. The clothing had been bagged up and sent for forensic tests, and traces of cocaine were later found on T-shirts.

It transpired that the police knew these two passengers. The man had recently been released from prison and the woman was the girlfriend of a known Jamaican drug dealer in London. They had apparently kept themselves to themselves on board, and had gone ashore twice in Vigo, returning before the ship sailed. The itinerary had been changed because of problems in Casablanca, which may have been the reason for their premature departure in Cadiz.

Within a few hours approximately twenty kilos of cocaine were found hidden away, very amateurishly, in the deck head of a galley locker. The customs rummage squad, with a couple of dogs, searched the ship for the remainder of the day, but nothing more was found. We sailed that evening for Harwich, where we were to commence our northern cruising season the next day. Customs were in the terminal, watching the crew take their shore leave and searching bags. Nothing more was found. Before we sailed, however, one of our Jamaican bar waiters failed to return to the ship. He had left over $5000 in an envelope tucked under his mattress. This was found by his cabin mate, another Jamaican who had been with us for years, who passed it on to the hotel director. With it was a note that asked for the money to be passed to his family if he failed to return. He didn't, and nothing was heard from him again, either on board or from ashore.

We passed up into the North Sea at an average speed of a little less than 14 knots, our destination the entire Norwegian coast all the way past the Arctic Circle and up to the North Cape, over one thousand miles. A great deal of our journey would be completed inside the shelter of some magnificent fjords. Picking up two local pilots, we passed Kopervik and Haugesund at breakfast time of the second morning, sailed into Hardangerfjord and up to the Bondhusbreen glacier by lunchtime. This type of cruising is all about scenery. We pray for good weather to show the countryside off at its best, but of course we don't always get it. This day was not so bad, and the ship was held off the glacier for over thirty minutes while the passengers took their photographs. All day we were in the fjords, and we only went back out to sea later in the evening after we had passed through the fjords on the outskirts of Bergen.

The following day was Ålesund, a charming small town at the entrance to the Geirangerfjord. Passengers had all day to go on tour or stretch their legs before we sailed again in the evening, this time to take the outside route in order to discharge 'grey' water legally. In the morning we picked up a further pilot and entered again below Rørvik, where the road bridge passes just a metre or so above our masthead. The weather had deteriorated and the remainder of the day was murky, to say the least, with light rain at times blocking the spectacular views. However, by the time we arrived at Svartisen glacier later in the afternoon, a clearance had come through. This glacier, probably the most famous on the coast of Norway, is just north of the Arctic Circle. We lowered a lifeboat so that the ship's photographer could take some pictures of the ship with the glacier behind.

The following day was described in the brochure as 'cruising the Lofoten Islands', which is OK, but I do like to get in close. We passed into a small inlet with the village of Leknes at its head, where I took the ship almost alongside the small dock, as next year we were scheduled to make a call there and run a morning tour. I wanted to see if we 'fitted'. She would, provided there was little wind, as half the ship would be projecting into the harbour with only a mooring buoy to take the bow lines. Later in the afternoon we passed into Trollfjord, which always has a tremendous 'wow' factor with the passengers. The fjord is approximately a mile in length, but it is so narrow that, once in, it is impossible to turn around until the far end is reached. Here there is less than four hundred metres between the sheer walls in which to rotate the ship through one hundred and eighty degrees. Although it might have looked difficult to the passengers, in fact it was a relatively straightforward manoeuvre, as there was not a breath of wind.

Later that day we passed the pilot station at Lødingen, where our pilots were changed, and we finally went out to sea via the Andanes pilot station. The whole coast is covered by various pilot stations, and in one voyage we can board up to ten pilots to assist us on our way. The next day was Tromsø, the 'capital' of the north, followed by Honningsvåg, a tiny port just twenty-nine miles south of the most northern point in Europe. The weather had finally changed for the better, with blue skies but strong offshore winds that made securing to the tiny jetty an interesting manoeuvre. We sailed at nine thirty in the evening. It was relatively calm but rather cold as we passed close under the towering cliffs of North Cape at midnight, the sun still visible about fifteen degrees above the horizon. For this trip at least, this was truly the land of the midnight sun.

In Hammerfest the next day we employed a local diving team to weld a small steel plate to the bottom of the hull. A water ballast tank had kept filling, even though we pumped it out. Ballast lines, joints and flanges were checked, but in the end it turned out to be tiny hole directly through the striker plate under the sounding pipe in the tank. Over the years the plate had worn through as a result of the carpenter dropping the sounding line down the pipe to check the amount of ballast water in the tank. Sailing was delayed an hour when we had to land a lady who had unfortunately fallen and broken her hip. Passing through the inside route because of adverse weather outside, we had two pilots during the night. They changed at Tromsø, and the second finally left at Lødingen at seven the following morning.

Tuesday 1 July found us in Trondheim, a bustling little city and one that news of our drug seizure had already reached. Sixteen customs officers with dogs came aboard to search the ship. The passengers, who were unaware of preceding events, thought it quite routine and spent much time petting the spaniels, which were, so I discovered, trained for their drug detection role in the UK. Nothing was found, and we left on schedule.

At 0400 hours the following morning a pilot boarded just south of Ålesund to take us up into the Geirangerfjord, a distance of 59 miles. Most Norwegian cruises visit this spectacular fjord, with its majestic scenery. We anchored at the head near the village of Merok, and the passengers were taken ashore by tender. Many were taken way up into the mountains, above the cloud line, where snow could be expected even in the middle of summer. The best views, however, are from just three hundred metres or so up – the fjord fills one's vision, and the anchored ships look like toys floating on a boating lake.

We were having our own problems, however. The shore tender we had arranged was not giving us the service we required and it took a few phone calls to sort the problem. Our own number 3 tender suffered a broken propeller shaft coupling; this was temporarily repaired, but failed again just as the boat was to be lifted on board. A slipping clutch of the lifeboat davit winch caused an hour's delay to departure, and then a coil in the anchor windlass motor failed. This resulted in a very slow heaving of the anchor and further delay. We had to take the ship about twelve miles around to Hellesylt and pick up our all day-tour passengers.

Fortunately we managed to arrive at the same time as the coaches and there was little further delay in their boarding.

After holding the ship in place for over an hour using engines and thruster, we headed back down the fjord. The pilot finally disembarked off Breidsundet at 2130 hours, a long day for all of us involved with the ships operation. By 0530 I was back on the bridge to pick up the next pilot of the island of Fedje, some 28 miles north of Bergen, where we berthed shortly after 0800 hours. Apart from repair and installation of bridge equipment the day was quiet, and we sailed on schedule for the five-hundred-mile journey back across the North Sea to Harwich – where yet more customs officers came on board to search the ship. Fingerprints had been detected on the drugs found two weeks ago, a match was found amongst the crew, and I was advised that a Jamaican pastry chef would be taken ashore under arrest.

The Baltic

There were two Norwegian cruises, the itinerary being the same for both, and the total distance we travelled in the four weeks was just over six thousand miles. On Saturday 19 July we sailed from Harwich for the Baltic; there were three scheduled cruises, and I would be in command for the first two. I had been fortunate to be master on the three cruises to the Baltic in 2002, so I knew what to expect and looked forward to many of the ports we would be visiting.

The first cruise would take us to Oslo in Norway, Gothenburg and Stockholm in Sweden, Helsinki in Finland, St Petersburg in Russia, Tallinn in Estonia, Copenhagen in Denmark and the Dutch city of Amsterdam before returning to Harwich. The second cruise would substitute Gdynia in Poland for Amsterdam, which, along with Gothenburg, was another maiden call for our company – and one which was of course popular with the few Polish officers we had on board.

Oslofjord was a welcome sight after crossing five hundred miles of the North Sea, even though I had to be on the bridge by four in the morning. Passing through the narrows at Drøbak is particularly scenic, with the old wartime defences still visible on the island opposite. The chart shows the wreck of the Second World War German battleship *Blucher*, which was sunk during the initial invasion, hit by a land-fired torpedo, while attempting to penetrate up to Oslo during the hours of darkness. We docked at the Akershus pier, just five minutes' walk from the city. At Gothenburg, however, we were over thirty minutes from the town, and the walk was too much for many of our older passengers. Many rarely take a taxi, as they are not prepared to pay the fare. Seventeen customs officers and their two dogs visited us; they failed to find anything apart from a small stash of cigarettes in a crew member's locker. Before we left, a charming American-style girl marching band came and entertained passengers from the dockside.

Although our harbour pilot left us before 1830 hours, I was back on the bridge for midnight, as we had to pass through the Sound, the relatively narrow gap that separates Denmark from Sweden. Fortunately there is not too much ferry traffic between Helsingør in Denmark and Helsingborg in Sweden at that time of night, but even so it is necessary to have all your wits about you. Passing Copenhagen the sea becomes very shallow and I needed to reduce speed to less than 12 knots in order to maintain steerage and avoid squat, that particular phenomenon which pulls the stern down deeper into the water and can cause grounding. A buoyed channel took over half an hour to pass through, and at times the echo sounder showed just a metre or two of water under the keel. By 0300 hours we were back into deep water and I could finally get some rest. Fortunately the next day was spent cruising so an early start was not required.

We entered the archipelago off Stockholm at 0430 hours, and the course through the islands took us through forty-five miles of narrow channels separating hundreds of low-lying islands, all of which seemed to have at least a few houses. Like the Norwegians, the Swedes often have a flagpole nearby; if they are 'at home' their national flag in the shape of a long burgee is flying. They obviously are not too concerned about burglars, as a flagless pole would be a fairly obvious suggestion to the criminal fraternity. Pulling into Stockholm itself is a delight, as the ship sails round the last island to reveal this most beautiful of cities in all its glory. It is one of the most elegant of ports.

By 1700 hours we had to be ready to sail, in order to follow the big ferries of Viking and Silja Lines out of the archipelago once more to cross the Gulf of Finland and pick up the Helsinki pilot shortly before 0900 the following morning. The entrance past the old fort, built originally to keep the Russians out, is very narrow indeed and has a small change of course, requiring precise helm orders from the pilot. The big ferries were already docked inside the inner harbour, so we berthed a little further out, but still within twenty minutes' walk of the city centre. This harbour and its approaches freeze over completely in the winter, and the port employs massive icebreakers to ensure navigation can continue.

The approach to St Petersburg is through a twenty-eight-mile long channel. The pilot was picked up at 0430 hours and we proceeded fairly slowly towards the small island of Ostrov Kotlin, dominated by the cathedral in Kronshtadt and a large naval port. During Soviet times this island was apparently out of bounds to civilians. The military fortifications were in a terrible state of repair and the docks, with their many redundant naval craft, looked a sorry state. The pilot, speaking English in a deep-throated accent, assured me that there were a few ships and a submarine still in active service. They looked mothballed to me, but nothing was quite as it seemed in this land. We passed into the working port of St Petersburg at 0640, with only three more miles to go, but because of the speed restriction it took another hour before we were docked on the passenger berth on Ostrov Vasilyevsky. The passenger terminal was a product of the communist sixties; a now tired-looking hotel clad in aluminium or stainless steel sits above. I wasn't sure if foreigners used the hotel, but on the first floor there was a bowling alley and a large bar where some of the lads went in the evening. During the morning we received yet another visit from customs, this time seven officers and two dogs. It appeared that the ship now had a reputation throughout Norway and the Baltic – but still nothing more was found.

The city of St Petersburg is one of those places that every traveller should visit. It was built from a master plan prepared by Peter the Great exactly three hundred years before our visit. I always tell the passengers that it has a kind of shabby splendour. Many of the faded stucco buildings, particularly those facing the River Neva, had been spruced up or cunningly disguised for the anniversary celebrations. Pot-holed roads, along with the tram-lines, had been covered over by new tarmac.

During a visit the previous year I had managed to obtain from a market vendor an ex Soviet Mig fighter pilot's leather helmet, which I had actually worn, much to the passengers' amusement, when we had sailed. This year I intended to get another, but with the original throat microphone. So on our first voyage I made a recce and found the same guy, and he promised to try his best for the next call. We sailed on the evening of the following day, Sunday 27 July. It was Russian Navy days so there were a few naval craft moored on berths in the river. I had asked the agent to find out whether I could take the ship up the River Neva on departure. He asked why, and I explained that it would be a thrill for the passengers to see the city from the river before we had to turn and make our way to sea. He said he would write a letter to the harbourmaster, but told me just before we sailed to ask the pilot when he boarded. I did, and he again asked why. I explained again, and he said he would ask the harbourmaster.

I expected nothing, but was pleasantly surprised when we were given the go-ahead. I reversed the ship off the berth and went stern-first into the river a quarter of a mile away. The pilot took over the con and we proceeded slowly towards the Lieutenant Schmidt Bridge, the first and possibly the busiest crossing point for road traffic. The bridges on the river, closed during the day, remain open for barge traffic during the night, and it is then possible to go all the way to Moscow and further by water. As we approached, I took over the con again and turned the ship through one hundred and eighty degrees, sounding three long blasts as we went. The traffic, including a tram, stopped to see the spectacle of this large passenger ship turning in such a narrow space. I played 'Land of Hope and Glory' on the deck speakers and the passengers, as well as the sailors on some of the Russian ships, were suitably impressed. 'The icing on the cake,' one later said.

The pilot was finally landed just before 2100 hours, and within twelve hours we were on our berth in Tallinn; two other large cruise ships already docked. The old town here is charming, and it is hard to believe that in recent memory Estonia was part of the Soviet bloc. Any image of communism had been completely shed, cafés were bustling, shops were full of local 'collectables' and the streets were heaving with people. Regular ferry services operate from Sweden and Finland, and there was obviously thriving business between the countries.

Copenhagen followed two days later, the Sound being navigated in daylight this time. A surveyor from International Maritime Security came aboard for a two-day audit of our security arrangements. For some reason known only to themselves, the port authority allows ships to leave and enter the port without a pilot – very unusual in this day and age, when any way of taking a fee or otherwise making money is ruthlessly pursued. Dawn on Friday 1 August found us approaching the locks of the North Sea Canal at IJmuiden. The ship had to rise just half a metre or so, because of the tide, and the process took no more than twenty minutes. These locks are far bigger than those of the Panama Canal, but even so the ship handler needs to know his stuff and the way a closed basin of water can affect the manoeuvring capabilities of his vessel. The passage up to Amsterdam took over two and a half hours. Speed had to be reduced, both to avoid damage to the bank and also to reduce the wake effect on other craft that were berthed nearby. Our berth was just past the main railway station, and the canal in this area was very busy, with every size of watercraft going about their business, seemingly in one great melee but apparently in some degree of order that only the skippers understand. The passenger terminal was smart, modern and obviously quite functional, and I wondered why we still have such outdated tarted-up sad structures in the UK.

I landed one crew member with a grumbling appendix, and another new joiner was refused as we found out he was a haemophiliac. We left the berth shortly after 1800 hours, passed back down the canal, and entered the lock at 2000 hours. This time we had company, a large self-propelled barge and the cruise liner *Silver Cloud*, but there was still room to spare. The North Sea was crossed without incident, and at 0545 hours the Harwich pilot boarded. Just in time we were alongside, as we had an older passenger whose lungs were filling with fluid, and an ambulance sped him away for emergency admission. Three thousand miles had been covered in two weeks.

The next cruise followed a similar pattern, except for the change in a couple of ports. In Oslo we landed a passenger who had suffered a heart attack while we crossed the North Sea the day before. I dismissed two Thai crew members after they had decided not to work (they said they had been misled by their agent and were not prepared to do the utility job they had been allocated). In Stockholm thirty customs officers boarded with three dogs – they still didn't find anything. In Helsinki the pilot was very complementary about my 'driving' skills after I had docked the ship without any apparent effort in a gusty offshore wind. But again it was St Petersburg that I looked forward to the most.

The call started well. The Russian pilot was unusually talkative for four thirty in the morning – with bad breath and beaming smile, he kept saying he should be going down below 'for dancing!' The harbourmaster's son Piotr, who was with our agency, took me into town to pick up my leather helmet. In the end I bought two at $30 each. A little negotiation brought down the price and, in a rush of unexpected generosity, the trader gave me a Russian naval officer's hat that turned out to be a perfect size for my son. I persuaded another trader to let me buy an old military barograph for $35; he was an amusing character with a scrappy beard who muttered partly in Russian and partly in a deep guttural English, pleading poverty and fiercely bashing his calculator at the same time as searching for an old plastic bag in which to place his latest sale.

Before we left another passenger had to be landed, this time with unexplained fainting spells. Yet again I managed to convince the authorities that we should cruise the Neva before heading to sea. This time I think our agents must have heard of my previous musical exploits, for both Sergei and Gennardy were on the nearby dock to watch the turn by the bridge, but this time we gave 'Land of Hope and Glory' to the German passenger ship *Berlin* berthed nearby. I'm not sure whether it was the music the passengers were impressed with, or the mere six metres of water we had spare as our stern passed the *Berlin*.

Our maiden call at Gdynia went without a hitch, Roy Dearman, my relief, came aboard for a four-day handover and yet another passenger was hospitalised, this one with internal bleeding and diabetes. Our last day at sea was marred by the death of an elderly passenger who had died in his cabin of a suspected heart attack. Regrettably, when so many passengers are carried, over time there are bound to be one or two that pass away.

I left the ship on 16 August. In just two months we had been visited by over one hundred customs officers from four different countries.

Command seminar 2000: passenger ship evacuation – a master's worst nightmare

I read the following paper to a large audience of colleagues and other interested parties at the International Command Seminar held at Trinity House, London, in May 2000. The paper was later reproduced in the Nautical Institute magazine Seaways.

In 1912 a large liner, reported by the media to be unsinkable, went to the bottom of the Atlantic after a collision with an iceberg. The damage caused by the iceberg allowed sea water to enter sufficient watertight compartments to cause progressive flooding above the bulkhead deck. The loss of life which has made the tragedy so enduring was caused not only by insufficient lifeboats, but also because many of the poor souls who entered the water quickly succumbed to the effects of hypothermia.

A one-off, perhaps? You may ask, 'Is this really likely today, with all the technical improvements that have been made over the years, the ever-increasing number of SOLAS regulations, and the apparently endless inspections carried out by Classification Society, US Coast Guard and Port State Control, to name but a few?'

I can name you a few relatively recent examples of passenger ships which have been evacuated and where another master might say, 'There but for the grace of God go I.'

In 1963 the Greek cruise vessel *Lakonia* caught fire off the Canaries. One hundred and twenty-eight people lost their lives, again many as a result of hypothermia.

The *Prinsendam*, 330 miles off Alaska in 1980 – she had an uncontrolled engine-room fire and the ship eventually sank as a result of the effects of water ingress from the fire-fighting operations. All 524 passengers and crew abandoned the ship into lifeboats and life rafts, and were subsequently rescued by the US Coast Guard. Even using thirteen aircraft, three Coast Guard cutters and three commercial vessels it took twenty-one hours to complete the rescue.

In 1986 the *Admiral Nakhimov* sank in the Black Sea after a collision just seven miles from the coast, with a loss of 423 of the 1,234 passengers and crew.

The *Oceanos*, off South Africa in 1991, where the master reported he had difficulty launching lifeboats due to the rough weather. Eventually all 580 crew and passengers were rescued with the aid of thirteen helicopters of the South African Defence Force and three nearby merchant ships.

More recently the *Sun Vista* – which sank after a fire in the engine room while sailing off the coast of Malaysia. Here all passengers and crew evacuated the ship using the survival craft, but into the calm waters of the Malacca Strait.

And I would not like to have been the hapless master of the *Norwegian Dream*. I'm sure he must have since considered on more than one occasion that if the container ship had gone into the side of his vessel in way of the watertight bulkhead adjacent to the engine room, the outcome might have been very different.

––––––

So what are the differences between our large modern vessels and the *Titanic*?

We have lifeboats or, as we refer to them nowadays, survival craft, to cater for all.

Or do we? The rules changed to ensure that there would always be a factor of 25% extra capacity for the ship's maximum complement, passengers and crew. There must be lifeboat capacity for at least 37.5% of the total complement on each side of the ship. In this case, the remaining 50% requirement can be made up by life rafts, which must be capable of being launched from either side and of course have hydrostatic releases.

A significant percentage of these life rafts need to be davit-launched, although the recent introduction of evacuation chutes, as fitted to P&O's new *Aurora*, has provided an alternative to the, I believe, slow and cumbersome davit launching system.

But here is the question – what happens if, in severe weather, the master is unable to launch safely the boats on the windward side?

One must appreciate that few masters with any common sense would consider putting boats into the water during their weekly crew drill, if there was any degree of 'chop' on the surface of the dock. The thought of putting a fully loaded lifeboat into an ocean with anything more than a force 2 or 3 blowing fills me with great apprehension, unless of course there is a good lee – the kind of lee you might allow when embarking a pilot.

When all power is lost, my experience has shown that a passenger vessel will come to settle with the wind and sea on the beam. There is a lee side, which may be suitable to get boats away relatively safely, but what of the other side? I would suggest that it is, at best, optimistic to believe a safe and successful launching will be achieved with any of the windward-side boats.

We therefore still have a scenario where possibly 12.5% of the total complement on board will not have a survival craft to embark into, and that is assuming that those life rafts stowed, perhaps in racks, on the windward side can be carried over to the lee side or can be otherwise launched satisfactorily. Those 12.5% will therefore have to eventually enter the water should the vessel sink. On a large modern cruise vessel such as the new *Voyager of the Seas* belonging to Royal Caribbean Cruise Line, a ship of 142,000 gross tonnes and having a capacity of 5,021 souls, this will mean a figure of **at least 627**. They will be entering the water with a standard lifejacket that may keep them afloat but will in no way protect them from the effects of hypothermia, which I shall return to in due course.

Even if the master says **'Damn and blast it – send them away!'** what will be the outcome? The rules have changed in that, for ships built since 1986, lifeboats must be of the partially enclosed type and have automatic simultaneous off-load release hooks that release as soon as the weight of the boat is fully off both hooks. The coxswain of the boat can choose to release 'on load', but can you imagine the effect of a fully loaded lifeboat dropping into a boiling sea and being thrown against this wall of steel? None of these petrified passengers are strapped in. Even if the boat survives upright and intact, I really don't believe many of the passengers will, and therefore the risk to passengers is considerable.

Of interest at this point is the fact that, according to SOLAS, marine evacuation systems are required to be tested up to a Beaufort wind strength of force 6 and a significant wave height of three metres. Lifeboats and davit-launched life rafts have **never** had a requirement to be tested in adverse weather conditions.

The answer may be, apart from regulating that the vessel must have sufficient survival craft capable of being launched on either side for the entire vessel complement, that the rules should stipulate that there must be an independent power supply for the thrusters, allowing the master, in the event of a total loss of power from the main machinery spaces, to swing the ship through 180 degrees, thus making the windward side the lee side. He could then choose, at least in theory, to lower the boats and rafts on one side and then swing the ship to lower the other side when it gains the lee. I'm not sure, however, whether panicking passengers would either understand or even allow him the privilege of making this decision. The success of this manoeuvre would not necessarily lie in the seamanship, but in the skill of his communication beforehand.

Changing tack, if I may – you are aware that in theory the degree of damage stability and fire protection provided in modern ships should provide sufficient time to launch the survival craft. **What is that time for Class 1 passenger ships? Thirty minutes.**

Surely any experienced sailor with a modicum of common sense will realise that this is a practical impossibility. Over 5,000 people into life rafts and lifeboats, lowered to the water and away from the ship's side in thirty minutes? **Why do we accept this nonsense?**

As a practical master I would consider even a time of two hours to be highly optimistic. Not only does the master have to recognise the need to evacuate, he has to sound the general alarm, the passengers need to become aware of the urgency of the situation, then they have to be guided to their muster station and counted into the boats. The muster station leaders need to reassure those panicking passengers so that there is an orderly embarkation. Will they all fit? With the greatest respect, I would say it is very difficult to ensure that you fill within thirty minutes a 140-place lifeboat with 140 obliging little Filipino crew on a drill, yet alone the average American or European of what may be considered 'normal' size in a real emergency.

SOLAS damage stability rules are based on floodable length, and the degree of subdivision must be at least two compartments, but may be higher. Of course we are assuming that, in the event of a collision, all watertight doors will not only be closed promptly by the officer on the bridge, but that they will in fact all close. Passenger vessels are constructed with main vertical zones that have fire-rated boundaries, thus ensuring that an uncontrolled fire will take a great deal of time to spread throughout the whole ship. We again assume that all the fire doors will close when the release is activated on the bridge. Even on the most well-run ship, particularly as age and time takes its toll, it is quite possible that between five and ten per cent of these doors may not close immediately and full integrity will then be lost – perhaps just at that crucial position where the fire may be 'stretching its legs'.

We should not forget the *Scandinavian Star*, where fire-zone integrity was lost. Fire ravaged the vessel and many passengers were lost.

I thankfully acknowledge the compulsory introduction of sprinklers on all passenger ships by the year 2002. These have saved the day on many occasions. However, it is still a requirement to have only a one-shot extinguishing system in the machinery spaces. In a recent boiler room fire on Carnival Cruise Lines *Tropicale* the fire was not controlled by this system. Surely it cannot be considered an extravagance to insist that there should be two chances of flooding the technical spaces with the primary extinguishing agent. Let's face it, can we be sure that all the flaps and dampers protecting the engine spaces will close automatically? The difficulty of testing the generator-room flaps with the ship in service is known to the experienced master, so can he rely on 100% gas-tight integrity at the press of a button? The master of the *Tropicale* believed the reason his one-shot system failed was because of a small gap in a bulkhead allowing oxygen into what should have been a sealed boiler room.

I have recently been made aware of the welcome news that machinery spaces will be required to have an additional water-based or equivalent secondary fire extinguishing system. This will be for new ships after 2002 and existing ships by 2005.

There is still a requirement, depending on length, to have a maximum of only three fire pumps. I would suggest that it should be compulsory for there to be a fire and ballast pump within each watertight compartment capable of being run independently from the main generators.

Returning to the subject of hypothermia. Let us assume that we may have a considerable number of souls in the water – can we prevent or even delay the effects of water at a temperature below that of the human body having its inevitable effect – i.e. **death**?

In November of last year the Chinese ferry *Dashun* caught fire and foundered in heavy seas off the port of Yantai. The weather conditions prevented any nearby vessels going to her assistance and only twenty of the 312 passengers were found alive. Hope quickly faded for the others because of the high winds and freezing conditions.

There is an answer. The immersion suit is readily available but is considered expensive. They are already carried on board ships, but in very small numbers. The rules regarding insulated immersion suits say that they must prevent the body's core temperature dropping more than two degrees Celsius after a period of six hours in water at a temperature of between zero and two degrees Celsius.

The cruise companies that are now building 3,000-plus passenger vessels should be able, simply because so many suits would be required, to bring the price down to a relatively minor cost. Perhaps it may be considered that a suit without inherent insulation, which meets SOLAS Regulation 32 and is therefore classified as a lifejacket, would be appropriate considering the trading patterns of these large ships.

Alternatively the Nordic countries have introduced the 'thermal protective lifejacket'. This jacket covers torso and head, and is designed to protect against heat loss as well as ensuring a turning function and a suitable floating angle when the wearer is at rest. A spray hood or face shield is designed to avoid heat loss from the face and drowning from water spray. The jacket is expected to extend the wearer's consciousness from perhaps fifteen minutes to more than three hours. I understand the IMO subcommittee on ship design and equipment are considering whether it should become standard for ro-ro passenger vessels.

This piece of equipment would of course be a step in the right direction, particularly for ferries in northern waters. However, for a large passenger ship foundering many hundreds of miles from land, perhaps on a trans-ocean positioning voyage, is three hours' protection long enough?

Should the rules change and it becomes a requirement to carry some sort of immersion suit, then I believe the equipment could be placed in a sealed package that a passenger need not open unless it is required in an emergency. Video programmes on the in-house TV would educate the passenger on how to don the suit, and a practical demonstration by a member of the crew at the passenger muster would reinforce their knowledge, in much the same way the airlines promulgate their safety procedures.

The SOLAS regulations as they stand, in my opinion, have not matched the technological developments of modern lifesaving aids, and certainly do not allow for the present rapid rise in large cruise-ship passenger capacity. I know other cruise-vessel masters share my concerns. If we do not act to ensure a higher degree of survivability, we may end up with major loss of life, followed shortly by hastily thought-out and inappropriate regulations – repercussions not so very different from those following the events of 1912.

In conclusion – I consider this forum should forward my observations and suggestions to the Maritime Safety Committee of the International Maritime Organisation so that they may add to further discussion.

I believe there is at least a need to have the following:

1. Side thrusters which have an additional and independent power source, capable of swinging the bow through 180 degrees in heavy weather.

2. Increased subdivision to ensure the vessel will stay afloat for between three and six hours, thus allowing the safe abandoning of the vessel.

3. A minimum three-compartment ship.

4. A replacement for the archaic lifejacket which will keep the passenger afloat with head clear of the water, and which will offset the effects of hypothermia for at least six hours in cold water.

Considering the different nationalities and skills we have to work with, plus the training which never seems to stop, our crews are only human and they do well. But they cannot prevent disasters from happening. However, given a modern ship with realistic safety measures, they may be able to reduce needless waste of human life.

One of the aged mates I sailed with in Clan Line many years ago said to me, 'Son, if it's going to work at sea, it's got to be Jolly-Jack-proof' – I don't believe the present rules are 'Jolly Jack' proof.

There is little need for the black boxes we shall all be required to install within the next few years, if they will only tell us the facts we already know, and which will show us the problems we could have prevented – but didn't, because we did not use our present knowledge to bring in practical, common-sense regulations now.

I understand the Maritime Safety Committee of IMO are meeting this week, and that one of the papers under discussion will be that of the secretary general William O'Neil. The emphasis of that paper is that the IMO should consider undertaking a global consideration of safety issues pertaining to passenger ships, with particular emphasis on large cruise ships. Not before time, gentlemen.

Saga

A fter leaving Sun Cruises I was lucky enough to have several offers of employment, and, after little deliberation, I accepted the position of master on board the classic *Saga Rose*, originally built in 1965 as the *Sagafjord*.

Saga had been cruising for eight years with the *Saga Rose*, and had chartered the smaller *Saga Pearl* for two summer seasons. The company then bought the *Caronia*, ex *Vistafjord*, from Cunard in 2004 and renamed her *Saga Ruby*. With the permanent addition of the near sister ship another experienced master was required, so I left the UK after a few months' leave and signed on the *Saga Rose* when she arrived in Auckland in early March. I relieved one of the two permanent masters in order to complete the 2005 world cruise. He was to relieve the previous master, who had already transferred his command to the new vessel. The two ships quickly developed great passenger loyalty and have since cruised worldwide during the winter and out of the UK from spring to the end of each year. There are very few places around the globe that the ships have not been, from Greenland and Spitsbergen in the north to Antarctica in the south. We are all very proud of our ability to go anywhere and yet consistently give our passengers great service in comfort and safety.

Within the first eighteen months on board I had visited many ports and areas which were new to me. I had been around the world and travelled from top to bottom. The masters in Saga are tasked by the company to write a diary of sorts which could be published on the Saga website, and these were referred to as the 'Captain's blog'. The Nautical Institute also asked me to write a column for their monthly magazine, so I offered them edited versions of the 'blogs' for Antarctica and Greenland, with some further material added by way of introduction. I reproduce those articles here, in the hope that they may give the armchair traveller something of the sense of 'being there'.

Cruising Antarctica

Article published in the Nautical Institute Magazine Seaways,
August 2006

This year, 2006, is the third *Saga Rose* has visited the Antarctic Peninsula as part of her World Cruise. The ship is owned and operated by the British company Saga, which offers services such as holidays and insurance to the over-fifties.

In order for the vessel to travel to the Antarctic the company had to be granted a permit by the Foreign and Commonwealth Office of the British Government. (The UK is a signatory to the Antarctic Treaty of 1959.) In addition, Saga is a full member of the International Association of Antarctic Tour Operators (IAATO), which has very strict guidelines and operating procedures for visitors to the region.

Risk assessment had taken place by an independent company of marine consultants, the approved search and rescue plan was lodged with the Falmouth Maritime Rescue Coordination Centre and a medical emergency contingency plan was contracted with a Chilean company which had bases on the mainland and King George Island.

I am myself an experienced master, and at the time we first visited Antarctica I had more than fifteen years in command on passenger vessels. I also had Captain Chris Elliott on board to assist and advise. Chris had just retired from thirty-eight years with the British Antarctic Survey, master for the last thirty. In addition, the vessel carried an expedition leader, Dr Beau Riffenburgh, who is based at the Scott Polar Research Institute in Cambridge. Dr Riffenburgh is the editor of *Polar Record* and had completed over a dozen field trips to the Arctic or Antarctic. Dr

Liz Cruwys, assistant expedition leader, and five other lecturers made up the team of very experienced additions to the vessel's normal complement.

Saga is very much aware of its responsibilities with regard to environmental management and the safety of their passengers while its vessel is in the region.

A tried and tested routine to run passengers ashore in the five Polar Circle (PC) boats carried on board was initiated at each landing. All passengers had been thoroughly briefed before arrival and at no time were more than 100 persons allowed on shore at one time. Emergency contingency equipment for that number of persons was landed ashore with the first boat to leave the vessel. During the vessel's stay in the region a comprehensive waste management plan was enforced.

In this article I have tried to give an impression of what it is like to take a cruise ship into Antarctica. It is based on my 'Captain's blog', and starts with a fairly typical day at sea.

———

We approached Admiralty Bay from the east, having reduced speed a few hours before. Icebergs and sea ice had been present since 0400 hours but not a hindrance to navigation. The sky was overcast, but not heavy, the land grey and forbidding. Glaciers could be seen in the distance and as we entered the bay a sleety shower passed through and took away our view.

Even though the charts are relatively good, I approached the anchorage with caution, always confirming with our ice pilot that my navigation was acceptable. The deep water slowly shoaled and eventually, when we were just three-tenths of a mile off our intended landing point, instructions were given to 'walk' the anchor out. By 0740 we were anchored and the first Polar Circle boat lowered to send the expedition team ashore. The operation takes organisation and Simon, the staff captain, along with the other senior officers had made their preparations well.

The first eight passengers left the ship at 0845, by which time

Saga Rose in Antarctica

the shore party had made the initial set-up. The nearby Polish scientific station, Arctowski, had been informed and was on hand to talk with our only Polish officer. They even have a small shop for tourists to buy a few souvenirs. From then on our five Polar Circle boats were running throughout, ferrying groups of eight at a time until over 430 passengers had visited the shore, seen the seals and penguins, but always knowing that they had to take care to avoid any damage to this fragile environment. The scenery all around is spectacular, with many glaciers just a few miles away. Brash ice floated past the ship, and adult seals could be seen teaching their young how to swim and fish.

During our first stop in Antarctica we were able to extend our hospitality to a couple of the Polish scientific team. I went across and was shown their living quarters and one of the labs, all very clean and business-like. The young radio officer told my wife and me that he was to be there for a year, but felt privileged to be given such an opportunity.

Our schedule is tight and I needed to be away as soon as possible in order to be able to slow down if conditions deteriorated. By 1600 hours all passengers were back and we had hoisted the last of our five PC boats back on board. Three propeller guards and a propeller had been damaged on the stony landing; they will be repaired during the night. The anchor had held without difficulty throughout our stay, with the ship being held in position by a current coming from one direction and the wind another.

By 1700 hours we had left the bay and were heading southwest towards the Gerlache Strait. I had gained a precious two hours; even so, maximum speed was set while conditions remained clear and calm. We had 204 nautical miles to travel during a night where darkness would not fall. In the distance icebergs could be easily seen, but it was not until the early hours of Saturday that speed was reduced. Our second staff captain, a Russian named Max, was backing up the bridge team from midnight and he was joined later by Chris, the Antarctic ice pilot. Speed was further reduced after 0300 as the sea ice started to increase and some alterations of course were required.

We were set to arrive at Waterboat Point at 0600 hours for a long intensive day, but nothing could have given us a clue as to how magnificent a day it was going to be.

I returned to the bridge before 0500 as we approached the Bryde Channel south of Lemaire Island. The Antarctic mainland was in front of us and it was awe-inspiring with the dark rugged mountains rising to over 5,000 feet. Snow fields and glaciers came down to the sea and smaller icebergs were everywhere to be seen.

Entering Paradise Harbour our speed was down to just a few knots as we crept towards Waterboat Point. With a following wind and an unknown current I had to place the ship close enough to the landing to operate a safe boat service. We drifted slowly with the ice until passing the Chilean González Videla base. There is no suitable anchorage, so the ship would have to be manoeuvred constantly during our visit. To the north there was an area of clear water and this is where I elected to turn and 'park'. With just a few engine movements and a push or two from the bow thruster we held position for nine hours, stemming the wind and current.

The passenger operation started just after 0700 hours and we were constantly aware that, to comply with our Antarctic permit, there should be no more than 100 people ashore at any one time. The base personnel made us very welcome, again opening their little shop in order to sell Antarctic patches, certificates, maps, etc. Gentoo penguins were everywhere and appeared totally unafraid of their human visitors. The adults were feeding and protecting their young from the marauding skuas who every now and again took dives at the colonies – which reacted with much flapping and screeching. Quite comical in a way, but we were also able to witness first hand the harsh reality of nature as a chick was taken.

The passengers were, in many cases, totally overwhelmed by the grandeur of nature that surrounded them. One gentleman said he could not think of words to describe what he was seeing. No one came back without intimating at least that the day had been a big 'Wow!'

Passengers and crew were all back on board by 1500 hours so, once the boats were secured, we set off for Port Lockroy.

We crossed the Gerlache Strait and headed for Wiencke Island, dodging large ice floes on the way. There seemed to be no way through this tremendous wall of rock and ice reaching up to 4,700 feet in front of us. As we closed the land an opening began to show itself to the south – the entrance to the Neumayer Channel, through which we would shortly be passing.

The channel is just a mile wide and continues for over eight miles, passing several large glaciers on the way. On either side the steep sides towered above us until we eventually came out into the greater daylight off Port Lockroy. This little British station is now a museum, but was built during the Second World War to secretly monitor enemy activity in the area.

We had to wait for a short time while another small passenger ship prepared to leave the bay and Goudier Island, on which the base is located. We took the opportunity to send away a PC boat in order to collect the base team. The boat was having difficulty in getting through the brash ice and so we followed them in, giving directions. From our greater height we could see the leads. The team of one lady and two men were eventually brought to the ship, took a shower, changed clothes and were introduced to the passengers in the Grand Ballroom. They told us that up to three passenger ships a day call at the base to see the museum and the Gentoo colony on the island.

Our mail was sent back with the team. It might take up to six weeks to reach home, by which time we expect to be in Australia! By 2100 hours we were back in the Neumayer heading north to Half Moon Island. An interesting aside is that it was the grandfather of Rhys James, our second officer, who helped to originally construct the base. Simon made sure he went over in the boat to take a quick visit.

By 0700 on Sunday, our final day in Antarctica, we were a few miles off Livingston Island and turning into the McFarlane Strait, going around the grounded iceberg that was conveniently marking the shallows to port. Half Moon Island looks as one might expect and we approached the entrance from the northeast, anchoring in the sheltered waters of the small bay. The chinstrap penguins could be heard easily in the silence of the morning, chattering and squawking in the rookeries less than a quarter of a mile away.

We were greeted on the radio by the commander of the Argentine Camara base located at the head of the bay, and some of his team were invited on board to sell their souvenirs. I in turn visited his base with a small gift and was given coffee and a guided tour. As it was a Sunday they were preparing a barbecue, but this had to be done inside the large working building, as open fires are no longer allowed outside on the continent. My wife and I opted to walk the half-mile back to the boat landing; it was along a raised crescent of large rounded stones and was not easy. Passing the odd seal and enjoying the silence, we eventually arrived among our red-coated passengers busy photographing the hundreds of penguins perched all over the higher rocks.

Now and again one would pass between them, either heading home or back to the sea.

The day was mild, around eight degrees centigrade, and with no wind, hats and gloves were really not required. The operation was now working like clockwork, passengers and crew were well versed in the procedures of getting ashore and by 1500 hours the ship was again almost ready for sea. As we were ahead of schedule I figured we could give the passengers a small bonus before heading back across the 'Drake'.

By 1600 we were sailing from the anchorage and headed southwest, leaving the impressive cliffs of Livingston Island to starboard. Deception Island is a volcanic island with a flooded caldera that had its last major eruption in 1969; it lay some thirty miles ahead of us. Originally the island had been on the itinerary but for operational reasons had been dropped, but now we had time to spare, so Chris and I planned a course to take us to the entrance channel.

To enter we had to pass through Neptune's Bellows, a very narrow channel that required precise navigation. Chris piloted while I and the officer of the watch monitored the progress, relaying depth and radar information as required. Many of our passengers were on deck; as we passed Peter's Pillar and the cliffs to starboard less than a thousand feet away, it was yet another of those amazing 'Wow!' moments.

Once inside, the vista opened up. We took the ship into Whalers Bay, turning through 180 degrees at slow speed in order for the passengers to see the remains of the old whaling station and the ruined buildings of the British Antarctic Survey base that was destroyed in the last eruption. Even the hangar still stands from the days when the small ski-fitted aircraft, brought out on the supply ship, could fly in and out of the base. Now all looks desolate; where the snow has melted everything is covered with volcanic ash and an undulating black landscape is all that remains of the ice runway.

Within the hour we were returning through the Bellows,

equally impressive on the way out, particularly as a grounded berg appeared to be blocking our way until the final course was reached. The Drake Passage, and whatever weather it may have in store for us, lay ahead.

Cruising Greenland

Article published in the Nautical Institute Magazine Seaways,
October 2007

With the seemingly endless increase in the number and size of cruise ships it is perhaps inevitable that 'new' destinations are sought. Saga, since 2003, have been cruising at least once a year up to Greenland. In August 2006 I made my first visit, and it has become a lasting memory to add to those from my many years at sea.

Saga Rose was built in 1965 and is one of the few traditional passenger vessels still trading worldwide. Her elegant looks perhaps hide her reassuringly proportionate scantlings. A small comfort to any master who may be tasked to take his vessel to an area where icebergs are, at times, too numerous to count.

Here follows my diary – commencing six days into the voyage as we approached the Greenland coast and published at the time on the Saga website as the 'Master's blog'. I will add some of my unpublished recommendations offered to the company as a conclusion. These perhaps may be of more practical use to my Institute colleagues.

Friday 11 August: Qaqortoq, Greenland
By 0200 hours icebergs had been detected on the radar. No adjustments of course were required, however, as the nearest passed down the port side well over a mile away. The darkness turned into a long twilight and the visibility went up and down with the change in air temperature. The navigation bridge can become a strange place at times like these, an atmosphere of quietness

and attention, illuminated by the instruments and radars, and the icy waters have a distinct smell which pervades our space every time someone goes out to the bridge wing to visually check a target.

Smaller icebergs and bergy bits had to be negotiated as we passed up the twelve miles of Julianehåb Fjord to the anchorage. The anchor went down, somewhat in a rush, but in good time to commence our day's business.

A quarter of a mile away, Qaqortoq appeared as a busy collection of painted houses perched on low rocky treeless hills surrounding a small harbour. The higher up the hill, apparently, the wealthier are the occupants. The three thousand or so mainly Inuit inhabitants are connected to the rest of Greenland by boat or helicopter and the heliport is right there, close to the sea and a stone's throw from the centre of town. It is a busy place, and all day choppers seemed to be buzzing over our heads on a regular basis.

Saturday 12 August: at sea towards Ilulissat
The rain started to fall steadily after midday and there were few passengers ashore when the last tender returned. We sailed slightly before our scheduled departure time and, within an hour, were passing icebergs of up to 100 metres in length. They were all shapes, some fairly flat, others more angular, and all were producing their own fog which could be seen cloud-like above and drifting downwind, reducing the visibility even further.

Again the speed was reduced during the hours of darkness, but the visibility improved dramatically as we turned to the north and the barograph started to rise. The cool moist winds from the south veered as the front eventually passed through and the morning dawned much colder. Bands of grey sky, some more white than dark, lay like an upturned duvet on the snow-covered mountains of the west coast ten miles on our starboard beam.

A humpback whale of perhaps twelve or fifteen metres in length passed close down our starboard side, and that was enough to set seemingly everyone off on whale-watching duty for the rest of the day.

Sunday 13 August: Ilulissat

I returned to the bridge shortly before 0200 hours as Rhys, our navigator, was reducing speed for our approach to Disko Bay. Although the sun had set some four hours before, there was an eerie grey light which was sufficient to see the icebergs, a relief to any master. For the next four hours we cruised into the calmer waters, passing some very large bergs and having to take avoiding action from time to time.

By 0630 the face of Jakobshavn Isfjord was just a mile or so ahead and speed was further reduced to pass through bergy bits and other floating debris coming from the massive field of towering ice. As the bright morning sun reflected from the oily sea, *Saga Rose* gracefully sailed within a few hundred yards of spectacular ice towards her intended anchorage off Ilulissat.

With growlers all around, the port anchor was walked out and Steve, our Cornish staff captain, launched tender number 10. Dodging the ice floes, the boat was taken into the tiny port to set up our shore operation. Ilulissat is becoming a tourist destination for those that can afford to go there, but it still has that 'frontier town' feel. Our work here is challenging.

Throughout the day we kept the tenders running between ship and shore, and at times we had to get one of them to push a growler away from the pontoon as it drifted dangerously close by. Less than half a mile away, a horizon full of slowly moving icebergs appeared to be preventing our ship from ever being able to leave.

Monday 14 August: cruising – the Eqip Glacier

Of course, we did leave, and for an hour or so before dinner the ship was negotiated back along the face of the Isfjord. Our ice pilot Idar and I had planned the next day, but that night we would cruise slowly on one engine in the less 'busy' waters of Disko Bay.

The night was crystal clear so navigation was relatively easy, and by 0500 hours we were making an entry into Ata Sund. Twenty-nine miles ahead lay Eqip Glacier.

When still eight miles away the enormous size gave the impression it was much closer. We approached slowly, putting a tender down to confirm the soundings ahead. I need not have worried, for as we finally came to rest less than a quarter of a mile from the face, the sounder was still showing over 100 metres.

For two hours we sat there, listening for the great cracks and bangs of a living glacier and waiting for the ice falls to make their great splashes in the waters below. Rising to over 50 or 60 meters above us, it was a fabulous sight and very awe-inspiring. Thousands of photographs must have been taken before we left, but it was our tender, half a mile away further along the face, that put perspective to the scene. It looked so tiny.

The schedule meant that we had to leave shortly after 0900 hours, so again we passed through the brash and the growlers, heading back towards Disko Bay.

Tuesday 15 August:
heading south towards the Farewell Passage
After two beautiful blue-sky days, the forecast was not good for Nuuk the next day. While we were still passing the bergs of Disko Bay I elected to cancel the call and head directly for the Farewell Passage. The decision turned out to be the correct one, for by the following morning we had over 60 knots of wind blowing over the bridge top. Uncomfortable seas, but *Saga Rose* weathered them well.

With the extra time available I knew we could make the next day particularly special. I had over six hours inside 'The Passage' to work with, but still there was no confirmation from the Greenland coastguard that it was clear of ice at the entrance. The weather down there had been so bad the helicopter had been grounded.

All day in these Arctic seas we passed many icebergs and

growlers, but by now many of our passengers were starting to become quite accustomed to the scenery outside moving past as they sat in their comfortable chairs. It may be hard for those not here to believe some passengers were more intent on listening to the Tivoli Quartet than watching through the window on the opposite side as 150,000 tons of ice slid serenely by.

Wednesday 16 August: the Farewell Passage
No one could have convinced me that this day would be as special as it turned out. Navigation into 'The Passage' required concentration as we skirted closely past several bergs that were neatly positioned on our track line. Fortunately the weather was clear, so there was plenty to see for the mass of passengers gathered on the promenade deck below the bridge. The jagged mountainous scenery is spectacular, small glaciers drop down from the troughs between the summits, and waterfalls are numerous. A larger glacier came down almost to the water's edge, terminal, medial and lateral moraines clearly visible, a perfect specimen from my geography lessons all those years ago.

Before lunch we stopped off the tiny settlement of Augpilagtoq, lowered one of our Polar Circle boats and sent away a small team to carry the mail ashore. Over 400 postcards will eventually reach their destination with the rare Cape Farewell frank. Apparently most of the men were away sealing but a few Inuit locals came over in their boats and the passengers sent down sweets to them, while a handful of children played on the rocks nearby.

This tiny remote Greenland village is six hours by ferry from the nearest reasonably sized town, and most of the 150 or so people who live there have never been anywhere else. Remarkable.

After an hour we set off again, over thirty miles to go and the narrowest part of the fjord yet to come. There was a surprise in store.

The Farewell Passage continued

There were a couple of fairly tight turns to make before we reached Prins Christian Sund, both achieved without problem even though small ice and growlers had, at times, to be avoided. I had advised passengers that the narrowest part, Qornoq, was as narrow as 400 metres and almost three miles long.

As we approached Idar and I exchanged concerned glances. There was a very large flat berg which appeared to be blocking almost the full width of the channel. I became more concerned the closer we came. The radar showed virtually no clear channel remaining, and visually it was difficult to tell. Number 10 boat was hastily prepared and our safety officer Wesley was given instruction to take the boat up ahead, sound the channel close to the cliff face and ascertain if the berg had any underwater 'lip'.

There was immense interest below the bridge, with passengers almost clamouring to get a shot. Reports coming back to me were favourable, speed was increased and we headed for the gap. Like the lovely lady she is, *Saga Rose* slid elegantly past without the slightest chance of loosing her makeup. Great cheers rose from the passengers below, and the team on the bridge breathed again, seemingly for the first time in minutes.

After stopping to pick up the boat, when Wesley said he was mobbed by enquiring passengers on the deck, we continued on to the end of the Farewell Passage. By the evening we were back into the fog, with icebergs yet again all around.

Conclusion

The difficulties of navigating in these waters may perhaps be simplified to the problems of ice, fog and speed plus the ability of the bridge team to stay alert and avoid becoming complacent after many days of ice dodging.

We carried an experienced Danish Greenland ferry master as our coastal pilot, and he was on duty with us whenever we were in the busier waters, a source of knowledge and experience to assist my own deliberations. On the bridge, watches were doubled, with two pairs of eyes continually monitoring radars. Lookouts inside and outside the wheelhouse were tasked to specifically look directly ahead down the beam of the searchlight. There was virtually no other vessel traffic, but icebergs and growlers could be expected at any time while on the coast. With six out of the seven nights affected by reduced visibility a reduction to a 'safe speed' was often required.

Itinerary planners therefore need to consider that there must be flexibility in timings that allow the master, particularly during the hours of darkness, sufficient leeway to act responsibly yet still meet passengers' expectations. Because of the unpredictable weather, alternatives need to be built into the schedule.

Dwindling on-board fresh water and fuel oil as the days went by meant stability had to be carefully monitored. The problems of fresh-water capacity, consumption, manufacture and bunkering, along with garbage and grey water disposal, must therefore be fully investigated before even considering a voyage to this area, where there are few suitable berths and limited facilities.

In addition, companies considering Greenland for future itineraries should consider that the lack of suitability of existing radars to pick up small targets within the sea clutter at close range may require a specific ice radar with a lower scanner to be fitted. Windscreen wipers must be positioned where the lookouts will stand and actually work effectively, and a glass coating such as Rain-X may be an advantage. The vessel must have at least one powerful searchlight, fixed to shine directly ahead, and which does not irritatingly reflect back off any deck fitting.

Without doubt the Greenland coast is spectacular, but it should be remembered that, if preparation and execution are carried out without rigorous regard for safety, voyaging to these more remote places could come with a price any master or owner is not prepared to pay.

Philip Rentell

From his days as a cadet on the ageing training ship *Worcester*, Captain Philip Rentell's forty-year career has spanned the world's oceans and a huge variety of seagoing experience. He served as a junior officer on numerous freighters and liners, as the navigator of cross-Channel hovercraft, and then as first officer of the Cunard flagship *QE2*, on which he went to the South Atlantic with over 3,500 British troops and a volunteer crew of 650 during the Falklands War of 1982. Since leaving Cunard in 1990, he has been an English Channel and North Sea pilot, and has commanded a succession of cruise ships.

Philip Rentell is a Fellow of the Nautical Institute and a Younger Brother at Trinity House. In 1998 he published an earlier volume of memoirs entitled *Not Yet*, and he has also produced three small illustrated books on liners. In 2002 he obtained a law degree from the Open University, one of the first group of students to do so. He has held a private pilot licence for fixed wing aircraft, and in his spare time he has recently built an autogyro.

Captain Philip Rentell is currently master of the classic cruise liner *Saga Ruby*, and when he is not at sea he lives in Cornwall.

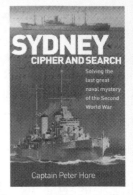
SYDNEY, CIPHER AND SEARCH
Solving the last great naval mystery of the Second World War

CAPTAIN PETER HORE

In November 1941 the Australian light cruiser HMAS *Sydney*, with a crew of 645, disappeared off the coast of Western Australia. Shipwrecked German sailors told an incredible tale of how their ship, the lightly armoured merchant raider *Kormoran*, had sunk the pride of the Australian navy. Almost at once conspiracy theories sprang up to explain the tragic loss of the ship and so many lives. Based on the author's decryption and interpretation of German coded accounts, interviews with German survivors, and other research, this book tells what really happened in the desperate fight to the death between the two ships, whose wrecks were finally located in March 2008.

> **'A fine piece of historical detective work which reads like a thriller'**
> Nicholas Rodger

> **'The amount of evidence-gathering, sifting, analysis and assessment is astonishing ... utterly convincing ... an exciting read'**
> Richard Woodman

Illustrated · ISBN 978-1-906266-08-0 pbk · £9.95, or £14.50 with companion DVD, + £1.05 p&p

WALKING ON WATER
A voyage round Britain and through life

GEOFF HOLT

In 1984, at the age of 18, Geoff Holt broke his neck in a swimming accident. He was left paralysed, his promising career as a yachtsman at an end. 23 years later to the day, Geoff became the first quadriplegic yachtsman to sail single-handed around Great Britain. This is Geoff's story of his life before and after the accident: how he learned to live with his disability, how he achieved astonishing success in spite of it, how he rediscovered the sea and helped to promote sailing for disabled people – and how he conceived and completed the dangerous circumnavigation. With a foreword by HRH The Princess Royal.

> **'This is a story tht will excite admiration from all sailors, disabled or otherwise'**
> Sir Robin Knox-Johnston

> **'Beautifully written and honest'**
> Dame Ellen MacArthur

Illustrated · ISBN 978-0-906266-09-7 pbk · £9.95, or £14.50 with companion DVD, + £1.05 p&p

AMPHIBIOUS ASSAULT
Manoeuvre from the sea
From Gallipoli to the Gulf – a definitive analysis

Edited by TRISTAN LOVERING MBE

In this uniquely authoritative study,
leading international military
and academic experts analyse 37
amphibious operations, from the 'how
not to do it' catastrophe of Gallipoli
in 1915 to the Al Faw landings in
Iraq in 2003. In between, there are
chapters on the Second World War in
Europe, North Africa, the Indian Ocean
and the Pacific; and on Korea, Suez,
Vietnam, the Falklands and the first
Gulf War. British, American, German,
Japanese and Soviet operations are all
included. With over 500 pages of text,

300 photographs and 95 maps, this definitive analysis of amphibious warfare in the twentieth
century and beyond will be invaluable to anyone with an interest in military history, as well as
to those who, as military practitioners or historians, study it professionally.

'Simply the best book on the subject'
Dr Eric Grove, Salford University

**'An indispensable "lessons learned" portfolio ... a key source
document ... for all informed students of twentieth century
maritime warfare'**
Lawrence Phillips, *The Royal Navy Day by Day*

'How I wish it had been available and read by many before 1982!'
Commodore Michael Clapp CB RN,
Commander Amphibious Task Group Falklands

'Outstanding'
Professor George W Baer, US Naval War College, Monterey

**'... required reading for all politicians who feel the urge to launch
amphibious forces against substantial enemies'**
Dr Philip Towle, Centre for International Studies,
University of Cambridge

With a foreword by CORRELLI BARNETT

Royalties from this book will go to the Royal Marines 1939 War Fund, Charity No. 248733

Illustrated · ISBN 978-0-9550243-5-1 pbk · £35.00 + £4.95 p&p
ISBN 978-0-9550243-6-8 pbk with slip case · £45.00 + £4.95 p&p

Discounts available on multiple orders

DIVER

TONY GROOM

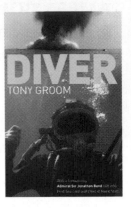

An honest, moving and sometimes hilarious account of a hair-raisingly exciting career, both in the Royal Navy and in commercial deep-sea diving – training the most unlikely of raw recruits ... handling unexploded bombs while under air attack ... living for months in a pressurised bottle with a voice like Donald Duck ... commuting to work through a hole in the floor in the freezing, black depths of the North Sea. Tony Groom joined the Royal Navy at the age of seventeen, determined to become a diver. As a member of the Fleet Clearance Diving Team, he found himself diving for mines, dealing with unexploded bombs and being shot at in the Falklands War. After leaving the Navy in 1985, he travelled the world as a commercial diver.

'The Royal Navy Clearance Divers, not the SAS, are the British mystery unit of the Falklands War'
Major General Julian Thompson

'Wide-ranging, illuminating and sympathetic ... this tale fills a massive gap and is long overdue'
Commodore Michael C Clapp

With a foreword by ADMIRAL SIR JONATHON BAND

Illustrated • ISBN 978-1-906266-06-6 pbk • £9.95, or £14.50 with companion DVD, + £1.05 p&p

SALVAGE: A personal odyssey

CAPTAIN IAN TEW

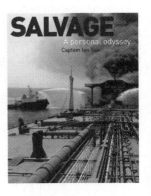

'No cure, no pay' is the rule. If a salvor is defeated by the elements, he receives nothing. It is not a business for the faint-hearted. Ian Tew joined Selco of Singapore in 1974. As tug captain and salvage master, he roamed the world, from the coast of Cornwall to the Southern Ocean, from the Gulf of Suez to the South China Sea. He tells of the challenges of ten tough years – a barge adrift in a hurricane – a freighter aground on a reef – a tanker hit by a missile in the Gulf. This gripping account of drama at sea is a tribute to the seamanship, courage and resourcefulness of the salvor.

'The often heroic work, sterling seamanship and amazing professionalism of salvage vessel crews often goes unnoticed and unsung by the wider world ... a vivid and insightful account'
Andrew Linington, Head of Communications,
Nautilus UK

Illustrated • ISBN 978-0-9550243-9-9 pbk • £19.95 + £1.05 p&p
ISBN 978-1-906266-00-4 hbk, signed limited edition • £24.95 + £1.05 p&p

THE LONE RANGER STORY
From salvage tug to super yacht

JOHN JULIAN

Lone Ranger worked as a salvage tug (then named *Simson*) and towed some of the largest oil installations ever built during twenty of the most challenging years in the history of the business. During the mid-1990s, she embarked on a second career as the world's pre-eminent expedition yacht, whether in Antarctic waters or the Caribbean and the Mediterranean, where her purposeful lines stand out among the pleasure craft. Now in her fourth decade, she is as supremely seaworthy as ever, with more long voyages in prospect, thanks to the vision and commitment of her owner and crew.

> **'A fascinating story, well told, about a vessel that has had two totally different but interesting careers spanning more than 30 years'**
> *Shipping Today and Yesterday*

Illustrated · ISBN 0-9550243-0-7 hbk · £19.95 + £1.05 p&p

SKELETONS FOR SADNESS

EWEN SOUTHBY-TAILYOUR

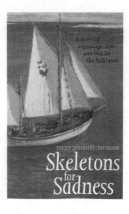

It is September 1980. Edward Casement, sailing with his crew towards Cape Horn and the Pacific in his ketch *Nomad*, calls in at the Falklands. Things do not go according to plan, and, having lost his crew, he ends up spending longer in the islands than he had intended, sailing on charter for the Governor in the company of an English nurse. In an atmosphere of growing intrigue, not all is as it seems, and then comes the Argentine invasion. A story of love, espionage, a yacht, and a war in the South Atlantic.

> **'A breathtaking thriller ... highly original and beautifully written'**
> Lt Cdr Tristan Lovering MBE RN

Illustrated · ISBN 978-0-906266-02-8 pbk · £9.95 + £1.05 p&p

AFTER YOU, MR LEAR
In the wake of Edward Lear in Italy
MALDWIN DRUMMOND

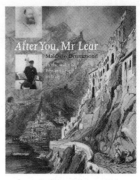

This is the story of a journey in search of the character and work of the Victorian polymath Edward Lear (1812–1888). Best known today as a nonsense poet and humorist, Lear was also a talented and celebrated topographical landscape painter. On the 150th anniversary of Lear's appointment as Queen Victoria's drawing master, Maldwin and Gilly Drummond set sail in their yacht *Gang Warily*, from near Osborne house, Queen Victoria's home in the Isle of Wight. They cross the Channel, navigate the rivers and canals of France to the Mediterranean, and follow the coast of Italy from Lear's adopted home at San Remo south as far as Calabria. A fascinating account of a voyage of discovery, richly illustrated, and including some of Lear's own most accomplished drawings and paintings, as well as the author's photographs and sketches, and new insights into the life and work of a remarkable man.

Illustrated • ISBN 978-0-9550243-7-5 pbk • £18.95 + £1.05 p&p
ISBN 978-0-9550243-8-2 hbk, signed limited edition • £29.95 + £1.05 p&p

ICE BEARS AND KOTICK
PETER WEBB

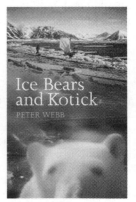

This is the story of an impossible boat journey that two men made for the fun of it. They rowed through pack ice and survived polar bears, starvation and capsize, and in doing so they completed the first circumnavigation of the Arctic island of Spitzbergen in an open rowing boat. Along the way they learned about themselves and about life, and experienced a wilderness that will most likely disappear before the century is out. This is a story for small-boat sailors, lovers of ice and snow, and anybody who knows anybody who wanted to run away to sea.

'An evocative tale of good, old-fashioned adventure amid one of the bleakest landscapes on earth ... vividly and thoughtfully written, an inspiration'
John Ridgway – first transatlantic oarsman

Illustrated • ISBN 978-0-906266-03-5 pbk • £9.95 + £1.05 p&p

JOSEPH CONRAD: MASTER MARINER

PETER VILLIERS

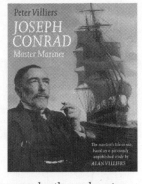

Before he published his first novel in 1895, Joseph Conrad spent 20 years in the merchant navy, eventually obtaining his master's ticket and commanding the barque *Otago*. This book, superbly illustrated with paintings by Mark Myers, traces

his sea-career and shows how Konrad Korzeniowski, master mariner, became Joseph Conrad, master novelist. Alan Villiers, world-renowned author and master mariner under sail, was uniquely qualified to comment on Conrad's life at sea, and the study he began has been completed by his son, Peter Villiers.

'A book that finally does justice to Conrad's time at sea'
Traditional Boats and Tall Ships

Illustrated with 12 paintings in full colour by Mark Myers RSMA F/ASMA
Illustrated · ISBN 0-9547062-9-3 pbk · £14.95 + £1.05 p&p

CRUISE OF THE *CONRAD*

A Journal of a Voyage round the World, undertaken and carried out in the Ship JOSEPH CONRAD, 212 Tons, in the Years 1934, 1935, and 1936 by way of Good Hope, the South Seas, the East Indies, and Cape Horn

ALAN VILLIERS

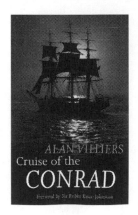

In 1934 the Australian sailor and writer Alan Villiers set out to fulfil his life's ambition – to obtain, equip and sail a full-rigged ship around the world, and enthuse others with his own love of sail before the opportunity was lost for ever. He was successful. His record of that extraordinary journey, more odyssey than voyage, was first published in 1937. In this new edition, complete with a short biography of Alan Villiers and richly illustrated with his own photographs, it will inspire a new generation of sailors and sea-enthusiasts.

'No other book like this will ever be written'
The Sunday Times

With a foreword by Sir Robin Knox-Johnston · Illustrated with photographs
Illustrated · ISBN 0-9547062-8-5 pbk · £12.95 + £1.05 p&p